D1108648

FROM

RESOLUTION

TO

REVOLUTION

THE MESSAGE OF ASHURA

Reflections on religion, ethics, culture,
family, youth, and citizenship.

Sayed Moustafa Al-Qazwini

Islamic Educational Center of Orange County
3194-B Airport Loop Drive
Costa Mesa, California 92626 U.S.A.
Telephone: (714) 432-0060
Fax: (714) 432-0070

Website: www.iecoc.org
E-mail: info@iecoc.org

First U.S. Edition 2011

The Library of Congress Cataloging-in-Publication Data
Al-Qazwini, Moustafa
From Resolution to Revolution/Moustafa Al-Qazwini
p. cm.

ISBN: 978-0-615-49336-7

Book Layout and Design by the Islamic Publishing House [www.iph.ca]

Printed in Canada by Friesens Corp.
www.friesens.com

Table of Contents

In the Name of God, the Most Gracious, the Most Compassionate

Introduction

This book is a compilation of a progressive lecture series delivered over a three-year span in London, England, from 2005 to 2007 (1426-1428 AH) during the Ashura season. The series given reflect a number of spiritual, social, and individual struggles that resonate within every person, and further seek to provide spiritual direction to those challenges.

Since the lectures were inspired by the character and sacrifice of the grandson of Prophet Muhammad, Imam Husayn b. Ali, peace be upon them, whose life was taken in the midst of his prime years, highlighting the years of youth, in particular Muslim youths living in the West, will predominate most of the themes throughout the book.

The raising of ethical character is the platform by which the brick and mortar of practice and faith sets the foundation for attaining human perfection. The combined elements of faith and practice are used to understand and resolve issues dealing with Muslim youth, in areas such as youth leadership, family, marriage, personal and spiritual refinement based on the Qur'an and the ways of Prophet Muhammad, and the imams (the Ahlul-Bayt) that followed him.

The age of discovery and reflection begins to surface in the formidable years and as maturity develops, proper Islamic guidance, nurturing and role models play crucial roles in the spiritual, intellectual, and self-development process. Without proper guidance, the young generation can easily detour.

Muslims and non-Muslims alike will be able to see a reflection of their own human struggle and experiences unfold throughout the book. Although the words spoken are directed towards a youth audience, other readers will also benefit by understanding the youth of our time. Their experiences, challenges, and direction requires a unique approach in defining and solving social and religious issues that pertain exclusively to them.

With the correct guidance, the potential and contribution of the Muslim youth living in the West in becoming influential Muslim leaders is something to be anticipated. Their abilities will not only affect the Muslim communities in the West, but all around the world as well, including non-Muslims. The Muslim youth generation in the West has better opportunities and privileges at their disposal, than other young Muslims not living in the West. Prestigious institutes for higher learning, heightened thoughts, and economic advantage are some of the critical elements that give them a cornerstone advantage. Their sincere concern for public engagement and commitment to social issues provides an assurance of their dedication and capabilities.

Muslim youth in the West are facing immense challenges and are under tremendous pressure when it comes to issues of identity, conformity, and religiosity. They desire to be religiously educated and practicing; and they anticipate more from Muslim scholars to identify with their situations and provide rational and proper guidelines. This book hopes to shed light on some of these issues and bring forth modern solutions.

Citations from the Holy Qur'an and lessons drawn from Islamic history illuminate throughout the book, and form the central themes and guidance for our comprehension of the purpose of life. Understanding what the Divine expects from us is crucial to our spiritual success. How do we strengthen our relationship with Him? What is the significance of the prayer and why should we repent? How do we maintain ethical gender-relations? Refining spirituality through the ways of the Divine is the key source by which Muslim solutions are sought for issues, such as the direction of life, social and family structure, and leadership.

For hundreds of years, Muslims have traditionally held sacred the first ten days of Muharram (Muharram is the first month in the Islamic calendar). These hallowed days turn into ten nightly vigils known as the commemoration leading up to Ashura. In Arabic, Ashura means tenth, and many Muslims recognize the 10th of Muharram (61 AH) as being the date that the grandson of the Prophet Muhammad, Imam Husayn, was brutally martyred. Ashura is a landmark event - on the surface, it marks the anniversary of the martyrdom of Imam Husayn, his family, and 72 companions in the year 61 AH in Karbala, Iraq, but there are many deeper lessons to learn from this great tragedy.

Although the events of Ashura seem tragic, the underlining outcome was that it became a timeless example for revolutionary change. Ashura is not just about one young and brave man who stood before an army and tyrant and refused to comply with oppression, but it is a guidance that forces people to reflect and question their own principles in life. The message of Ashura sets the stage for social and personal reform, and I hope that this book will inspire the reader for such changes.

The event of Ashura provides an outstanding opportunity for Muslims to better understand their religion. The commemoration of it every year not only provides an avenue for Muslims to discover the beauty of Islam and the sacrifice of notable Muslims, but more importantly, Ashura awakens and stirs the soul to recognize itself. This season is a catalyst for Islamic renaissance and self-reform in every age and place.

The love for Prophet Muhammad is the heart line of every Muslim; and the love that was expressed by the Prophet to his grandson, Imam Husayn represents a link to unify and strengthen the various schools of thought within Islam. Imam Husayn and the commemoration during the days of Ashura should initiate opportunities for open dialogue and sincere connection amongst Muslims.

In keeping with the message of Ashura alive, the followers of Ahlul-Bayt worldwide commemorate this occasion with a series of ceremonies, rituals, and lectures. Although some of these programs have been merely cultural in the past, today they have evolved and adapted to a more modernized intellectual remembrance and awakening. In some parts of the world, many have sanctified the traditional and cultural processions of Ashura, while others have disapproved them.

Traditionally, the commemoration nights of Ashura recapture the historical and heart-breaking events that led and occurred on that 10th day of Muharram, and in my lectures series I did present the storyline but chose not to include them in this written work. I preferred to keep the objective of Imam Husayn's message in a more contemporary and constructive production.

A very close friend and colleague, the late Sayed Mohammad Ridha Sharazi, who passed away in June 2008, was the inspiration behind this book. His words of encouragement initiated the spoken words to being written down and thus I dedicate this book in his honor and memory.

Of course, this book would not have seen the light without the assistance of many loyal friends and companions in the Muslim community in North America. Foremost, I am indebted to Sister Fatma Saleh whose markings and suggestions throughout the book played a crucial role in its development and deliverance. Much appreciation also extends to Shaykh Saleem Bhimji and Sister Arifa Hudda in the editing, design and printing; and Sister Amina Inloes in the initial compilation of the book. I would also like to express a deep gratitude to the financial contributor who preferred to remain anonymous. May Allah reward and grant them all success and honor in this life and in the Hereafter.

I humbly appeal to my Lord to accept my sincere efforts in presenting this work and to forgive me for any of the shortcomings within these pages. It is to Him that I am most thankful to and it is Him that I yearn to please.

I ask the readers to keep me in their prayers and thoughts. May God bless you all.

Please note: It is customary in Islam that when the name of Allah, Prophet Muhammad, the other prophets, or imams (descendants and successors of Prophet Muhammad) is enunciated, the following phrases are mentioned: Allah - "Glorified and Exalted is He (*Subhannah wa-tallah*)"; Prophet Muhammad - "Peace be upon him and his family"; after the names of prophets, imams from the family of Prophet Muhammad and his daughter - "Peace be upon him/her." With great respect, admiration, recognition, and praise, I have omitted the mentioned phrases for the sake of continuity.

Sayed Moustafa Al-Qazwini
March 2011 / Rabi al-Thani, 1432
Orange County, CA, USA

Part One

London, England
2005 CE / 1426 AH

Dignity & Honor
Chapter 1

﴿يَا أَيُّهَا النَّاسُ اعْبُدُواْ رَبَّكُمُ الَّذِي خَلَقَكُمْ وَالَّذِينَ مِنْ قَبْلِكُمْ لَعَلَّكُمْ تَتَّقُونَ الَّذِي جَعَلَ لَكُمُ الأَرْضَ فِرَاشاً وَالسَّمَآءَ بِنَآءً وَأَنْزَلَ مِنَ السَّمَآءِ مَاءً فَأَخْرَجَ بِهِ مِنَ الثَّمَرَاتِ رِزْقاً الَّكُمْ فَلاَ تَجْعَلُواْ لِلَّهِ أَنْدَاداً وَأَنْتُمْ تَعْلَمُونَ﴾

O mankind! Worship your Lord, who created you and those who were before you, so that you may be God conscious. He who made the earth a place of repose for you, and the sky a canopy, and He sends down water from the sky, and with it He brings forth crops for your sustenance. So do not set up equals to God, while you know. (2:21-22)

THE ESSENTIAL COMPONENTS WHICH DISTINGUISH THE HUMAN BEING from an animal are three: the power to reason, free-will, and an innate sense of honor. While each of us hold the inborn potential to use these faculties to raise ourselves above the level of the angels, we also run the risk of plummeting lower than the lowest of God's creation if we neglect to use these three traits correctly.

The existence and significance of our free-will and intellect is something we recognize instantly. We are born with the ability to choose our own course in life and have been designed with outstanding powers to discover, resolve, and reason. Yet, we may not always understand our inborn sense of honor, even though God created us with honor and dignity. We are His best of creations and we far exceed any other creation in existence, "We bestowed honor on the sons of Adam...and conferred upon them special favors, above a great part of Our creation."[1]

Thus, each and every one of us is highly valued by God and that is why when He created Adam, God asked the angels to prostrate before Adam as a sign of recognizing the honor and dignity of the human being. Therefore, we have to recognize our self-worth and uphold it in honor.

$$﴿وَلَقَدْ خَلَقْنَاكُمْ ثُمَّ صَوَّرْنَاكُمْ ثُمَّ قُلْنَا لِلْمَلآئِكَةِ اسْجُدُواْ لِآدَمَ فَسَجَدُواْ...﴾$$

Certainly We created you, then We formed you, then We said to the angels, "Prostrate before Adam." So they [all] prostrated... (7:11)

This is not to say that acknowledging our self-honor is a form of arrogance, because arrogance is a form of abomination. However, we need to be extremely cautious not to showcase ourselves above others, as this is a form of arrogance which must be avoided. Arrogance is the illusion that we are the only ones of value, as evinced by Satan, the founder of arrogance.

$$﴿قَالَ مَا مَنَعَكَ أَلاَّ تَسْجُدَ إِذْ أَمَرْتُكَ قَالَ أَنَاْ خَيْرٌ مِنْهُ خَلَقْتَنِي مِنْ نَارٍ وَخَلَقْتَهُ مِنْ طِينٍ﴾$$

Said God, "What prevented you from prostrating when I commanded you?" "I am better than him," he said. "You created me from fire and You created him from clay." (7:12)

---

[1] *Al-Qur'an*, 17:70

Stressing the value of the human, over 1,400 years ago Islam prohibited infanticide. In the pre-Islamic era, people used to kill their children out of fear of poverty and deprivation.

$$﴿وَلاَ تَقْتُلُوٓاْ أَوْلاَدَكُمْ مِّنْ إِمْلاَقٍ نَّحْنُ نَرْزُقُكُمْ وَإِيَّاهُمْ﴾$$

...you shall not kill your children due to penury - We will provide for you and for them... (6:151)

Anthropologists summarize that infanticide has been seen in various forms and in many civilizations from the Greeks to the Persians, from the Indians to the Chinese and the Europeans. The Arabs in the pre-Islamic era had seen their share of child infanticide, especially if it was a female. Muslim historians cite various reasons; however, the prime factor was related to poverty or to prevent dishonoring the reputation of the family. Thankfully, prohibition of female infanticide was eradicated by Islam.

In the verse just cited, God reminds us that it is He who sustains and provides for our livelihood. In fact, God indicates something even deeper - He provides sustenance for the parents because of their children!

A story has been mentioned in which a man complained to the sixth Imam, Jafar as-Sadiq that he was poor. The Imam instructed him to get married. The man thought that perhaps the Imam did not understand that the reason why he was not married was because he was poor. However, the Imam understood his complaint the first time and again instructed the man to get married. The Imam was indicating to the man that God would provide him a better life for the sake of his wife and children if he gets married!

In a misguided attempt to prove their worth, many people chase after wealth and power - this is a wrong approach. Acquiring masses of wealth will not give you dignity. Even in society, those who amass great riches but do not know how to use it are mocked; seeking accolade through material means only results in derision.

True honor emanates from one source and that is the Creator. The closer we align ourselves with the source of dignity, the more we are transformed by it. Imam al-Hasan al-Mujtaba advises us, "If you seek honor without kinsmen or awe without power then take yourself away from the humiliation of disobeying God to the honor of obeying Him."[2]

Training our souls to be what God wants us to be will bring us honor, and through following His commands, we will avoid the lower actions that bring about disrespect, and by working to please the Creator, we will free ourselves from the need to lower ourselves in order to seek acceptance from the created; and finally, it goes without saying that He will grant His honor as a gift to His true servants.

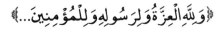

Honor belongs to God and His Apostle, and the faithful... (63:8)

In contrast, many people, particularly today, try to fulfill their need for social acceptance through their physical appearance. Especially in the West, we find an extreme emphasis on physique, youthful appearance, clothing, and material goods. The commercial tendency of society has conditioned a great number of people into believing that one's value lies in their appearance and possessions. Only if you purchase more will your life then improve. Unfortunately, this sort of thinking is a fallacy and a trap designed to exploit the vulnerable. However, while this trend has spun out of control today, it is nothing new as it was also rampant among the hypocrites who claimed Islam but secretly fought the Prophet.

---

[2] *Bihar al-Anwar*, Al-Allamah Al-Majlisi, v. 44, p. 138

﴿وَإِذَا رَأَيْتَهُمْ تُعْجِبُكَ أَجْسَامُهُمْ وَإِنْ يَقُولُوا تَسْمَعْ لِقَوْلِهِمْ كَأَنَّهُمْ خُشُبٌ مُّسَنَّدَةٌ...﴾

When you look at them, their exteriors please you; and when they speak, you listen to their words. They are as (worthless as hollow) pieces of timber propped up (unable to stand on their own). (63:4)

These hypocrites looked impressive. They had burgeoning muscles and intimidating physiques, but they devalued all of those gifts by using them to oppose the truth. Despite knowing that the moral character of the Prophet was flawless, still his enemies made it their life's mission to destroy his cause, and in doing so, they sank beneath the level of animals.

﴿لَهُمْ قُلُوبٌ لاَّ يَفْقَهُونَ بِهَا وَلَهُمْ أَعْيُنٌ لاَّ يُبْصِرُونَ بِهَا وَلَهُمْ آذَانٌ لاَّ يَسْمَعُونَ بِهَا أُوْلَـئِكَ كَالأَنْعَامِ بَلْ هُمْ أَضَلُّ أُوْلَـئِكَ هُمُ الْغَافِلُونَ﴾

...they have hearts with which they do not understand, they have eyes with which they do not see, they have ears with which they do not hear. They are like cattle; rather they are more astray. It is they who are the heedless. (7:179)

Animals do not think, reason, or believe like humans, they also do not fight the natural order of their existence; they live according to their nature. Those who opposed the Prophet not only neglected their natural faculties of reason, but they intentionally plotted against the progress of their own societies as well. They harbored in mindless, self-indulgence, thus denying their human potential - the potential that led the Prophet to declare, "A single believer is dearer to God than the Ka'bah."[3] Had people understood their true worth, they would have never fought against the Prophet.

---

[3] *Bihar al-Anwar*, Al-Allamah Al-Majlisi, v. 64, p. 71

The manner in which the opponents of the Prophet devalued themselves was similar to what was described by Sharif al-Radhi, the compiler of *Nahjul Balaghah* (*Peak of Eloquence*) in a discussion between himself and an atheist during the Abbasid era. The atheist was maintaining that severing the fingers of a thief encroached upon his human value. Sharif al-Radhi replied that the value of a human was in his soul and not in his hands. As long as a person used his hands for honest deeds, they were invaluable. However, once he used them to steal (out of greed, not need) then they became worthless - the soul was what gave them their value.

We can learn from such impostors that recognizing our own sense of honor is paramount to our human development. When we respect ourselves, we will consider it beneath our honor to do any wrong actions. When we lack self-respect then nothing can restrain us from committing immoral action.

Consider the state of the Muslim nation under the Umayyad rule.[4] Although, many people recognized the immoral position taken by the regime in opposing the grandson of the Prophet, Imam Husayn, still they yielded and allowed themselves to be bought for a paltry sum. They imagined the wealth and honor that the Umayyad rulers were promising them would bring them true honor. However, it was not so.

---

[4] The Umayyad dynasty (661-750) established a system of hereditary succession for the leader of the Muslim world. The Umayyads, headed by Abu Sufyan, were a largely merchant family of the Quraysh tribe. They had initially resisted Islam, not converting until the last few months of the Prophet's life. Umayyad rule was divided between two branches of the family: the Sufyanid (reigned 661–684), descendants of Abu Sufyan, and the Marwanid (reigned 684–750). The Sufyanids, notably Muawiyah (b. Abu Sufyan) (reigned 661–680) centralized his caliph authority in Damascus. Muawiyah administered the death of Imam Hasan, and his son Yazi also administered the death of Imam Husayn, which eventually led to the start and end of the Umayyad rule.

True honor lies with God; therefore, in rising up to oppose the grandson of the Prophet, they disgraced themselves for all of eternity.

We must recognize our own worth in order to prevent ourselves from being used or misguided. In addition, we also have to recognize our worth in order to worship God the way that He wants us to. A hadith says, "Whoever knows himself will then know his Lord."[5] True humility does not come from an abased servant who has failed in his pursuit of the illusions of this world; rather, it comes from an esteemed servant who knows his worth and is willing to submit himself to God. After all, we need to recognize our own worth before we can submit to God.

Many of our forms of worship are two-dimensional. If they are done for anyone other than God then they bring nothing but derision. However, if they are done solely for the pleasure of God then they earn praise, not only from the Creator but even from others. Prayer (*salat*) is a prime example of this. It is beneath human dignity to put our face on the ground for anyone except our Creator. If we were to prostrate ourselves for anyone other than to God, then we would find nothing but scorn within society. Yet we find peace when we put our face on the ground for God, and in turn, others respect that gesture as well. An act which in other situations would be considered as degrading is seen as honorable.

If our intentions are not genuine and sincere then our efforts will be futile. Take for example the people who murdered Imam Husayn. These were people who prayed but without sincerity. Umar b. Sa'd was the commanding officer of the armed forces of the Umayyad dynasty whose army murdered Imam Husayn and his close companions on the day of Ashura[6] (Muharram 10, 61 AH), they were an

---

[5] *Bihar al-Anwar*, Al-Allamah Al-Majlisi, v. 2, p. 32 and *Tafseer Al-Razi*, Al-Fakhr Al-Razi, v. 1, p. 91

[6] Ashura, being the 10th day of Muharram. It is recognized as "the day" in which the events and tragedy at Karbala occurred.

unfortunate example of the hadith that reads, "If someone prays and his prayers do not keep him away from evil or shameful deeds, then his prayers will only distance him from God."[7]

The men in the army were not intoxicated when they killed the grandson of the Prophet, they were people who prayed, but the lack of sincerity in their prayers was what damned them.

$$\text{﴿فَوَيْلٌ لِلْمُصَلِّينَ . الَّذِينَ هُمْ عَنْ صَلَاتِهِمْ سَاهُونَ ۞ الَّذِينَ هُمْ يُرَاءُونَ﴾}$$

Woe to them who pray, those who are heedless of their prayers, those who show off... (107:4-7)

Pilgrimage is similar. When a person makes the pilgrimage of Hajj they are stripped of all ordinary accruements and are subjected to difficult conditions. A person is wrapped in two small pieces of coarse cloth. They have to eat and sleep in the desert with millions of devotees. They are exposed and tried by the sheer volume of the crowd, all clustered and pressured to move together from one ritual act to the other. Under normal circumstances people would avoid such an experience. However, because it is for the sake of God, the faithful rush towards it. Rather than degrading them, and despite all of its difficulties, the Hajj uplifts people. Practitioners of other religions envy Muslims and wish that they had a similar practice themselves. The scenes of white-clad pilgrims worshipping in unison add to Islam's dignity in the human eyes.

It is hard to believe that only fifty years after the Prophet's death a select few were able to devalue the message of God and turn it into a game to be used for political gain. Imam Husayn rose up to change that - he was the human embodiment of dignity for humanity.

---

[7] *Bihar al-Anwar*, Al-Allamah Al-Majlisi, v. 79, p. 198 and *Kanzul Ummal*, Al-Muttaqi Al-Hindi v. 7, p. 525

The responsibility of Imam Husayn to preserve Islam is similar to the responsibility given to Amir al-Mumineen Imam Ali b. Abi Talib. In the final revelation, God completed Islam by saying, "Today, I have perfected your religion for you."[8] God would not have commanded the Prophet to deliver this verse had Imam Ali not been capable of carrying out that trust. Imam Husayn also bore the same responsibility. Without him, Islam would have become a worthless set of rituals.

Before leaving for his final journey, Imam Husayn made his intentions very clear. He declared that, "They have given me two options - fighting or humiliation; and I would never choose humiliation."[9] His honor lay in upholding the message of God, even if that meant being martyred. Therefore, he pronounced, "I see death as nothing but happiness and living under tyrants as nothing but affliction."[10] He knew that death would be more dignified than to live a life of humiliation because in death, the soul remains, but humiliation extinguishes both - a dignified life and it obliterates the soul after death.

Like Prophet Muhammad, Imam Husayn was a man of peace, however when circumstances forced him to take defense, he was the first to stand for what was right and sacrificed himself and his kinsmen in the process. He recognized that death was just a transition, an exodus from one state of being to another. He knew that suffering for the sake of God in this world would bring nothing but divine grace, whereas succumbing to worldly fears would lead to nothing but loss in this world and in the next.

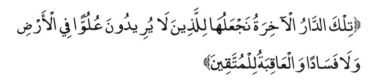

﴿تِلْكَ الدَّارُ الْآخِرَةُ نَجْعَلُهَا لِلَّذِينَ لَا يُرِيدُونَ عُلُوًّا فِي الْأَرْضِ وَلَا فَسَادًا وَالْعَاقِبَةُ لِلْمُتَّقِينَ﴾

---

[8] *Al-Qur'an*, 5:3
[9] *Bihar al-Anwar*, Al-Allamah Al-Majlisi, v. 45, p. 8
[10] *Bihar al-Anwar*, Al-Allamah Al-Majlisi, v. 45, p. 8

This is the abode of the Hereafter which We shall grant to those who do not desire to domineer in the earth nor to cause corruption, and the outcome will be in favor of the God-conscious. (28:83)

Unlike Umar b. Sa'd and the others, Imam Husayn was not blinded into thinking that the temporary gains of this world would give him honor. He stood on the principle of Prophet Muhammad in that true honor comes from sacrificing yourself for God; and this is what distinguished him from his enemies.

Imam Husayn gave his life for clear-cut reasons - to revive the Muslims and bring them back to their true religion. Even today, his sacrifice resurrects our souls, not by absolving us of sin, but by awakening us into reflection. That is why the followers of Imam Husayn hold dearly the first ten days of Muharram - they are the days of reflection and revolution, not just mourning.

Although crying can be one of the highest forms of the manifestation of human emotion, still some people criticize the lovers of Imam Husayn because of their excessive mourning for him. Tears are a natural reflection for any person when tragedy hits. Despite their infallibility, prophets and imams (the Twelve successors to the Prophet) were no exception to this rule, in fact, our tears pale in comparison to theirs. When the Prophet had to follow the funeral procession for his young son Abraham, he turned to one of the mountains in Madinah and said, "O mountain, if you had to bear my suffering, you would have shattered to pieces."[11] Despite the fact that his heart was filled with tranquility and the remembrance of God and a poignant awareness of His will, he was still human. Through the ways of the Prophet, we are assured that when there is a cause to mourn, it is a natural and accepted human concept.

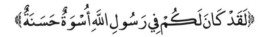

---

[11] *Mustadrak Al-Wasael*, Al-Mirza Al-Noori, v. 2, p. 386

In the Apostle of God there is certainly for you a beautiful pattern of conduct... (33:21)

At least three times in recorded history, it has been narrated that the Prophet wept for Imam Husayn. The first time was when he was born and the Prophet took the newborn from the midwife, Um al-Fadhl Bint al-Harith, kissed him and wept. Um al-Fadhl asked if anything was wrong with the baby to which he replied, "Nothing, he is perfect. However, a portion of my community will murder him and still hope for my intercession!"[12]

The collector of Prophetic sayings, al-Bukhari narrates from Abu Hurayrah that several years later Abu Hurayrah and some companions were walking through the alleyways of Madinah with the Prophet when they saw Husayn playing with a group of children. The Prophet went to catch him and Husayn playfully ran away. The Prophet left his companions and continued to chase Husayn. When he finally caught him, he kissed him and said crying, "Husayn is from me, and I am from Husayn. May God love whoever loves Husayn."[13] That was the second time he cried for Husayn though Husayn was still very young.

The third episode was narrated by Um Salamah, the wife of the Prophet and she reports that while the Prophet was lying on his deathbed:

> I opened the door and found Husayn sitting on his grandfather's chest. The Prophet was holding a piece of clay in his hand and weeping. When I entered, the Prophet turned to me and said, "Um Salamah, here is some soil from Karbala so keep it with you. I have just received it from Gabriel. He gave it to me and told me, 'Verily, this is your son that will be

---

[12] *Al-Irshad*, Sheikh Al-Mufeed, v. 2, p. 129
[13] *Musnad Ahmad*, Ahmad b. Hanbal, v. 4, p.172 and others

murdered.' Keep it in a bottle, and when you see it turn to blood, then you will know what has happened."[14]

Muslims are following the practice of the Noble Prophet when they mourn for Imam Husayn. They are also following the practice of the imams who used to invite poets to recite poetry to express their grief for the Imam. Once, a famous poet went to visit Imam Ali al-Ridha at his house and he narrated that:

> When I arrived there, I saw that the Imam appeared very saddened. He was flanked by his companions and disciples in a heartrending gathering. When I looked at the Imam questioningly, he said, "Do you not know what days these are? They are the days of mourning and sadness for us but of joy and happiness for our enemies. These are the days of Ashura and Muharram. Whoever cries or heartens others to mourn for Husayn will be fully rewarded by God. So I ask you to recite some poetry lamenting on my grandfather Imam Husayn."[15]

So he began to recite some of his famous Arabic poetry, which has survived until the present day.

May God allow us to be among those who follow the Sunnah of the Prophet and remember Imam Husayn. May we be given the opportunity to recall the sacrifices he made to preserve the integrity of the message of the Noble Prophet and the Islamic teachings.

---

[14] *Bihar al-Anwar*, Al-Allamah Al-Majlisi, v. 44, p. 247
[15] Ibid

The Tactics of Satan

Chapter 2

﴿أَلَمْ أَعْهَدْ إِلَيْكُمْ يَابَنِي آدَمَ أَنْ لاَ تَعْبُدُوا الشَّيْطَانَ إِنَّهُ لَكُمْ عَدُوٌّ مُبِينٌ. وَأَنِ اعْبُدُونِي هـٰذَا صِرَاطٌ مُسْتَقِيمٌ. وَلَقَدْ أَضَلَّ مِنْكُمْ جِبِلاًّ كَثِيراً أَفَلَمْ تَكُونُوا تَعْقِلُونَ﴾

Did I not exhort you, O children of Adam, saying, "Do not worship Satan. He is indeed your manifest enemy. Worship Me. That is a straight path? Certainly he has led astray many of your generations. Did you not use to apply reason?" (36:60-62)

GOD AFFIRMS THAT SATAN IS AN AVOWED ENEMY OF MANKIND AND EVEN worse, that his strategies are enigmatic - people cannot detect his assaults because they are very subtle. "Satan flows through the veins of the son of Adam like blood,"[16] the Prophet warned. Just as we do not feel the blood running through our veins, we also do not recognize Satan's presence in our souls until he has completed his work and impelled us to act on his evil desires. Therefore, it is imperative for us to become aware of his tactics in order to combat them.

It is worth asking, why did God create Satan in the first place if he is so evil? To begin with, we must understand that Satan was not created

---

[16] *Al-Kafi*, Sheikh Al-Kulayni, v. 8, p. 113

evil. Satan comes from the *jinn*[17] creation and he worshipped God in Heaven for many years. Through this devotion, Satan permeated into the ranks of the angels. However, when he was tried with the smallest test, he crumbled and plummeted to ignomiry.

$$﴿وَلَقَدْ خَلَقْنَاكُمْ ثُمَّ صَوَّرْنَاكُمْ ثُمَّ قُلْنَا لِلْمَلَائِكَةِ اسْجُدُوا لِآدَمَ فَسَجَدُوا إِلَّا إِبْلِيسَ لَمْ يَكُنْ مِّنَ السَّاجِدِينَ﴾$$

Certainly We created you, then We formed you, then We said to the angels, "Prostrate before Adam." So they [all] prostrated, except Iblis[18]: he was not among those who prostrated. (7:11)

In that fateful moment, Satan committed three irredeemable crimes - arrogance, envy, and rebellion. Interrelated, these three crimes became the mother of all evils on earth, beginning with the murder of Abel (by his own brother Cain), and these became the first tools that Satan used to carry out his promise to mislead humanity.

Had Satan not felt that he was superior to Adam, he would not have rebelled against God. Therefore, arrogance was the first - but not the last of his crimes.

$$﴿قَالَ فَاهْبِطْ مِنْهَا فَمَا يَكُونُ لَكَ أَن تَتَكَبَّرَ فِيهَا فَاخْرُجْ إِنَّكَ مِنَ الصَّاغِرِينَ﴾$$

"Get down from it!" God said. "It is not for you to be arrogant therein. Be gone! You are indeed among the degraded ones." (7:13)

Arrogance is deadly - in the heavens, on earth, and most importantly, inside us. The Prophet warned that, "Whoever has the smallest speck

---

[17] A smokeless flame creation made by God that has the ability of free-will; some *jinns* can be good or evil.

[18] Iblis is another name for Satan.

of arrogance in his heart will never enter Paradise."[19] No one can calculate the misery caused by those who consider their race or culture superior, such a view has produced untold suffering and injustice. Racism continues to be a pernicious evil globally, and even in the most advanced and prosperous countries, they have yet to root out the scourge of racism from their societies.

On another front, the Prophet has been quoted to have said that, "Pride causes depression."[20] Although pride may seem initially exhilarating but it is really a delusion. No one truly enjoys being proud because people that are full of pride are usually alone and isolated. A proud person cannot appreciate others and it blinds them of self-reflection and recognition of error. It is a destructive weapon wielded by Satan.

Out of arrogance came Satan's second offense which was envy. Since he thought that he was superior, he could not accept to see the angels bow to someone else (other than him) and jealousy consumed him until he rebelled against God. A tradition from the Prophet says, "Envy eats up your good deeds the same way that fire burns wood,"[21] and in another Prophetic saying we are told, "Envy is the worst disease."[22]

Left unchecked, envy can destroy a person. Therefore, we need to learn from Satan's example and guard ourselves against it; but if we cannot, then at least we have to guard ourselves from acting upon it. We have to control envy and not allow it to control us until we can purge it from our hearts, otherwise arrogance and envy will lead to Satan's third sin - rebellion against God.

Interestingly, God does not just say that Satan "did not bow" but adds that "he refused to be of those who bow down."[23] There is a

---

[19] *Bihar al-Anwar*, Al-Allamah Al-Majlisi, v. 78, p. 186

[20] *Amalee Al-Sadooq*, Sheikh Al-Sadooq, v. 1, p. 395

[21] *Al-Kafi*, v. 8, p. 45

[22] *Ghurar Al-Hikam*, Al-Amidi, hadith 1378

[23] *Al-Qur'an*, 7:11

tremendous lesson for us to learn by this statement. From time to time we may commit a sin by procrastinating in regards to our religious duties, such as the prayers or fasting, but far worse would be if we adamantly refuse or despise to do the prayers, for this mirrors Satan's rebellious act against God. God does not want us to rebel against Him, and ultimately if we rebel against God we are in essence rebelling against our own selves.

Not only are the acts of neglect and rebellion against God a sin but to mock those who obey God is also a serious sin. This was something which was seen evident during the time of Prophet Muhammad when the Muslims began to practice their faith, and this is still evident in today's time.

For example, one can see the same dynamics with hijab (Muslim women attire). There are many Muslim women who do not wear hijab but acknowledge that they should and ask God for courage to do so. However, there are some Muslim women, even men, who know that hijab is an act of faith but they not only refuse to practice it, but they also despise it, and even worse, they resent others who practice it.

A young Muslim woman once came to the mosque and told me that she decided to embrace the hijab. I congratulated her and she went home. Sometime later, she came back to the mosque in tears. Her mother had refused to let her inside the house until she removed her hijab. The mother said that hijab represented backwardness and narrow-mindedness. The action of this mother is an example of a person who not only refuses God's orders but also ridicules others for following it, and the chastisement for such deeds is severe, as it is much worse than simply lacking the strength or inclination to wear hijab - it is the act of trying to prevent someone else from following the obligations laid down by God.

That was Satan's problem. Not only did he not want to bow, but he also did not want to be part of those who bow down to God. Although he had worshipped God for a long period, his faith was not secure because he betrayed the foremost ordination of faith which was submission to the Creator, thus he became the most despicable creature in existence.

In contrast, true faith comes when we submit unconditionally to the decree of God. It does not come from just praying, fasting, or occasional acts of charity. It comes when we dedicate our entire life to God, as Prophet Abraham said:

﴿قُلْ إِنَّ صَلَاتِي وَنُسُكِي وَمَحْيَايَ وَمَمَاتِي لِلَّهِ رَبِّ الْعَالَمِينَ﴾

Say, "Indeed my prayer and my worship, my life and my death are for the sake of God, the Lord of all the worlds." (6:162)

Prophet Abraham dedicated his entire life to God, not one hour a day, not eight hours a day, but 24 hours a day. Therefore, everything we do: working, eating, sleeping, and communicating needs to be dedicated to God and only then can we reach the level of true faith.

In fact, even our own emotions need to be for the sake of God alone. Although Satan, filled with arrogance and envy, failed that test miserably, we have the capacity to do better and implement the teaching of the Prophet which says that, "True faith rests on loving and hating for the sake of God."[24] We need to love those whom God loves and hate those whom God hates. Therefore, not only our actions, but even our emotions need to be for Him.

Clearly, no one has the right to argue with God. We are reminded of this point when He commanded the growing Muslim community during the Prophet's time by saying:

---

[24] *Al-Kafi*, v. 2, p. 125

﴿فَلاَ وَرَبِّكَ لاَ يُؤْمِنُونَ حَتَّى يُحَكِّمُوكَ فِيمَا شَجَرَ بَيْنَهُمْ ثُمَّ لاَ
يَجِدُوا فِي أَنفُسِهِمْ حَرَجًا مِّمَّا قَضَيْتَ وَيُسَلِّمُوا تَسْلِيمًا﴾

But no, by your Lord! They will not believe until they make you a judge in their disputes, then do not find within their hearts any dissent to your verdict and submit in full submission. (4:65)

By extension, it is also not proper to argue with the authentic Sunnah of the Prophet. Of course, we can question why certain religious injunctions are the way they are, but we cannot offer our own interpretation.

Both Sunni and Shia Muslims maintain that they are following the Prophet; one through the Companions, and the other through the Ahlul-Bayt (family of the Prophet). Although, the perception of some schools of thought have maligned the Shia as "innovators," when in fact they contend that it is the absolute submission to the Qur'an and Prophet that characterizes the Shia school of thought. Case in point, other traditions, in the process of legislation, permit *istihsan*, which is legislating something because it is pleasing to some. This form of legislation permitted "reforms" to religious injunctions made by some of the caliphs after the Prophet Muhammad. Cases of human reasoning against divine injunction exemplifies human tendency to put their preferences over God. Satan convinces some people that they know better than what the Prophet knew. Thus devotees, have to avoid incorporating into religion what they favor, otherwise they will be following their own religion and not God's. Nevertheless, some people, particularly today, succumb to this temptation presented by Satan and pick and choose what they like of the religion of God.

A select few people are truly fortunate as they have reached the level where Satan can no longer influence them.

﴿إِنَّ عِبَادِي لَيْسَ لَكَ عَلَيْهِمْ سُلْطَانٌ إِلَّا مَنِ اتَّبَعَكَ مِنَ الْغَاوِينَ﴾

Indeed, as for My servants you do not have any authority over them, except the perverse who follow you. (15:42)

However, Satan approaches the rest of us in a very clear manner.

﴿وَاسْتَفْزِزْ مَنِ اسْتَطَعْتَ مِنْهُمْ بِصَوْتِكَ وَأَجْلِبْ عَلَيْهِمْ بِخَيْلِكَ وَرَجِلِكَ وَشَارِكْهُمْ فِي الْأَمْوَالِ وَالْأَوْلَادِ وَعِدْهُمْ وَمَا يَعِدُهُمُ الشَّيْطَانُ إِلَّا غُرُورًا﴾

"Instigate whomever of them you can with your voice; and rally against them your cavalry and your infantry, and share with them in wealth and children, and make promises to them!" But Satan promises them nothing but delusion. (17:64)

This verse outlines his four primary methods of attack: his voice, his cavalry, wealth and children, and his false promises.

Satan speaks to all of us and some of us heed to his call. In addition to his ordinary whispers, commentators ascribe two more meanings to the phrase "Satan's voice" and they are music (songs) and seductive speech.

God, in the Our'an purports to the prohibition of music (songs) that are immorally enticing, provocative, or aimless by using the phrases "avoiding false speech (*qawl al-zur*)" and "avoiding vain talk (*laghw*)":

﴿وَالَّذِينَ لَا يَشْهَدُونَ الزُّورَ وَإِذَا مَرُّوا بِاللَّغْوِ مَرُّوا كِرَامًا﴾

Those who witness no falsehood (zur), and if they pass by futility, they pass by it with honorable (avoidance). (25:72)

﴿وَالَّذِينَ هُمْ عَنِ اللَّغْوِ مُعْرِضُونَ﴾

[The believers are those] who avoid vain talk (laghw). (23:3)

Some scholars today exempt certain types of music from these verses, but maintain that any music (song) which alludes to immoral, indecent, or violent thoughts would be considered as "vain talk." Many music, especially today are futile, they do not carry a social or positive message, instead they mainly propagate unrealistic romantic fantasies, and even more, many popular lyrics are full of vulgarity and indecency. Some people would never think of saying such words in their day to day talk, but they have no problem listening to them in a song. When you listen to musical lyrics, the brain is lulled into blindly absorbing them. They become a part of you, whether you like it or not; and without you even realizing it, they impose on the sanctity of your heart and mind.

If unconsciously your heart becomes filled with something impure, it may interfere with your ability to remember God. As a person of faith, it is a daily struggle to be in a state of purity, thus vigilance is needed. Try not to be naïve by thinking that negative music will not have an effect on you. I once heard someone say, "I can't get that song out of my head. I keep singing it all day long!" You may think nothing of it when you are listening to a certain song but when it comes time to focus, your mind will be elsewhere and you may not be able to concentrate, especially when the time comes to stand before God and offer Him your sincere prayers. As human beings, we do not have a switch to turn these influences on and off at will.

Therefore, in order to mend yourself, you need to try to remember God (not only during prayers) all the time, and one should try to avoid distractions because the sanctity of the heart cannot be restored in a matter of seconds. If you really need to listen to something, then listen to the words of your Creator, which is the Noble Qur'an. It brings peace to the soul and leads you towards what is right, and instead of harming your spirit, it will bring you inner peace and a spiritual cure.

It is clear how Satan uses songs to reach out to people, and along with that, commentators also ascribe the "seductive tone of people" to the phrase "voice of Satan."

$$ ﴿ فَلاَ تَخْضَعْنَ بِالْقَوْلِ فَيَطْمَعَ الَّذِي فِي قَلْبِهِ مَرَضٌ وَقُلْنَ قَوْلاً مَعْرُوفًا﴾ $$

...do not be complaisant in your speech, lest he in whose heart is a sickness should aspire, and speak honorable words. (33:32)

Some people may not realize how their voices are being heard by others, and therefore one should not be too forthcoming with strangers. Even with your co-workers or classmates you should maintain a level of proper conversational demeanor (*qawlan ma'rufa*). Try not to be too complaisant in your speech or else the one who has ill intentions might act upon them. Bypass speaking freely about sensitive or private issues to others with whom you do not share a close affinity with, and even if they are close friends of the opposite gender, do not enter into matters of intimacy.

Nowadays, this aspect of Satan's work has been facilitated by the Internet and mobiles, especially through social network sites. People think Internet chatting, texting or Tweeting is purely innocent without recognizing of the possible dangers lurking. How often does a father assume that his son is doing his homework in his bedroom, but instead he is chatting with the wrong people? Satan can work just as easily online and via mobiles as he can in person.

After warning us about Satan's voice, God warns us about his infantry. When referring to "Satan's infantry," Muslim commentators give this phrase several meanings. One is violence or an unjust use of force, whether it is military might or domestic violence, it is a tool of Satan. It solves nothing and only breeds more violence.

Lastly, the Prophet said, "A woman who displays herself immodestly is a soldier of Satan."[25] Contrary to the Western ideology, a woman's body is not a show to display openly. It is a gift that should be honored, respected, and protected. What does a woman accomplish by showing herself off? Are women really adding dignity to themselves or benefiting society when they are immodestly dressed? There are some women who do not care and say that it is a man's responsibility not to stare at them, and of course this is true, but to some extent.

We should keep in mind that the Prophet said, "Cast down your eyes, and you will see wonders."[26] From this saying, we understand that God has granted those who cast down their gaze the ability to see mysteries that others cannot imagine. Men and women have a great responsibility to protect themselves and the health of society at large.

Many times, we do not realize the ramifications of Satan's enticements. How often does he entice us to do something destructive while dangling the illusion of benefit in front of our eyes? We do not realize that his promises are false until it is too late because he is superb in his last tactic of "false promises," as mentioned in verse 17:64.

A classic example of Satan's deceit is the Bani Umayyad dynasty. Tens of thousands of Umayyad soldiers rode out against the grandson of the Prophet, Imam Husayn on the plains of Karbala. The soldiers used to pray - in fact, on the day of Ashura they performed their prayers! Still, Satan misled them with false promises of richness, and even convinced some of them that they were murdering Imam Husayn for the sake of God. After the massacre, one of the soldiers was seen clutching the black drape of the Ka'bah and imploring, "O God, forgive me!" The soldiers of the Bani Umayyad were Muslims, but they had been possessed by Satan and his false promises. Before their martyrdom, Imam Husayn explained to his son Ali al-Akbar what had happened to

---

[25] See translation (*tafseer*) of Qur'an, 17:64
[26] *Bihar al-Anwar*, Al-Allamah Al-Majlisi, v. 101, p. 41

the soldiers on the opposing side, "Satan encircled and engulfed these people until they forgot the remembrance of God."[27]

Since over a thousand years have elapsed since Imam Husyan was murdered, some people question as to why we continue to shed tears for him. They say, would we not honor his memory better simply by holding only lectures? Most definitely, the lectures do provide a way to spread the knowledge of Islam and awareness of what happened to him; however, the memorial sessions allow us to rediscover and keep alive who he was and what he sacrificed. Thus, when we cry, we share our pain with him and the other members of the Ahlul-Bayt. Crying is an expression of human empathy; and when we cry, we feel what they felt and relive their sufferings. By crying, we demonstrate and build our solidarity with the Holy Household.

In order to understand a fraction of what the Prophet and the Ahlul-Bayt endured, we have to try and put ourselves in their position. If you are not affected by their sacrifice then it might be hard to fully understand what it means to be a follower of Islam. Demonstrating our loyalty towards Ahlul-Bayt by mourning is invaluable and the rewards for it are inconceivable.

There is nothing wrong with one expressing their grief; the prophets of God expressed their grief by crying. We see it in the story of Prophet Jacob when he lost his son Joseph. For years, Prophet Jacob cried of the separation from his son even though he had 11 other sons.

﴿وَتَوَلَّى عَنْهُمْ وَقَالَ يَا أَسَفَى عَلَى يُوسُفَ وَابْيَضَّتْ عَيْنَاهُ مِنَ الْحُزْنِ فَهُوَ كَظِيمٌ . قَالُوا تَاللَّهِ تَفْتَأُ تَذْكُرُ يُوسُفَ حَتَّى تَكُونَ حَرَضًا أَوْ تَكُونَ مِنَ الْهَالِكِينَ﴾

---

[27] *Maqatil of Imam Al-Husayn*

And he turned away from them and said, "Alas for Joseph!" His eyes had turned white with grief, and he choked with suppressed agony. They said, "By God! You will go on remembering Joseph until you wreck your health or perish." (12:84-85)

From the story of Joseph and other such Qur'anic narratives we see that it was in the nature of the prophets to express their love and connection to God thru tears.

$$\text{أُوْلَـٰٓئِكَ ٱلَّذِينَ أَنْعَمَ ٱللَّهُ عَلَيْهِم مِّنَ ٱلنَّبِيِّينَ مِن ذُرِّيَّةِ ءَادَمَ وَمِمَّنْ}$$

$$\text{حَمَلْنَا مَعَ نُوحٍ وَمِن ذُرِّيَّةِ إِبْرَاهِيمَ وَإِسْرَاءِيلَ وَمِمَّنْ هَدَيْنَا}$$

$$\text{وَٱجْتَبَيْنَآ إِذَا تُتْلَىٰ عَلَيْهِمْ ءَايَاتُ ٱلرَّحْمَـٰنِ خَرُّوا۟ سُجَّدًا وَبُكِيًّا}$$

They are the ones whom God has blessed from among the prophets of Adam's progeny, and from [the progeny of] those We carried with Noah, and from among the progeny of Abraham and Israil, and from among those We guided and chose. When the signs of the All-Beneficent were recited to them, they would fall down weeping in prostration. (19:58)

The prophets also conveyed their love for Imam Husayn by crying. The first to ever cry over the tragedy of Imam Husayn was the Prophet Muhammad. Imam Ali b. Husayn Zain al-Abideen narrates that the Prophet cried for Husayn several times, when Husayn was born and lastly before the Prophet left this world.

Many prominent historians narrate that the companions were sitting in the Mosque of the Prophet when the Prophet entered with tears in his eyes. They asked him, "O Prophet of God, what happened?" The Prophet replied, "Gabriel was with me a few moments ago and told me how I will lose my son."[28] This event happened 50 years before the martyrdom of Imam Husayn!

---

[28] *Kanzul Ummal*, v. 7, p. 106 and other sources

The Ahlul-Bayt also mourned for him and we are told in the books of history that for 35 years, Imam Ali b. Husayn Zain al-Abideen cried continuously. When he ate, tears would mix with his food. One day, one of his disciples, Abu Hamzah (Thabit b. Dinar) was sympathizing with him and asked, "O son of the Messenger of God, why don't you stop crying? It has been a long time. Remember that your family is reputed to being murdered. Your family has been honored with martyrdom."

"May God reward you," the Imam replied. "My father and grandfather and all the imams from my descendants will be murdered. But whenever I look at my aunts and sisters, I remember them on the afternoon of Ashura running from tent to tent as the enemies shouted, 'Burn the tents of the oppressors!'"

The Prophet Muhammad has been quoted as saying, "Lengthy mourning is not recommended, except for Imam Husayn."[29] When God takes one of our loved ones, we must be content within ourselves with His decree. Of course, it is natural to cry, but our mourning should not go on excessively, for a hadith says, "Whoever is not pleased with My decree and is not patient with My trials should find another Lord other than Me."[30] However, the Prophet made one exception - Imam Husayn. He will continue to be remembered until the end of time, for in the words of the Prophet, "A special love for Husayn is rooted in the hearts of the believers." In addition he said, "In the hearts of the believers, the heat of sorrow and pain over the martyrdom of Imam Husayn will never be diminished." These are the words of the Prophet. These feelings are eternal, and the remembrance of Imam Husayn will continue forever.

---

[29] *Al-Fusool Al-Muhimmah*, Al-Amili, v. 3, p. 257
[30] *Al-Jami' Al-Sagheer*, Al-Suyooti, v. 2, p. 235

Death and Dying

Chapter 3

﴿وَجَاءَتْ سَكْرَةُ الْمَوْتِ بِالْحَقِّ ذٰلِكَ مَا كُنْتَ مِنْهُ تَحِيدُ. وَنُفِخَ فِي الصُّورِ ذَلِكَ يَوْمُ الْوَعِيدِ. وَجَاءَتْ كُلُّ نَفْسٍ مَعَهَا سَائِقٌ وَشَهِيدٌ. لَقَدْ كُنْتَ فِي غَفْلَةٍ مِنْ هٰذَا فَكَشَفْنَا عَنْكَ غِطَاءَكَ فَبَصَرُكَ الْيَوْمَ حَدِيدٌ﴾

Then the agony of death brings the truth: "This is what you used to shun!"
Then the Trumpet will be blown: "This is the promised day." Then every soul
will come accompanied by a driver and a witness: "You were certainly
oblivious of this. We have removed your veil from you, and so your sight is
acute today." (50:19-22)

LIFE MAY SEEM PERMANENT, BUT WE WERE NOT CREATED TO REMAIN
here. The Qur'an tells us, "Everything shall perish except for the face of
God," (28:88) and "Every soul shall taste death." (29:57) Young or old,
we will all face the reality of death.

﴿وَمَا هٰذِهِ الْحَيَاةُ الدُّنْيَا إِلَّا لَهْوٌ وَلَعِبٌ وَإِنَّ الدَّارَ الْآخِرَةَ لَهِيَ الْحَيَوَانُ لَوْ كَانُوا يَعْلَمُونَ﴾

The life of this world is nothing but diversion and play, but the abode of the
Hereafter is indeed Life, had they known! (29:64)

We were not created to live in this world, but rather to be transformed to the Hereafter. The worldly life is finite; even the universe is limited. Every day, millions of people arrive and millions of others depart from this world. We are trapped here and our only route out is the one that God has prescribed which is the separation of the soul from our body. Although unnerving, we must undergo that journey, for without it, we will never reach our final destination.

Our worldly life only forms a fraction of our total existence. Before we came into this world, we lived in the spiritual world.

﴿وَإِذْ أَخَذَ رَبُّكَ مِن بَنِي آدَمَ مِن ظُهُورِهِمْ ذُرِّيَّتَهُمْ وَأَشْهَدَهُمْ عَلَى أَنفُسِهِمْ أَلَسْتُ بِرَبِّكُمْ قَالُوا بَلَى شَهِدْنَا أَن تَقُولُوا يَوْمَ الْقِيَامَةِ إِنَّا كُنَّا عَنْ هَذَا غَافِلِينَ﴾

When your Lord took from the Children of Adam, from their loins, their descendants and made them bear witness over themselves, [He said to them,] "Am I not your Lord?" They said, "Yes indeed! We bear witness." [This] lest you should say on the Day of Resurrection, "Indeed we were unaware of this."
(7:172)

Although we did not have physical bodies, our souls made a covenant with God. Then, He sent us to be physically born, and this is where we are now. We live in this world, then we will die, and our souls will be sent to the "in-between world" called *alam al-Barzakh*, and finally, we will face Him and reach our ultimate home.

﴿كَيْفَ تَكْفُرُونَ بِاللَّهِ وَكُنتُمْ أَمْوَاتًا فَأَحْيَاكُمْ ثُمَّ يُمِيتُكُمْ ثُمَّ يُحْيِيكُمْ ثُمَّ إِلَيْهِ تُرْجَعُونَ﴾

How can you be unfaithful to God, [seeing that] you were lifeless and He gave you life, then He will make you die, and then He shall bring you to life, and then you will be brought back to Him? (2:28)

The Prophet said that in this life people are asleep, and once we die, we will wake up. Life after death will be a completely new experience. It is told by the Prophet that the dead hear so clearly that the tapping of footwear on the graves reaches their ears. For this reason, after the Battle of Badr the Prophet walked among the dead ones of Quraysh, looking at them and calling out to them by name, "O Utbah! O Shaybah! O Waleed!" Curious, one of his disciples asked him if he was talking to the dead. He replied, "By God, your hearing is not more powerful than theirs. If God had permitted them, they would have answered as well."[31]

If only death was the end of our journey; and if death was nothing but annihilation, then we would have no reason to fear the grave. However, we fear the grave because we are uneasy of what is to come. In *Dua Abu Hamzah al-Thumali*, narrated by Imam Zain al-Abideen, we read, "I cry over the removal of my soul. I cry over the tightness of my grave. I cry over the interrogation of the grave." What we may face in the grave is real, and since every person will succumb to death, we should prepare ourselves for it. It is written in *Nahjul Balaghah* that Imam Ali cautioned:

> If you could experience what those who died before you are experiencing now, you would be shocked and confused. You would listen and obey God's commands much more. However, it is hidden from you; but soon, the curtain will be lifted from you.

At the moment of death, the first thing that we will experience is *sakrat al-mawt* which is known as the "intoxication of death."

---

[31] *Al-Ghadir*, Al-Amini, v. 10, p. 42

﴿وَجَاءَتْ سَكْرَةُ ٱلْمَوْتِ بِٱلْحَقِّ ذَٰلِكَ مَا كُنتَ مِنْهُ تَحِيدُ﴾

Then the agony of death brings the truth: "This is what you used to shun!"
(50:19)

Shock may paralyze some of us as we behold the Angel of Death. Our
bodies will no longer be able to respond to our commands but we will
continue to sense what happens around us. We may try to cry out for
help but to no avail; our tongues will no longer move. We will be fully
conscious as our soul is taken out from our body. We will be in pain
and unable to express it. We will be completely incapacitated. This
could be the distressful moment of our existence, according to Imam
Zain al-Abideen. The Prophet said:

> If you could hear what the deceased were saying (to the
> person washing the dead body then), you would never agree to
> wash their bodies again because as they are being washed,
> they are pleading, "O the one who is washing my body, be kind
> to me, for by God, as I was dying, whenever my soul would
> leave one of my limbs, it felt as if that limb was being
> amputated. So, please I cannot bear any more pain; have mercy
> on me!"

Everyone will experience that moment, even the believers. A hadith *al-
Qudsi* (God's saying) reads:

> If I decide to forgive a guilty person and admit him to Paradise,
> then I need to purify him in his (or her) lifetime. So sometimes,
> I test him with health and sometimes with poverty; sometimes
> with the loss of a friend or relative. If he averts these, then I
> test him at the time of death and make it as such that when he
> dies, he dies pure and immaculate. Then, I can forgive him and
> admit him into Paradise.

A man, whose brother was in such a situation, dying a slow, agonizing death, came to Imam al-Sadiq to plead for help. His brother had been near death for three days and was in severe pain, but his soul was still clinging to his body. He was unable to pass beyond the extraction of the soul at the larynx, so Imam al-Sadiq advised him to move his brother to his prayer mat in the same place that he used to offer his prayers, and to recite *Surah Ya Seen* and *Surah al-Saaffaat* next to him. By doing this, it would alleviate his pain and ease the process of death.

Through all of this fright shines a huge ray of hope. Prophet Muhammad promised, "Whoever's last words are *la ilaha illa Allah* (there is no god except the (one true) God) enters Paradise."[32] Of course, these words need to be the full embodiment of one's practice and life, and not just mere words. However, some cannot even utter these last words no matter how hard they try. Therefore, we should remind a dying person about God's mercy, blessings, and forgiveness as to ease the agony and fear of death by reciting the *talqeen*,[33] the dictation before death, part of which is a reminder for us as well, in which the dying person is but a forerunner and we shall soon follow the same journey. Right before the burial, we need to recite a second *talqeen* to assist the dead person with the questioning by the two angels.

Some of you may be thinking that you are too young to worry about death, but death knows no age. Walk through any cemetery and you will see the graves of many young people who died in their teens. The Angel of Death does not discriminate against age. When our time comes, we need to be ready, even at a tender age.

It is said that once the Angel of Death transformed himself into a human being in order to visit Prophet Solomon in Jerusalem. Prophet Solomon had a man over as a guest at the time in his home. The Angel of Death instantly recognized the man because he was scheduled to

---

[32] *Al-Amalee*, Sheikh Al-Sadooq, p. 634
[33] Full *talqeen* can be found in the index

take the man's soul the following day - but in India. After the angel left, the man became startled and sensed who he was. The man pleaded with Prophet Solomon to use his power to help him escape from there. Since God had subjugated the wind to Prophet Solomon, he felt obliged to aide him and sent the man to a far away land. The next day, when the Angel of Death returned, Prophet Solomon asked him what had happened. "O Prophet of God," the Angel of Death replied, "I was scheduled to take that man's soul today but in India. When I saw him with you in Jerusalem, I was shocked because he was supposed to be in India!" Even though the man was attempting to flee from death he met up with his fate in India as decreed by God.

﴿أَيْنَمَا تَكُونُواْ يُدْرِككُّمُ الْمَوْتُ وَلَوْ كُنتُمْ فِي بُرُوجٍ مُّشَيَّدَةٍ﴾

Wherever you may be, death shall overtake you, even if you were in fortified towers. (4:78)

However, if you are prepared, you would not fear your last moments. "Whoever loves God will love to meet God,"[34] the Prophet said. If you truly love God, He will give you a glimpse of your place in Paradise, and despite the anxiety of death, He will shower you with much mercy at the time of death that you will be eager to leave this world.

﴿يَا أَيَّتُهَا النَّفْسُ الْمُطْمَئِنَّةُ ۞ ارْجِعِي إِلَى رَبِّكِ رَاضِيَةً مَّرْضِيَّةً ۞ فَادْخُلِي فِي عِبَادِي ۞ وَادْخُلِي جَنَّتِي﴾

"O soul at peace! Return to your Lord, pleased, pleasing! Then enter among My servants! And enter My Paradise!" (89:27-30)

---

[34] *Al-Kafi*, v.3 p. 134

There are a select few people whose level of spirituality is greatly distinguished that await for death, because they understand it as a transitional stage from this lower world to the permanent abode. Ali b. Abi Talib once said, "I don't care whether death comes to me or I go to death; I welcome it. I am yearning for death (meeting my Lord) more than a baby yearns for its mother's breast."[35]

Imam Husayn expressed the same thought. In Mecca, he proclaimed, "Death has been decreed for the son of Adam. It encircles him the same way that a necklace encircles a woman's neck. I long to see my forefathers the same way Jacob longed to see his beloved son, Joseph."[36] He was waiting to be reunited with the Messenger of God and the rest of his family. God offered him martyrdom and he yearned to the calling of his Lord will full submission.

---

[35] *Majma'ul Bahrain*, Sheikh Al-Torayhi, v. 4 p. 238
[36] *Bihar al-Anwar*, Al-Allamah Al-Majlisi, v. 44 p. 366

Challenges for Muslims in the West
Chapter 4

﴿نَحْنُ نَقُصُّ عَلَيْكَ نَبَأَهُمْ بِالْحَقِّ إِنَّهُمْ فِتْيَةٌ آمَنُوا بِرَبِّهِمْ وَزِدْنَاهُمْ هُدًى. وَرَبَطْنَا عَلَى قُلُوبِهِمْ إِذْ قَامُوا فَقَالُوا رَبُّنَا رَبُّ السَّمَاوَاتِ وَالْأَرْضِ لَنْ نَدْعُوَ مِنْ دُونِهِ إِلَـٰهًا لَقَدْ قُلْنَا إِذًا شَطَطًا﴾

We relate to you their account in truth. They were indeed youths who had faith in their Lord, and We had enhanced them in guidance, and fortified their hearts when they stood up and said, "Our Lord is the Lord of the heavens and the earth. We will never invoke any god besides Him, for then we shall certainly have said an atrocious lie." (18:13-14)

MAINTAINING OUR MUSLIM FAITH AND IDENTITY IN THE WEST IS A constant challenge for us. The invitation to prohibited acts summons us from every direction, and if we try to live a morally upright life, then we usually end up becoming a minority within a minority. Although upholding the tenets of any religion within a secular society is difficult, Muslims face the additional challenge of living not only in a non-Islamic society, but one which is continuously becoming more and more secular.

Unfortunately, some Muslims succumb to the pressures around them and eliminate all outward aspects of their religion. A woman stops wearing hijab; a man stops praying; another person begins to drink alcohol, and so on. Therefore, Muslims need to continuously guard themselves to prevent this loss of faith. Our spiritual survival depends upon preserving our Islamic values in the face of challenges.

One of the greatest challenges for the Muslims in the West is social integration, such that it does not compromise our Muslim identity.

Without a doubt, it is normal to want to make friends with classmates, co-workers and neighbors, even if they do not share the same belief system. Nonetheless, some may try to argue that Islam does not permit the befriending of non-Muslims and some even extend this to include Christians and Jews. They cite the following verse to support their argument:

﴿يَاأَيُّهَا الَّذِينَ آمَنُوا لَا تَتَّخِذُوا الْيَهُودَ وَالنَّصَارَى أَوْلِيَاءَ بَعْضُهُمْ أَوْلِيَاءُ بَعْضٍ وَمَنْ يَتَوَلَّهُمْ مِنْكُمْ فَإِنَّهُ مِنْهُمْ إِنَّ اللَّهَ لَا يَهْدِي الْقَوْمَ الظَّالِمِينَ﴾

O you who have faith! Do not take the Jews and the Christians for friends: they are friends of each other. Any of you who take them as friends is indeed one of them. Indeed God does not guide the wrongdoing folk. (5:51)

When reading this verse out of context it may seem that God is instructing the Muslims not to befriend the Jews and Christians, however if we carefully study the contextual and historical aspect of this verse, we see that this is not the case at all. In this verse, God is directly speaking to the Muslims living in Madinah during the time of the Prophet not to associate with some of the Jews and Christians that were fighting against them (the Prophet and the Muslim community).

When it comes to causing strife, God even instructs us to avoid our parents and children if they oppose our faith.

﴿يَٰٓأَيُّهَا ٱلَّذِينَ ءَامَنُوٓاْ لَا تَتَّخِذُوٓاْ ءَابَآءَكُمْ وَإِخْوَٰنَكُمْ أَوْلِيَآءَ إِنِ ٱسْتَحَبُّواْ ٱلْكُفْرَ عَلَى ٱلْإِيمَٰنِ وَمَن يَتَوَلَّهُم مِّنكُمْ فَأُوْلَٰٓئِكَ هُمُ ٱلظَّٰلِمُونَ﴾

O you who have faith! Do not befriend your fathers and brothers if they prefer faithlessness to faith. Those of you who befriend them - it is they who are the wrongdoers. (9:23)

Similarly we read in the Bible, in Matthew 10:35-36, "For I am come to set a man at variance against his father, and the daughter against her mother, and the daughter-in-law against her mother-in-law. A man's foes shall be they of his own household."

Clearly, Islam (under normal circumstances) encourages interfaith relations.

﴿لَّا يَنْهَىٰكُمُ ٱللَّهُ عَنِ ٱلَّذِينَ لَمْ يُقَٰتِلُوكُمْ فِى ٱلدِّينِ وَلَمْ يُخْرِجُوكُم مِّن دِيَٰرِكُمْ أَن تَبَرُّوهُمْ وَتُقْسِطُوٓاْ إِلَيْهِمْ إِنَّ ٱللَّهَ يُحِبُّ ٱلْمُقْسِطِينَ﴾

God does not forbid you in regard to those who did not make war against you on account of religion and did not expel you from your homes that you deal with them with kindness and justice. Indeed God loves the just. (60:8)

As long as people are not fighting against you - either physically or ideologically - you can befriend them. However, if they taunt you for wearing hijab or mock you for praying, then they are not your true friends. Surely, true friends will try and share their traditions and culture with you, but will not try to manipulate or impose their beliefs upon you - true friends will respect you for who you are.

Unfortunately, during our life journey, we may encounter some people whose mission is to convert others. They seek friendship merely to win you to their side, and in fact, some evangelical groups systematically target Muslims and even invite their children to camps to persuade them to leave their religious beliefs - such people must be avoided at all cost! They may seem friendly, however time and experience has shown that they do not have your best interest at heart.

Incidentally, these cautions hold just as true for some Muslim friends. Regardless of what religion our friends profess, first and foremost, we need to ensure that they exert a moral influence upon us.

Both modern psychologists and religious sources confirm a fundamental principle which states that friends have an influence on you - an influence which is sometimes more profound than that which our families can exert upon us. Imam Ali has said, "A person follows the religion of his friend, so be aware of who you befriend."[37]

We understand that negative peer-pressure is a dangerous threat at any age, and indeed even the most intelligent and independent person cannot help but become influenced by others. The acceptance of such forms of peer-pressure is actually a part of human nature; therefore, we must be extremely selective in choosing our friends - do not choose friends randomly. On this quest for seeking out good friends, one should look for those who exhibit positive social and moral traits and avoid all of the others.

﴿وَاصْبِرْ نَفْسَكَ مَعَ الَّذِينَ يَدْعُونَ رَبَّهُمْ بِالْغَدَاةِ وَالْعَشِيِّ يُرِيدُونَ وَجْهَهُ وَلاَ تَعْدُ عَيْنَاكَ عَنْهُمْ تُرِيدُ زِينَةَ الْحَيَاةِ الدُّنْيَا وَلاَ تُطِعْ مَنْ أَغْفَلْنَا قَلْبَهُ عَنْ ذِكْرِنَا وَاتَّبَعَ هَوَاهُ وَكَانَ أَمْرُهُ فُرُطًا﴾

Content yourself with the company of those who supplicate their Lord morning and evening, desiring His Face, and do not lose sight of them, desiring

---

[37] *Al-Kafi*, v. 2 p. 375

*the glitter of the life of this world. And do not obey him whose heart We have
made oblivious to Our remembrance, and who follows his own desires, and
whose conduct is [mere] profligacy. (18:28)*

Someone who is heedless of God's remembrance; someone who follows
his or her own lower desires; and someone who is immoral is indeed a
dangerous friend. These characteristics will rub off on us and thus we
must follow the advice of the Qur'an and avoid becoming friends with
people who display such traits.

The qualities which a potential friend possesses are so critical that
Prophet Muhammad was once asked for advice on whom to befriend
and he replied, "Do not sit with the dead." When he was asked who
"the dead" were, he replied, "Every wealthy person who lives
extravagantly without concern for others."[38] Such people are lost and
are wasting their lives, and the more time that one spends with such
people, the more dangerous it can become for that person and they may
end up destroying their life as well. Instead, we need to seek out
friends who understand what is important in life, since the short life of
this temporal world is full of challenges, we must spend our time with
people who can help us create a positive perspective.

The brief enjoyments of this life are fast fleeing and that is why the
Prophet advised, "Save pleasure for Paradise and sleep for the grave."
Islamic sources constantly advises us to avoid people who seek only to
enjoy the "false things" of life, and that we need to spend our time with
those who understand the deeper meanings of our existence.

﴿وَمَا هَـٰذِهِ الْحَيَاةُ الدُّنْيَا إِلَّا لَهْوٌ وَلَعِبٌ وَإِنَّ الدَّارَ الْآخِرَةَ لَهِيَ
الْحَيَوَانُ لَوْ كَانُوا يَعْلَمُونَ﴾

*The life of this world is nothing but diversion and play, but the abode of the
Hereafter is indeed Life, had they known! (29:64)*

---

[38] *Al-Khisal*, Sheikh Al-Sadooq p. 228

Beyond mere friendship, there are some Muslims that want to marry outside the faith of Islam. You must remember that any differences - educational, cultural, and most importantly, religion could become a tremendous source of marital conflict. Such differences may remain dormant in the first few years after marriage, however once children arrive, such ideological differences are bound to surface. The father will want to take his children to the mosque while the mother wants to take them to a different house of worship. The father wants his daughter to be chaste, but the mother may think that she should be allowed to date. The children themselves will not know what to think and "who to be" and will consider themselves part-Muslim and part-non-Muslim. There is no such thing as "half" a belief. One must either believe that Muhammad was a prophet or not; and that either Jesus is God or not - there can be no compromise on such beliefs.

Many times, children who grow up in such households are forced to assimilate into two contradictory ideas because they think and are taught that both parents "are right." Therefore, we need to realize that children must be our primary concern in life as they are our most important responsibility and the ones who will carry forth our legacy.

We also need to remember that we need to take care of ourselves spiritually. Developing our spirituality is a lifelong challenge even in the best of circumstances, and even more so when we live in a non-Islamic society. Thus, if we come home to a non-Muslim spouse, then we seriously run the risk of limiting our religion and its influence on our lives.

﴿وَلاَ تَنكِحُوا الْمُشْرِكَاتِ حَتَّى يُؤْمِنَّ وَلَأَمَةٌ مُؤْمِنَةٌ خَيْرٌ مِنْ مُشْرِكَةٍ وَلَوْ أَعْجَبَتْكُمْ وَلاَ تُنكِحُوا الْمُشْرِكِينَ حَتَّى يُؤْمِنُوا وَلَعَبْدٌ مُؤْمِنٌ خَيْرٌ مِنْ مُشْرِكٍ وَلَوْ أَعْجَبَكُمْ أُوْلَئِكَ

يَدْعُونَ إِلَى النَّارِ ۖ وَاللَّهُ يَدْعُو إِلَى الْجَنَّةِ وَالْمَغْفِرَةِ بِإِذْنِهِ ۖ وَيُبَيِّنُ
آيَاتِهِ لِلنَّاسِ لَعَلَّهُمْ يَتَذَكَّرُونَ ﴾

Do not marry idolatresses until they embrace faith. A faithful slave girl is better than an idolatress, though she should impress you. And do not marry [your daughters] to idolaters until they embrace faith. A faithful slave is better than an idolater, though he should impress you. Those invite [others] to the Fire, but God invites to Paradise and pardon, by His will, and He clarifies His signs for the people so that they may take admonition. (2:221)

A believing partner will invite his or her spouse to God and help them lead a peaceful life, and the exact opposite would happen if a person marries a disbelieving partner. If we cannot avoid being influenced by our friends (whom we see for a few hours every day at school, at work, or in a social environment), then certainly we cannot avoid being influenced by our spouse (whom we are around on a regular basis). Therefore, trying to maintain our belief in such a marriage will become a constant battle, especially if one's spouse does not respect Islam. Eventually one partner will end up giving up their belief system altogether.

The issue of compatibility in marriage is something that must be taken seriously (even Muslim marriages). It is vital for a believer to marry someone who gives the same amount of importance to religion that you do. Sometimes the husband is practicing but his wife is not or vice versa; the wife wants to wear hijab but her husband refuses; sometimes the wife wants to attend a humanitarian function but her husband wants her home to serve him. Sometimes, one spouse is a follower of one school of thought while the other is of another, and in this specific situation, there may not be broadmindedness for the other belief system. In such circumstances, differences may increase hence we should try to weed out the sources of potential conflict before the marriage - not during it. That is why it is critical to examine the level of compatibility during the time of spouse selection. This provides a much better chance of having a harmonious marriage which in turn will lead to having stable children and a loving home as well.

Nowadays, religion is given little importance in society. For some, religion has become a once a week activity. A non-Muslim preacher once visited our Islamic center and made the following observation, "You Muslims may have small centers while we have large ones; however your work seems more fruitful than ours. Spirituality is absent in our centers, people come merely for amusement."

Many people who live in the West do not have time for spirituality because they are either too busy in the pursuit of money or preoccupy their time with trivial entertainment, and interestingly enough this is actually one of the reasons why more and more people are coming into the faith of Islam. Many reverts to Islam say they felt empty inside; they had attained the "American dream" - a good job and "everything" that comes with it - a house, car and other material possessions, however they still felt as if something was missing. When they came into the fold of Islam and became a Muslim, that void was filled by an encompassing remembrance of God.

﴿الَّذِينَ آمَنُوا وَتَطْمَئِنُّ قُلُوبُهُم بِذِكْرِ اللهِ أَلَا بِذِكْرِ اللهِ تَطْمَئِنُّ الْقُلُوبُ﴾

Those who have faith, and whose hearts find rest in the remembrance of God. Look! The hearts find rest in God's remembrance! (13:28)

﴿يَا أَيُّهَا النَّاسُ أَنتُمُ الْفُقَرَاءُ إِلَى اللهِ وَاللهُ هُوَ الْغَنِيُّ الْحَمِيدُ﴾

O mankind! You are the ones who stand in need of God, and God - He is the All-Sufficient, the All-Laudable. (35:15)

Without a doubt, spirituality is essential for everyone - whether one recognizes its importance or not. Modernity lures us into the danger of thinking that we do not need God; when we have a beautiful home, a huge savings account, and an abundance of friends and family - why do we need God in our lives? Why do we need prophets and imams in our lives when we live in "modernity" and can study contemporary psychology or philosophy at the universities?

The answer is that we need them because no matter how advanced or "modern" our world may seem, we must remember that its very existence is tenuous - we are clinging to a rapidly spinning, fragile world. Eventually, one day this world will come to an end, in fact, it would only take one single natural disaster to render all of our technology and knowledge useless. Therefore, as human beings, we need God in our lives in order to progress and advance forward. That is not to say that science and technology are not valuable, rather on the contrary they are, however they cannot help us through our spiritual difficulties. We need the guidance of God to help us through difficult times and to show us how He wants us to grow, for surely we were meant to live with God and if we expel Him from our lives, then we will never find true and everlasting happiness.

It is said that one day, Prophet Jesus and his disciples passed by a leper who had become blind and paralyzed. His people had abandoned him, and he had no food or shelter. When Prophet Jesus asked him how he was, he replied that he was doing well and that was because his heart and tongue had never ceased to remember God. Prophet Jesus told his disciples that this was true faith.

Therefore, it does not matter how much money you have, or the size of your house, or your zip code address, rather what matters is the size of your heart. A hadith *al-Qudsi* reads, "My heavens and My earth cannot contain Me, but the heart of My believing servant can (hold Me)."[39] Therefore, when you have God in your heart, you have everything.

---

[39] *Bihar al-Anwar*, Al-Allamah Al-Majlisi, v. 70 p. 60

"O God! One who did not recognize You achieved nothing! But one who recognizes You has achieved everything,"[40] Imam Husayn recited these words on the day of Arafat (the 9th of the Islamic month of Dhul Hijjah). These powerful words carry a message for us even today - over 1,300 years after he uttered them! We must not be deceived by material goods, for in all honesty, if success was measured in riches then all of the prophets sent by God would have been utter failures.

Just look at one of the greatest messengers of God, Prophet Moses and what he did when he was hungry. Rather than indulging in lavish dinners and various types of food, he merely gathered food from the brush. His success had nothing to do with wealth, what he ate, how he dressed, or the grandeur of his home - it simply came from a deep faith and conviction in God.

As Muslims in the West, we need to be proud of our faith and must not feel that we need to hide our belief. People will respect us more for praying or wearing hijab and hold sacred our ways. Nonetheless, there will always be some ignorant people who will mock us, however they are small in number and weak in hearts. I was at the airport one time traveling to another region when the time for the prayer set in. I went and performed my prayers, and after finishing them, an American man came up to me and complimented me on my courage to pray in public after the incident of 9/11.

We really do not have to worry about what others think, as long as God appreciates us, we will be prosperous. According to a tradition, once God falls in love with us, He will then ask the angels to fall in love with us; and once the angels fall in love with us, He will then ask the devout people on earth to love us as well. Regardless of where we live, either in the East or the West, we should continue to strive to maintain who we are and what we believe in and sooner or later, we will see the blooming fields of Islam.

---

[40] *Du'a Arafah*, Imam Husayn

The Ideal Approach to God
Chapter 5

Featured Themes:
Who are the Ahlul-Bayt; Verse 33:33; The Event of Mubahilah; The Cloak;
Ghadir Khum; Traditions concerning the Ahlul-Bayt

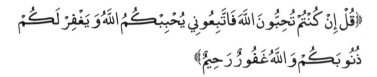

﴿قُلْ إِنْ كُنْتُمْ تُحِبُّونَ اللَّهَ فَاتَّبِعُونِي يُحْبِبْكُمُ اللَّهُ وَيَغْفِرْ لَكُمْ
ذُنُوبَكُمْ وَاللَّهُ غَفُورٌ رَحِيمٌ﴾

Say, "If you love God, then follow me; God will love you and forgive you your
sins, and God is All-Forgiving, All-Merciful." (3:31)

ONE OF THE PRIME CRITERION IN LOVING SOMEONE IS TO HONOR AND
respect their wishes, for when we truly love someone, we go to great
lengths to prove our devotion to them. Therefore, obedience is actually
an affirmation of love and honor. Without the emotion of love, we may
not be affected or stirred to do much in life and it is these two issues
which God has intertwined in His Book when He says to us that if we
love God then we follow whatever He has commanded us to do.
Furthermore, if we love God we should also be ready to love the
Prophet; if we love the Prophet, then we would show this love by
following him, and by following the Prophet, not only do we express
our love to him, but we are in turn loving and obeying God as well.
Therefore, we need to instill the love of and following of the Prophet in
our own hearts and in the hearts of our children, just as the Prophet
has been quoted as saying, "No one can attain true faith until I am more

beloved to him than his own soul, his parents, his children, and all of mankind."[41]

However, our responsibility does not end at that because the Noble Prophet has also told us that, "Love God and love me because you love God. Love my family because you love me."[42] We need to love the Prophet's family (the Ahlul-Bayt) with the same intensity that we love him and this is something which God tells the Prophet in the Qur'an to instruct the people to do, "No reward do I ask from you for this except the love of those near of my kin."[43] It is also for this reason that the Prophet has advised, "Train your children in three things: recitation of the Qur'an, love for your Prophet, and love for his family."[44] These three traits: love for God, love for the Prophet, and love for the Ahlul-Bayt form the essence of true Islam and are inseparable from one another.

Nevertheless, a question arises that if the Ahlul-Bayt are so important, then why are they not mentioned in the Qur'an by name? In fact, many verses were revealed about them, however we must understand the context of revelation of each of these verses in order to comprehend which verses they are. For instance, God addressed the Ahlul-Bayt specifically in this verse:

$$\text{﴿إِنَّمَا يُرِيدُ اللَّهُ لِيُذْهِبَ عَنْكُمُ الرِّجْسَ أَهْلَ الْبَيْتِ وَيُطَهِّرَكُمْ تَطْهِيرًا﴾}$$

Indeed God desires to repel all impurity from you, O People of the Household (Ahlul-Bayt), and purify you with a thorough purification. (33:33)

The importance of this verse cannot be underestimated, for surely God here is declaring that all of the members of the Ahlul-Bayt (who are a

---

[41] *Al-Amalee*, p. 414
[42] *Bihar al-Anwar*, Al-Allamah Al-Majlisi, v. 27 p. 105
[43] *Al-Qur'an*, 42:23
[44] *Kanzul Ummal*, hadith 45410

specific group) are immune from all forms of imperfection. Therefore, it is vital to discover *who* God is referring to as the Ahlul-Bayt.

Some people believe that the Ahlul-Bayt refers to the wives of the Prophet and cite the beginning of the verse as proof; however, this view falls apart when we look at the wording of the verse in Arabic. Initially in the verse God speaks to the wives of the Prophet, He addresses them in the feminine plural, however later in the verse when He addresses the Ahlul-Bayt, He speaks to them in the masculine plural. Therefore, He is not speaking to the wives of the Prophet anymore.

In addition, it has been mentioned by numerous scholars that this verse, which describes the Ahlul-Bayt as being "purified," cannot refer to the wives of the Prophet because the actions of some of them were not in line with the spirit of this verse and being "*tahir*" (pure of all acts of abomination), since we know that some wives of the Prophet conducted themselves in such a way that God Himself reprimanded and rebuked them. For example, in *Surah al-Tahreem*, God revealed to the Prophet:

$$﴿يَاأَيُّهَا النَّبِيُّ لِمَ تُحَرِّمُ مَا أَحَلَّ اللَّهُ لَكَ تَبْتَغِي مَرْضَاةَ أَزْوَاجِكَ وَاللَّهُ غَفُورٌ رَحِيمٌ﴾$$

O Prophet! Why do you prohibit [yourself] from what God has made lawful for you, seeking to please your wives? And God is All-Forgiving, All-Merciful. (66:1)

$$﴿عَسَى رَبُّهُ إِنْ طَلَّقَكُنَّ أَنْ يُبْدِلَهُ أَزْوَاجًا خَيْرًا مِنْكُنَّ مُسْلِمَاتٍ مُؤْمِنَاتٍ قَانِتَاتٍ تَائِبَاتٍ عَابِدَاتٍ سَائِحَاتٍ ثَيِّبَاتٍ وَأَبْكَارًا﴾$$

It may be that if he (the Prophet) divorces you, his Lord will give him in [your] place wives better than you: [such as are] muslim, faithful, obedient, penitent, devout and given to fasting, virgins and non-virgins. (66:5)

Al-Bukhari, in his collection of traditions from Prophet Muhammad, writes that Abdullah b. Abbas, one of the most prominent companions of the Prophet, asked Umar b. al-Khattab which wives did this verse refer to and he replied that it referred to Hafsa and Aishah.[45]

More notably, there is a tradition which tells us who the Prophet meant by the Ahlul-Bayt and many books of hadith, including *Sahih al-Bukhari* and *Sahih al-Muslim*, as well as various books of *tafseer*, such as those written by al-Razi and al-Zamakhshari relate a hadith known as the "Hadith of the Cloak."

According to this lengthy tradition, one day the Prophet gathered with Ali, Fatima, Hasan, and Husayn underneath a cloak in one of the rooms of the house belonging to his wife, Um Salamah. At that point in time, Gabriel came bearing this verse:

$$﴿إِنَّمَا يُرِيدُ اللَّهُ لِيُذْهِبَ عَنكُمُ الرِّجْسَ أَهْلَ الْبَيْتِ وَيُطَهِّرَكُمْ تَطْهِيرًا﴾$$

Indeed God desires to repel all impurity from you, O People of the Household (Ahlul-Bayt), and purify you with a thorough purification. (33:33)

The Prophet then related the revelation, prayed for these members of his family and declared, "O Lord, these are my Ahlul-Bayt." Hearing this Um Salamah asked the Prophet if she could be part of the Ahlul-Bayt too, but the Prophet politely refused by saying, "You too are (on the path of) good."[46] From this event we understand that it was the will of God, and that the Ahlul-Bayt are limited to only these five individually - namely the Prophet, Ali, Fatima, Hasan and Husayn.

---

[45] *Sahih al-Bukhari*, "Book on the Interpretation of the Qur'an," hadith 4531; *Sahih al-Muslim*, "Book on Divorce," hadith 2694
[46] *Al-Amalee*, Sheikh Al-Toosi, p. 525

In order to emphasize who the Ahlul-Bayt are and who this verse was in reference to, for nearly six months after its revelation, the Prophet would stop outside the house of Ali and Fatima, which was adjacent to his own house and the mosque and greet them every morning as the "Ahlul-Bayt" and he did so to reaffirm that his Ahlul-Bayt were these specific individuals and no one else.

Another event known as *Mubahilah* also clarified who falls under the category of the Ahlul-Bayt.

Although the Prophet had several wives and daughters, when he was commanded to take his sons and women to meet with the Christian monks of Najran (a region in the southern Arabian Peninsula), he only took Ali, Fatima, Hasan, and Husayn.

﴿فَمَنْ حَاجَّكَ فِيهِ مِنْ بَعْدِ مَا جَاءَكَ مِنَ الْعِلْمِ فَقُلْ تَعَالَوْا نَدْعُ أَبْنَاءَنَا وَأَبْنَاءَكُمْ وَنِسَاءَنَا وَنِسَاءَكُمْ وَأَنْفُسَنَا وَأَنْفُسَكُمْ ثُمَّ نَبْتَهِلْ فَنَجْعَلْ لَعْنَةَ اللَّهِ عَلَى الْكَاذِبِينَ﴾

Should anyone argue with you concerning him (referring to Prophet Jesus), after the knowledge that has come to you, say, "Come! Let us call our sons and your sons, our women and your women, our souls and your souls, then let us pray earnestly and call down God's curse upon the liars." (3:61)

Through a careful review of the books of *tafseer*, one will notice that the Qur'an *does* mention who the Ahlul-Bayt are.

In addition to revealing who the Ahlul-Bayt are, the Qur'an also praises them in several instances.

God revealed an entire chapter of the Qur'an for the occasion when Ali, Fatima, Hasan, and Husayn vowed to fast for three days out of gratitude to God. Each night, they prepared to break their fast when unexpectedly a needy person came to their door seeking assistance. On the first night, an indigent man came; the second night, an orphan; and the third night, a freed non-Muslim captive arrived at the doorstep. The members of the household (Ali, Fatima, Hasan and Husayn and their servant Fiddah) voluntarily gave all of their food away to those in need on all three nights - even Hasan and Husayn who were young children remained hungry for three days until the Prophet came and found the entire family extremely weak from hunger.

﴿يُوفُونَ بِالنَّذْرِ وَيَخَافُونَ يَوْمًا كَانَ شَرُّهُ مُسْتَطِيرًا ۞ وَيُطْعِمُونَ الطَّعَامَ عَلَى حُبِّهِ مِسْكِينًا وَيَتِيمًا وَأَسِيرًا ۞ إِنَّمَا نُطْعِمُكُمْ لِوَجْهِ اللهِ لَا نُرِيدُ مِنكُمْ جَزَاءً وَلَا شُكُورًا ۞ إِنَّا نَخَافُ مِن رَّبِّنَا يَوْمًا عَبُوسًا قَمْطَرِيرًا ۞ فَوَقَاهُمُ اللهُ شَرَّ ذَلِكَ الْيَوْمِ وَلَقَّاهُمْ نَضْرَةً وَسُرُورًا﴾

They fulfill their vows and fear a day whose ill will be widespread. They give food, for the love of Him, to the needy, the orphan and the prisoner, [saying,] "We feed you only for the sake of God. We do not want any reward from you, nor any thanks. Indeed we fear from our Lord a day, frowning and fateful." So God saved them from the ills of that day, and granted them freshness and joy. (76:7-11)

Most pivotally, the Qur'an also refers to the position of the Ahlul-Bayt as His successors to the Prophet.

﴿إِنَّمَا وَلِيُّكُمُ اللهُ وَرَسُولُهُ وَالَّذِينَ آمَنُوا الَّذِينَ يُقِيمُونَ الصَّلَاةَ وَيُؤْتُونَ الزَّكَاةَ وَهُمْ رَاكِعُونَ﴾

Your guardian (wali) is only God, His Apostle, and the faithful ones who maintain the prayer and give the zakat (alms-giving) while bowing down. (5:55)

There is some disagreement amongst the schools of thought about this verse 5:55, in particular to the word "*wali*" and its meaning. "*Wali*" in this context does not mean "friend," (as one of the multiple meanings that this word carries); but rather, it means "guardian." Both Sunni and Shia commentators agree that this verse refers directly to Ali b. Abi Talib who gave away his ring to a beggar while in the state of *ruku* during his prayer. However, in order to gloss over this verse, some Muslims confine the meaning of "*wali*" in this verse to "friend," and maintain that God revealed this verse just to tell us who our friends are, however for the Shia understanding, this verse is an explicit affirmation of Imam Ali's guardianship of the Muslim nation after the Prophet.

The role of Ali b. Abi Talib in being assigned as his successor and in guarding the message of Islam was extremely crucial that God Himself ordered the Prophet to convey to the masses, on a grand scale, that Ali would be his successor; in fact, God told the Prophet that if he did not inform the people, then the entire twenty-three years of revelation and the message of the religion of Islam would have been a waste.

$$﴿يَا أَيُّهَا الرَّسُولُ بَلِّغْ مَا أُنزِلَ إِلَيْكَ مِن رَّبِّكَ وَإِن لَّمْ تَفْعَلْ فَمَا بَلَّغْتَ رِسَالَتَهُ وَاللَّهُ يَعْصِمُكَ مِنَ النَّاسِ إِنَّ اللَّهَ لاَ يَهْدِي الْقَوْمَ الْكَافِرِينَ﴾$$

O Apostle! Communicate that which has been sent down to you from your Lord, and if you do not, then you will not have communicated His message, and God shall protect you from the people. Indeed God does not guide the faithless people. (5:67)

Although reluctant, since the Prophet knew that a few powerful figures around him would not approve, the Prophet heeded the command of God at a major event known as Ghadir Khum (which took place after Hajj, at a crossroad in the desert were the Muslims from various nations would separate from one another to make their way home), in front of thousands of Muslims, he irrevocably declared Ali as his successor. Only after Ali b. Abi Talib was appointed as the successor of the Prophet (at this final major event in the history of Islam) did God then perfect and prefer the message of Islam.

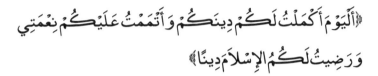

Today I have perfected your religion for you, and I have completed My blessing upon you, and I have approved Islam as your religion. (5:3)

It is vital for us to be aware of the importance of the Ahlul-Bayt and what their role is in the preservation and protection of Islam. The Prophet of Islam has said, "By the One who holds my soul in His hands, on the Day of Resurrection, no servant of God will be able to step forward without being asked about four things: 1. How did you spend your life; 2. How did you care for and utilize your body; 3. How did you accumulate and spend your wealth?" the last of which is, "love and loyalty to us, the Ahlul-Bayt."[47] Therefore, we will be questioned about them and we must prepare ourselves in this life to answer God in this regards.

Within the various verses of the Qur'an, God has given us the information we require to recognize and understand the significance of the Ahlul-Bayt. Nevertheless, some people refuse to accept these verses because they do not explicitly contain the names of who the Ahlul-Bayt are; however, we state with certainty that God did not need to mention their names because the job of explaining the Qur'an and elaborating on its finer points was the responsibility of the Noble Prophet.

---

[47] *Al-Amalee*, Sheikh Al-Toosi, p. 93

On more than one occasion the Prophet not only mentioned who his Ahlul-Bayt were, but he even named the twelve successors after him, described their characteristics, and this is a fact which both Sunni and Shia sources attest to.

The book of God is a book of principles, not explicit details: God tells us to pray, but He does not tell us how to pray; God tells us to pay charity, but He does not tell us how much to give; God tells us to follow the Prophet's successors, but He does not mention their names. He left these tasks to the Prophet to explain to us in detail. God tells the Prophet that He has given him the Book and it is his duty to teach it, thus He wanted us to recognize the magnitude of the Sunnah and commanded us to unconditionally follow the orders of the Prophet.

﴿وَمَا آتَاكُمُ الرَّسُولُ فَخُذُوهُ وَمَا نَهَاكُمْ عَنْهُ فَانْتَهُوا وَاتَّقُوا اللَّهَ إِنَّ اللَّهَ شَدِيدُ الْعِقَابِ﴾

Take whatever the Apostle gives you, and relinquish whatever he forbids you, and be wary of God. Indeed God is severe in retribution. (59:7)

God also wants us to understand that the Qur'an has a deeper meaning above the apparent reading of the verses.

﴿هُوَ الَّذِي أَنْزَلَ عَلَيْكَ الْكِتَابَ مِنْهُ آيَاتٌ مُحْكَمَاتٌ هُنَّ أُمُّ الْكِتَابِ وَأُخَرُ مُتَشَابِهَاتٌ فَأَمَّا الَّذِينَ فِي قُلُوبِهِمْ زَيْغٌ فَيَتَّبِعُونَ مَا تَشَابَهَ مِنْهُ ابْتِغَاءَ الْفِتْنَةِ وَابْتِغَاءَ تَأْوِيلِهِ وَمَا يَعْلَمُ تَأْوِيلَهُ إِلَّا اللَّهُ وَالرَّاسِخُونَ فِي الْعِلْمِ يَقُولُونَ آمَنَّا بِهِ كُلٌّ مِنْ عِنْدِ رَبِّنَا وَمَا يَذَّكَّرُ إِلَّا أُولُو الْأَلْبَابِ﴾

> *It is He who has sent down to you the Book. Parts of it are definitive verses, which are the mother of the Book; while others are metaphorical. As for those in whose hearts is deviance, they pursue what is metaphorical in it, courting temptation and courting its interpretation. But no one knows its interpretation except God and those firmly grounded in knowledge; they say, "We believe in it; all of it is from our Lord." And none take admonition (from it) except those who possess intellect. (3:7)*

Those who are "grounded with knowledge" and "understand the allegorical (*mutashabihat*) verses" are only the Ahlul-Bayt.

Like the Qur'an, the authentic Sunnah is perfect - everything that the Prophet said came from God and as the Word of God clearly states, the Prophet never erred.

$$\text{﴿وَمَا يَنْطِقُ عَنِ الْهَوَى. إِنْ هُوَ إِلَّا وَحْيٌ يُوحَى﴾}$$

Nor does he speak out of [his own] desire: it is just a revelation that is revealed [to him]. (53:3-4)

The books of history narrate that the Prophet had a companion who used to take notes of everything that he said, until one day someone told that companion to stop writing everything down because the Prophet was human and could make a mistake like anyone else. The Prophet replied that everything he said was the truth and instructed the man to continue writing his words.

Unfortunately throughout history, some people tried to suppress the Sunnah of the Prophet because they feared that it impinged on their hegemony. In particular, many of those who took over the caliphate tried to silence and remove the traditions about the merits of the Ahlul-Bayt, since they knew that such words from the Prophet threatened their power base. It is for this reason that the traditions of the Prophet went unwritten for over one hundred years after his death.[48] Historical records show that the reason why the first and second caliph prohibited the writing of the hadith was so that people would not get confused between the words of the Qur'an and the sayings of the Prophet. However, this is an elementary excuse because the people at that time were quite familiar with the esteemed style of the Qur'an, since they were experts in the science of poetry, and they were aware of the fact that the Qur'an had surpassed all poetic lines.

Even though the Prophet had commanded people to transcribe his sayings, the insight for recording the hadith amongst a specific sect of Muslims surfaced during the reign of Umar b. Abd al-Aziz. By that time, some hadiths had already been corrupted. In particular, two pivotal hadiths that were related to the Ahlul-Bayt were altered: "I am leaving behind two weighty things: the Qur'an and my Ahlul-Bayt,"[49] and "There will be twelve successors after me, and all of them will be from Bani Hashim." [50]In the first narration, "Ahlul-Bayt" was changed to "Sunnah." The reason for this alteration was clear because the ruling parties wanted to diminish the emphasis and role of the Ahlul-Bayt within society. In the second tradition, "Bani Hashim" was changed to "Quraysh." This too is clear since the people in political authority were not from the Bani Hashim and they wanted to maintain their legitimacy to rule.

If some individuals were brazen enough to alter the hadith, then they may even have attempted to tamper with the Qur'an as well, just like other previous Divinely-revealed books were altered, and thus had the Qur'an named the Ahlul-Bayt explicitly, some people may have tried to replace those names with the names of others. God did not will for His final revelation to be altered, and thus in order to protect its sanctity,

---

[48] Except for the followers of the Ahlul-Bayt, they never ceased recording the narrations of the Prophet.

[49] *Musnad Ahmad*, v. 3 p. 14

[50] *Musnad Ahmad*, v. 5 p. 92

He only referred to the Ahlul-Bayt by indication, and in this way He preserved the integrity of His message for the rest of history.

$$﴿إِنَّا نَحْنُ نَزَّلْنَا الذِّكْرَ وَ إِنَّا لَهُ لَحَافِظُونَ﴾$$

Indeed We have sent down the Reminder, and indeed We will preserve it (from corruption). (15:9)

Although the Qur'an does not name the Ahlul-Bayt directly, their contribution to Islam is unmatched, and their role is paramount in our lives. Therefore, we need to love and respect them the way the Prophet wanted us to, and the best way to do that is to follow the guidance which they have left behind.

$$﴿قُل لاَّ أَسْأَلُكُمْ عَلَيْهِ أَجْرًا إِلاَّ الْمَوَدَّةَ فِي الْقُرْبَى﴾$$

Say (O Muhammad), "I do not ask from you any reward for it (the 23 years of struggling to bring the religion of Islam) except the affection (love) for [my] relatives." (42:23)

Repentance: Turning Back to God

Chapter 6

﴿وَالَّذِينَ إِذَا فَعَلُوا فَاحِشَةً أَوْ ظَلَمُوا أَنْفُسَهُمْ ذَكَرُوا اللَّهَ
فَاسْتَغْفَرُوا لِذُنُوبِهِمْ وَمَنْ يَغْفِرُ الذُّنُوبَ إِلَّا اللَّهُ وَلَمْ يُصِرُّوا عَلَى
مَا فَعَلُوا وَهُمْ يَعْلَمُونَ﴾

And those who, when they commit an indecent act or wrong themselves,
remember God, and plead [God's] forgiveness for their sins - and who forgives
sins except God? - and who do not persist in what they have committed while
they know. (3:135)

EVERY DAY IS A NEW DAY TO TURN BACK TO GOD - NO MATTER WHAT WE
have done, God's mercy and forgiveness are always present. Even if we
are confident of our good deeds, we should still call upon God for His
forgiveness because no one could ensure direct entrance into Paradise.
Even our Prophet prayed, hence we too should pray to God to deal
with us through His grace, rather than His justice.

All of the prophets (despite the fact that they were all sinless)
constantly pleaded for God's forgiveness. Even the final Prophet
Muhammad used to stand at night and cry to his Lord until God
revealed to him:

﴿لِيَغْفِرَ لَكَ اللَّهُ مَا تَقَدَّمَ مِنْ ذَنْبِكَ وَمَا تَأَخَّرَ وَيُتِمَّ نِعْمَتَهُ عَلَيْكَ وَيَهْدِيَكَ صِرَاطًا مُسْتَقِيمًا﴾

That God may forgive you what is past of your sin and what is to come, and that He may perfect His blessings upon you, and guide you on a straight path. (48:2)

Prophet Muhammad engaged in such prayers and shed tears despite the fact that he was free of sin. Indeed, we can learn how to seek forgiveness by following his example. Ali b. Abi Talib has also given us many exquisite prayers, such as *Dua Kumayl* and *Dua Al-Sabah* to show us how to approach God.

When we study the lives of the prophets and the imams, we see that they continuously emphasized the importance of repentance because they understood how vital it is for us to repair our relationship with God.

﴿وَتُوبُوا إِلَى اللَّهِ جَمِيعًا أَيُّهَا الْمُؤْمِنُونَ لَعَلَّكُمْ تُفْلِحُونَ﴾

Turn to God in repentance all of you O faithful believers, so that you may be felicitous. (24:31)

Sometimes we forget how fortunate we are to live under the care of such a forgiving Lord. If our Lord was vengeful and full of anger, then we would have surely perished a long time ago. God tells us in a hadith *al-Qudsi* that He anxiously waits for wrongdoers to feel remorse and turn back to Him, and when they do repent, He then rejoices more than that person who was stranded in the middle of a desert, in the dark of the night who finally finds his companions after being all alone!

﴿إِنَّ اللَّهَ يُحِبُّ التَّوَّابِينَ وَيُحِبُّ الْمُتَطَهِّرِينَ﴾

Indeed God loves the penitent ones and He loves those who keep clean. (2:222)

Today, some religions teach that in order for a person to repent, one has to confess his sins to another human being; meaning that you have to share your guilt with a mere mortal and then only can you be forgiven of your sins. Other ideologies teach that simply believing in Jesus will save you - and one can enter Paradise just because you acknowledge him as your savior. However, Islam teaches otherwise, if we commit a sin, we should not tell anyone about it - not our spouse, parents, friends or even a religious scholar because God wants *us* to protect our own honor. We must keep in mind that one day, our closest friends may betray us, however God Almighty will never deceive His servants, and He wants to keep our secrets to ourselves and between us and Him alone. The only time we are permitted to mention our sin is in the case of a criminal offense, otherwise we should only share what we did with God and no one else. An example of this in our present world can be witnessed by a mother who covers up her child's weaknesses and faults in the presence of others, so as to not disgrace her child, but we believe that God will cover the sins of the believers even more so through His love and never-ending mercy.

However, we must realize that our repentance from sins must be quick because when we commit sins, it distances us away from God and since we cannot afford to remain away from Him, we must make amends immediately after sinning, otherwise this separation from God will cause us spiritual sufferings. Being cut off from God is much worse than being imprisoned in this world, for if we lose our connection with Him, then we will have nothing left.

Although we need to work very hard to avoid sinning and committing any acts against the laws of God, no matter how small they may be, but despite this reality it is part of the experience of life. Everyone, except the prophets and the imams, make mistakes. If we commit a sin using our body, then we are immediately aware of it; if we know we have used our hands to steal or our eyes to look at what is forbidden, then we know it is wrong. Knowing that we used our bodily gift, which He has conferred upon us, to disobey Him is a mistreatment of that gift, and thus we have to repent for those sins immediately.

Another category of sins which exist but are less obvious is the desire to commit a sin and this can be just as bad as committing the sin itself. Although we will not be punished for a mere thought of committing a sin; nonetheless, extreme caution must be exercised when the thought appears in our mind, lest God should test us and make the opportunity available for us to even 'attempt' to break one of His laws, and therefore we really need to try and suppress such thoughts.

The most elusive type of sin is forgetfulness or heedlessness of God - *ghaflah*. Although God is transcendent, He is also very near, but we sometimes forget His presence due to the satanic influences over our souls or our own misdeeds.

$$﴿وَلَقَدْ خَلَقْنَا الإِنْسَانَ وَنَعْلَمُ مَا تُوَسْوِسُ بِهِ نَفْسُهُ وَنَحْنُ أَقْرَبُ إِلَيْهِ مِنْ حَبْلِ الْوَرِيدِ﴾$$

Certainly We have created man and We know to what his soul tempts him, and We are nearer to him than his jugular vein. (50:16)

In a hadith *al-Qudsi*, God shares a beautiful thought with us that states, "...the heart of a believer is God's sanctuary." Therefore, by keeping Him in our hearts we are sanctifying ourselves, and we should keep ourselves free from sin. We need to constantly remember God in our minds, and when we do, He will then reside in our hearts.

We need to realize that being negligent of God could be perilous.

$$﴿نَسُوا اللَّهَ فَنَسِيَهُمْ﴾$$

They have forgotten God, so He has forgotten them. (9:67)

If we forgot God, then nothing can save us and artificial prayers will be of no avail. We must be cautious not to fall into the trap of being heedless of God, and try continuously to keep His remembrance alive within us.

All sins fall into two categories: major and minor. Despite the fact that no sin is insignificant because it is still a violation of a command of the Almighty, still God has promised us in the Qur'an:

$$﴿إِنْ تَجْتَنِبُوا كَبَائِرَ مَا تُنْهَوْنَ عَنْهُ نُكَفِّرْ عَنْكُمْ سَيِّئَاتِكُمْ وَنُدْخِلْكُمْ مُدْخَلاً كَرِيمًا﴾$$

If you avoid the major sins that are forbidden, then We will absolve you of your misdeeds, and admit you to a noble abode. (4:31)

As long as we avoid the major sins He will overlook the minor ones - of course, if we are not committing them intentionally.

While scholars debate about the exact number of the "major sins," God mentions three incontestable ones:

$$﴿وَالَّذِينَ لَا يَدْعُونَ مَعَ اللَّهِ إِلَـٰهًا آخَرَ وَلَا يَقْتُلُونَ النَّفْسَ الَّتِي حَرَّمَ اللَّهُ إِلَّا بِالْحَقِّ وَلَا يَزْنُونَ وَمَن يَفْعَلْ ذَلِكَ يَلْقَ أَثَامًا﴾$$

Those who do not invoke another god besides God; and do not kill a soul [whose life] God has made inviolable, except with due cause; and do not commit fornication. Whoever does these will encounter its retribution. (25:68)

Polytheism (*shirk*), murder, and fornication all merit the title of "major sin," and each one carries a severe penalty. Anyone who commits one of these three will receive a dual punishment because these sins are intertwined with some form of polytheism, which by far, is the worst sin.

﴿إِنَّ اللَّهَ لاَ يَغْفِرُ أَن يُشْرَكَ بِهِ وَ يَغْفِرُ مَا دُونَ ذَلِكَ لِمَن يَشَاءُ وَ مَنْ
يُشْرِكْ بِاللَّهِ فَقَدِ افْتَرَى إِثْمًا عَظِيمًا﴾

Indeed God does not forgive that any partner should be ascribed to Him, but He forgives anything besides that to whomever He wishes; and whoever ascribes partners to God has indeed fabricated [a lie] in great sinfulness. (4:48)

Although most people today are not guilty of outright polytheism, still some may occasionally harbor thoughts that resemble polytheism.

﴿وَمَا يُؤْمِنُ أَكْثَرُهُم بِاللَّهِ إِلاَّ وَهُم مُّشْرِكُونَ﴾

And most of them do not believe in God without ascribing partners to Him. (12:106)

For example, according to Imam as-Sadiq, if you lose your job and fear starvation, then you are committing a form of polytheism because God, not your manager is the one who sustains you. As long as we feel that our sustenance or our happiness depends on others, we are guilty of a form of polytheism, since God is the only true provider and everyone else - whether it is parents, teachers, relatives, or friends are just means for us.

﴿الَّذِي خَلَقَنِي فَهُوَ يَهْدِينِ. وَالَّذِي هُوَ يُطْعِمُنِي وَيَسْقِينِ. وَإِذَا
مَرِضْتُ فَهُوَ يَشْفِينِ. وَالَّذِي يُمِيتُنِي ثُمَّ يُحْيِينِ. وَالَّذِي أَطْمَعُ أَنْ
يَغْفِرَ لِي خَطِيئَتِي يَوْمَ الدِّينِ﴾

(The One) Who created me, it is He who guides me, and provides me with food and drink, and when I get sick, it is He who cures me; who will make me die, then He will bring me back to life, and who I hope, will forgive me my iniquities on the Day of Retribution. (26:78-82)

After polytheism, the next most severe crime is murder.

$$﴿وَمَنْ يَقْتُلْ مُؤْمِنًا مُتَعَمِّدًا فَجَزَاؤُهُ جَهَنَّمُ خَالِدًا فِيهَا وَغَضِبَ اللَّهُ$$

$$عَلَيْهِ وَلَعَنَهُ وَأَعَدَّ لَهُ عَذَابًا عَظِيمًا﴾$$

Should anyone kill a believer intentionally, his requital will be Hell, to remain in it [forever]; God will be wrathful to him and curse him and He will prepare for him a great punishment. (4:93)

The murderer will receive a double punishment such that he will die as a faithless person for taking the life of an innocent person, and not only will that person reside in Hell, but the curse of God (exclusion from His mercy) will descend upon him as well.

After murder, the next major sin is indulging in unlawful sexual relations. According to Prophet Muhammad, anyone who commits this sin will suffer three immediate consequences in this world and they are: the person's sustenance will be tightened, their lifespan will be shortened, and they will leave this world in disgrace. Society will not respect such a person and they will die faithless. Then, on the Day of Judgment, God will direct His wrath upon that person.

We cannot say that we have not been warned about the punishments, and even though God has promised to forgive us for our mistakes, He will also take us to account for our insincerity. He will not allow us to insult His status by sinning knowingly and then just assuming that we will be forgiven. If we have erred, then all that we can do is repent (*tawbah*). If we are truly sincere, then He will open up a way for us to return to Him.

$$﴿إِلَّا مَنْ تَابَ وَآمَنَ وَعَمِلَ عَمَلًا صَالِحًا فَأُولَٰئِكَ يُبَدِّلُ اللَّهُ$$

$$سَيِّئَاتِهِمْ حَسَنَاتٍ وَكَانَ اللَّهُ غَفُورًا رَحِيمًا﴾$$

Except those who repent, attain faith, and act righteously. For such, God will replace their misdeeds with good deeds, and God is All-Forgiving, All-Merciful. (25:70)

In order for our repentance to be accepted, first we need to admit our sin and seriously vow never to repeat it, for God will not accept our repentance if we just claim to be penitent. Rather, our remorse needs to come from our heart and at the last stage of repentance we need to do whatever we can to rectify our wrong doings. Although many times, we cannot compensate people for what bad we have done to them, however we have to at least try - if we stole something, we have to return it; if we slandered someone, we have to ask them for forgiveness. Most importantly, we have to do what we can to heal our own souls, for we are the first victims when we transgress against our Lord.

﴿وَإِذَا سَأَلَكَ عِبَادِي عَنِّي فَإِنِّي قَرِيبٌ أُجِيبُ دَعْوَةَ الدَّاعِي إِذَا دَعَانِ فَلْيَسْتَجِيبُوا لِي وَلْيُؤْمِنُوا بِي لَعَلَّهُمْ يَرْشُدُونَ﴾

When My servants ask you about Me, [tell them that] I am indeed near. I answer the supplicant's call when he calls upon Me. So let them respond to Me, and let them have faith in Me, so that they may fare rightly. (2:186)

From the verses of the Qur'an and the sayings of the infallibles we are told that the best time to repent is in the middle of the night - when everyone else is asleep, we should turn to Him and acknowledge what we have done wrong. Reflect on the acts that we have committed and their consequences, and then reach out for His mercy. Speak to Him and seek His forgiveness. Make a sincere effort to perform *Tahajud* (the Night Prayer), as we have been told that every good deed has a fixed reward for it other than *Tahajud* - for its rewards are limitless. We need to reflect upon our negative actions and in the darkness of the night, we should cry over what we have done; for the Prophet of Islam has promised, "Shedding one tear in the middle of the night extinguishes oceans of God's wrath." Indeed, the night prayer is one of the best ways to approach Him.

We close with a prayer from the Prophet on forgiveness:

> O God, You are my Lord; there is no god but You. You created me and I am your slave; and I am faithful to my responsibility to You and my promise to You, as best as I am able to be. I seek refuge with You from the ill of what I have done. I return to You with the blessings that You have bestowed, and I return to You with the sins that I have committed. So please forgive me, for no one forgives the sins except You.

The Empowering Prayers

Chapter 7

﴿كُلُّ نَفْسٍ بِمَا كَسَبَتْ رَهِينَةٌ ۝ إِلَّا أَصْحَابَ الْيَمِينِ ۝ فِي جَنَّاتٍ يَتَسَاءَلُونَ ۝ عَنِ الْمُجْرِمِينَ ۝ مَا سَلَكَكُمْ فِي سَقَرَ ۝ قَالُوا لَمْ نَكُ مِنَ الْمُصَلِّينَ ۝ وَلَمْ نَكُ نُطْعِمُ الْمِسْكِينَ ۝ وَكُنَّا نَخُوضُ مَعَ الْخَائِضِينَ ۝ وَكُنَّا نُكَذِّبُ بِيَوْمِ الدِّينِ ۝ حَتَّى أَتَانَا الْيَقِينُ ۝ فَمَا تَنْفَعُهُمْ شَفَاعَةُ الشَّافِعِينَ﴾

Every soul will be (held) in pledge for its deeds. Except the Companions of the Right Hand. (They will be) in Gardens (of Delight): they will question each other, and (ask) of the Sinners, "What led you into the fire of Hell?" They will say, "We were not among those who prayed; Nor were we among those who fed the indigent; But we used to talk vanities with vain talkers; And we used to deny the Day of Judgment, until there came to us (the Hour) that is certain." Then no intercession of (any) intercessors will profit them. (74:38-48)

ONE OF THE MOST FUNDAMENTAL FORMS OF COMMUNICATION BETWEEN us and God is the canonical prayer (*salat*). The prayer is our time to speak with God and remember Him throughout the day; but should we lose that vital link to Him, our lives will be deeply affected. All of our good deeds risk to be wasted, for there is a tradition which states, "Prayer is a pillar of religion. If it is accepted, then everything else is accepted. However, if it is rejected, then everything else will be rejected."[51] Without the prayer, we cannot rely on anything else that we do.

Although God always listens to His servants, prayer is the most effective way to reach Him. A tradition reads, "Prayer is the ascension of a believer."[52] Through our prayer, we can elevate ourselves to the highest status before God Almighty.

Unfortunately, many people, young and old alike, do not enjoy praying. They consider their prayers a burden and just go through the motions to appease others or to lessen their guilty conscience. They pray because they have to, not because they want to and they do not see much purpose in it. The fault is not in the prayer itself but in the person - if we do not put ourselves in the right frame of mind for the prayer, then we will find it uninteresting and not uplifting the way it should be.

Therefore, in order to enjoy our prayers, one of the most important qualities we have to cultivate is humility.

Those who humble themselves in their prayers. (23:2)

Humility is a constant state of mind; and it should not just set in at the time of prayers. If during the day, we waste time, use profanity, or behave irreverently, then we will not be able to develop the reverence of God when it is time to pray. If at night, someone flirts or chats on the Internet or phone with a stranger until dawn, then focusing on God during the morning prayer will be close to impossible. God is pure, and we can only reach Him when we have purified ourselves. If we contaminate our souls by infringing upon His limits, then we need to repent so we can re-establish our link with Him. Otherwise, there is

---

[51] *Al-Kafi*, v. 3 p. 268
[52] *Bihar al-Anwar*, Al-Allamah Al-Majlisi, v. 79 p. 303

no magic button to turn impiety into piety. Maintaining a spirit of humility is indeed a lifelong task.

In addition to guarding ourselves spiritually, we also have to guard ourselves physically and watch what we eat.

$$\text{﴿يَا أَيُّهَا الرُّسُلُ كُلُوا مِنَ الطَّيِّبَاتِ وَاعْمَلُوا صَالِحًا إِنِّي بِمَا تَعْمَلُونَ عَلِيمٌ﴾}$$

O apostles! Eat of the good things and act righteously. Indeed I know best what you do. (23:51)

Unlawful food (not halal or forbidden) will have an effect on our souls. Some people think that when they eat at non-halal restaurants the food will only affect their bodies; but in fact, it will affect their souls as well. We are not only what we eat physically, but even spiritually. The Prophet warned the community, "A single, unlawful morsel will prevent your supplications from being answered, and your prayers from being accepted."

As much as possible, it is better to avoid eating food prepared in restaurants, fast-food places, or cafeterias. If your family provides lawful (halal) food, then try to restrict yourself to what they have prepared. Whenever you eat outside, you never know where the food has been, what has been added to it, or who has had a hand in preparing it. Every year, Muslims discover that more and more of the food claimed as being "halal" are fraudulently labeled. We should not take this chance because eating unlawful food will directly affect our relationship with God.

Food does not become unlawful just because it is slaughtered incorrectly; it also becomes unlawful if it is purchased through illegitimate income. In order to prevent your food from harming you, you need to make sure that you are acquiring it through legitimate earnings as well.

When we are able to purify our body and soul, our reverence will become tangible. It has been recorded in history that when the time for prayers used to set-in, Imam Ali b. Husayn Zain al-Abideen would become pale and start to tremble. His family would ask him what was wrong, and he would reply, "Do you not know with Whom I am about to stand before? I am about to stand before the Omnipotent Power of the heavens and earth." If we keep in mind Who we are speaking to, then we will never be tired of our prayers or feel it as a burden.

However, lack of reverence can also show its traces. One day, when Imam Ali b. Abi Talib entered a mosque, he found a fidgety man praying and playing with his beard. When he finished his prayers, The Imam informed him that if his heart and soul were devout, then his reverence would have spread to his limbs. Since his heart was not present in his prayers, his body reflected his lack of attention.

In order to truly develop humility before God, we need to understand Him.

﴿إِنَّمَا يَخْشَى اللَّهَ مِنْ عِبَادِهِ الْعُلَمَاءُ إِنَّ اللَّهَ عَزِيزٌ غَفُورٌ﴾

Only those of God's servants having knowledge fear Him. Indeed God is All-Mighty, All-Forgiving. (35:28)

Due to the fact that the Prophet understood his Lord, he used to seclude himself before his mission in the cave of Hira in Mecca for one month or so at a time, to communicate alone with God. He enjoyed these times more than anything else because he knew with Whom he was talking to. After experiencing that communion, the glamour of life meant nothing to him. In fact, God had to advise the Prophet not to deprive his physical body from sleep in His remembrance.

We did not send down to you the Qur'an that you should be distress. (20:2)

The other prophets and imams were the same. Despite his immense involvement in society, Ali b. Abi Talib was described as someone who was estranged from the glamour of the world. He was said to be a person who sought solace with God in the solitude of the night; and he would spend hours speaking to God and never become bored. If we were acquainted with God, like the intimate friends of God were, then we would love to continue praying.

There is a famous story from Mashhad, Iran, in which there lived a young, beautiful princess named Gowhar Shah who built an elaborate mosque. After the last tile had been laid down, she wanted to be the first one to pray inside the mosque so she sent everyone home.

She was not aware that one of the laborers was curious to know what she looked like. Thinking that he would never have the chance to see the king's daughter again, he crept inside the mosque and hid behind some carpets. He was all alone there when the king's daughter entered. She looked around, marveling at the magnificent architecture, and began to pray.

He was spellbound for he had never seen a more beautiful woman in his entire life. By the time she finished her prayers and left the mosque, he had fallen deeply in love with her.

Thereafter, he lost all interest in eating or sleeping. When his mother, who he lived alone with, asked him what was wrong, he told her that he wanted to marry the king's daughter. She chided him because they barely had enough food to eat - how could he hope to marry a princess?

His situation became desperate. Finally, his mother took pity on him and decided to take the risk of approaching the king. One day, she made her way to the palace and stood in line to speak to him. When her turn came, she told the king that she had an important request and begged him not to refuse it. He promised to grant her whatever she wanted. She then told him that her son wanted to marry his daughter.

Silence fell. The king's aides thought that he would punish her. After a moment, he raised his head and surprisingly agreed that her son could marry his daughter, but on one condition. Drawing in her breath, she asked what that condition was. She assumed that he would name an impossible sum of money, but instead, he simply told her, "Tell your son that the king sends his regards, and if he stands for *Tahajud* (the Night Prayer) for 40 nights, then he can marry the king's daughter."

Thrilled, she rushed home and gave her son the good news. At first, he was skeptical. He did not understand what *Tahajud* had to do with him marrying the princess. His mother insisted and reminded him that the king had given his word in front of all of the people; and so he agreed to do it.

Since he did not know how to pray *Tahajud*, he rushed to a local *sheikh* to learn how to perform it, and then that night, he began the prayers. At first, it was very difficult for him. His mother had to wake him up because he was not accustomed to rising at that time in the middle of the night. As the days passed, he began to adjust to his new routine. He even began to look forward to his midnight session with God, rather than dread it.

The forty days passed, but they made no mention of it to the king. Concerned and slightly irritated, the king sent the mother an official letter of summons. When she came to the royal court, he asked her what had happened, and she replied that her son had fulfilled the agreement, but he did not mention anything again about marrying the princess.

Troubled, she returned home and asked her son what was wrong. Did he not know that his wait was over? Had he forgotten that he could now marry the girl of his dreams?

His reply was as follows, "I know that the forty days are over; but when I asked you to go to the king, my heart was empty. I was lonely.

Now, I have found a very dear friend. I can talk to Him every night, and He responds to me; thus I do not need anyone else."

This is a true story. God filled the emptiness in his heart through the prayers. Of course, this is not to say that you should abstain from marriage and do *Tahajud* instead. Rather, once a person has that connection with God, one would never want to give it up for anything else.

Hence, those who know their Lord in the true sense eagerly await their prayers. However, hearts that have been tainted by sins are distant from feeling God's nearness. The prayer is the nourishment of the soul, it is equivalent to food. When we are healthy, we enjoy eating, but when we are ill, we lose our appetite. When it comes to prayers, the virus is not in our bodies, but rather it is in our hearts.

﴿يُخَادِعُونَ اللهَ وَالَّذِينَ آمَنُوا وَمَا يَخْدَعُونَ إِلاّ أَنْفُسَهُمْ وَمَا يَشْعُرُونَ ۝ فِي قُلُوبِهِمْ مَرَضٌ فَزَادَهُمُ اللهُ مَرَضًا وَلَهُمْ عَذَابٌ أَلِيمٌ بِمَا كَانُوا يَكْذِبُونَ﴾

They seek to deceive God and those who have faith, yet they deceive no one but themselves, but they are not aware. There is a sickness in their hearts; then God increased their sickness, and there is a painful punishment for them because of the lies they used to tell. (2:9-10)

We have to keep ourselves spiritually healthy in order to maintain our enthusiasm for the prayers. If we lose our eagerness for the prayers, then it is a symptom that something is wrong.

Furthermore, in order to reap the benefits of communicating with God, we need to approach him with sincerity. A tradition says, "Prayer is not bowing or standing. Instead, it is your sincerity."[53] Therefore, the

---

[53] *Sharh Nahjul Balaghah*, Ibn Abil Hadid, v. 1, p. 325

essence of prayer is your sincerity. If you pray in order to show off, then your prayers are worthless. Unfortunately, some people pray to impress others while some even pray to impress themselves. Every form of worship can have a pitfall, and one of the pitfalls of the prayer is arrogance. Some people might let the lengthiness of their prayers get to their heads and imagine that those few extended minutes make them a noble person. They forget how small they are in comparison to the Creator, and how the entire purpose of the prayer is to instill humility in a person not pride. It is similar to the act of charity. God has warned us that we can destroy our charitable acts by mentioning them to the beneficiaries.

﴿يَا أَيُّهَا الَّذِينَ آمَنُوا لاَ تُبْطِلُوا صَدَقَاتِكُم بِالْمَنِّ وَالأَذَى كَالَّذِي يُنفِقُ مَالَهُ رِئَاءَ النَّاسِ وَلاَ يُؤْمِنُ بِاللَّهِ وَالْيَوْمِ الآخِرِ فَمَثَلُهُ كَمَثَلِ صَفْوَانٍ عَلَيْهِ تُرَابٌ فَأَصَابَهُ وَابِلٌ فَتَرَكَهُ صَلْدًا لاَ يَقْدِرُونَ عَلَى شَيْءٍ مِمَّا كَسَبُوا وَاللَّهُ لاَ يَهْدِي الْقَوْمَ الْكَافِرِينَ﴾

O you who have faith! Do not render your charities void by reproaches and affronts, like those who spend their wealth to be seen by people and have no faith in God and the Last Day. Their parable is that of a rock covered with soil: a downpour strikes it, leaving it bare. They have no power over anything of what they have earned, and God does not guide the faithless lot. (2:264)

Our worship should have nothing to do with worldly repute; otherwise, it will become worthless, and it will be as if we never did them at all.

Finally, we need to understand what we are saying in our prayers. While reverence comes from spiritual connection, awareness comes from intellectual understanding. On the most basic level, we need to know the meaning of the words which we recite in our prayers. Reciting incomprehensible syllables will not really help us much in this world or in the next.

As well, we need to ponder upon what we are saying. Although we repeat the plea "*ihdina sirat al-mustaqeem* (guide us on the straight path)" at least 17 times a day, oftentimes, we utter these words with our tongues, but not our hearts. We have to delve into the deeper meanings of what we are reciting. Each word and every gesture of the prayer has a deep meaning and great importance attached to it.

Even the phrase "Allahu Akbar (God is Great)" has insurmountable depth. One day, a man seated next to Imam as-Sadiq commented, "Allahu Akbar (God is the greatest)."

"God is the greatest?" the Imam asked him.

"Yes," he replied.

"Greater than who?" asked the Imam.

He paused for moment to think and then said, "Greater than everything."

"You have limited God by comparing Him to His creations," the Imam said. "God cannot be compared to anything in this universe."

The man asked, "So what does Allahu Akbar mean?"

"It means that God is too great to be described," replied the Imam.

Prayers have many aspects and depth. By reading the traditions on the prayers we can begin to contemplate and understand them better. The more we understand them, the more we will enjoy them and thank God for this priceless opportunity to turn our full attention towards Him.

Inter-Gender Relations

Chapter 8

Featured Themes:
Mixed Gatherings; Dating; Marriage; Spouse Selection

﴿وَمِنْ آيَاتِهِ أَنْ خَلَقَ لَكُم مِنْ أَنفُسِكُمْ أَزْوَاجًا لِتَسْكُنُوا إِلَيْهَا وَجَعَلَ بَيْنَكُم مَوَدَّةً وَرَحْمَةً إِنَّ فِي ذَٰلِكَ لَآيَاتٍ لِقَوْمٍ يَتَفَكَّرُونَ﴾

And of His signs is that He created for you mates from your own selves that you may take comfort in them, and He ordained affection and mercy between you. There are indeed signs in that for a people who reflect. (30:21)

ALMOST EVERYTHING FROM THE TINIEST PARTICLE TO THE LARGEST creature has been created in pairs and human beings are no exception to this rule. In fact, our creation is a bit more complex because we are more social beings, programmed to find companionship with one another. It is in our innate nature to find our other half, get married, and raise a family - this is part of the human cycle of life. God has created marriage for our benefit; and the sanctity of marriage provides a means of spiritual, emotional, and physical fulfillment for human beings.

﴿سُبْحَانَ الَّذِي خَلَقَ الْأَزْوَاجَ كُلَّهَا مِمَّا تُنْبِتُ الْأَرْضُ وَمِنْ أَنفُسِهِمْ وَمِمَّا لَا يَعْلَمُونَ﴾

> *Immaculate is He who has created all the kinds of what the earth grows, and of themselves, and of what they do not know. (36:36)*

Unlike other ideologies, Islam does not force us to suppress our natural desires. In fact, it sets the guidelines and criteria on how to best channel our natural instinct, while at the same time, also protects us from the dangers of promiscuity. Rather than allowing us to run uncontrolled and do whatever we feel like, Islam instructs us to control our desires in the most appropriate way. Ali b. Abi Talib says in *Nahjul Balaghah*, "Control your desires before they control you." Our Creator, Who knows what is best for us, has given us the correct way to handle our desires - and that is through the institute of marriage. Simultaneously, He has taught us how to behave with the opposite gender in order to avoid falling into inappropriate situations. He did this in order to protect us, as had there been wisdom in promiscuity, He would have permitted that, however He taught us how to limit the ways that we express our desires.

One of the most frequent questions asked is whether young Muslim boys and girls can talk to one another? Can they see each other or can they call, text, Facebook or Twitter people of the opposite gender? The answer to these varies according to the situation. In general, Islam has no problem with men and women interacting respectfully and responsibly in a decent setting, such as in an educational or spiritual setting. Take for example, the most sacred place on earth, which is the Ka'bah (Masjid al-Haram) in which men and women worship God side by side during Hajj season. He has permitted this because He knows that our intentions when we go there are solely for Him.

However, getting together just to waste time in private or public settings is not recommended. You might think you can go to a mixed wedding or birthday party or even a café and not run into problems, but God knows that even the best of us can be led into immoral actions. Usually the situation starts innocently, like studying and preparing for exams, but then the topic begins to drift off from the studying and onto private talk, and before you know it, emotions are connected, desires are stirred, and the unexpected can happen, but by then, it is too late. Therefore, He has not allowed attending these sorts of mixed gatherings, even if they are held in public setting or seem to appear innocent.

In order to prevent anything from happening in private, being alone with a non-*mahram* (non-family member) is not permitted. If a woman is not your mother, sister, wife, daughter, aunt or niece, then you should not be alone with her, even if she is your cousin. Satan has sworn that, "Whenever two non-mahram people get together, I will be the third one there, and I will not leave them until I impel them to commit adultery."[54]

You may not be aware of his presence, but he will be the third having the *shisheh* (tobacco water pipe), tea or coffee. Do not try to convince yourself that you are just studying together. It might begin with mathematics or theology, but it can very likely lead to something else. That is why God warns mankind in the Noble Qur'an that, "Do not approach adultery,"[55] not only is God telling us not to do it, but He insists - do not even get near it! Therefore, we need to avoid this road entirely.

A horrendous story is told about a thief who lived in Madinah during the time of the Prophet. He was not interested in stealing the wealth of the living; instead he preferred to steal the burial shrouds of the dead bodies. Whenever someone died, he would follow the funeral procession to see where the dead body was laid to rest. Then late at night, he would creep into that graveyard, unearth the deceased body, and take the shroud (*kafan*) to the market to sell.

He lived like this for a long time, until one day, the Prophet found him sobbing in the mosque. The Prophet asked him what was wrong. He

---

[54] *Mustadrak*, v. 14, p. 265
[55] *Al-Qur'an*, 17:32

replied that he had committed a terrible sin that God would never forgive him for.

"Is your sin greater than the heavens?" the Prophet asked.

He said it was.

"Is your sin greater than Earth?" the Prophet asked.

He said it was greater than that too.

"Is your sin greater than the oceans?" the Prophet asked.

He said it was even greater than them.

Finally, the Prophet asked him, "Is your sin greater than the mercy of God?"

"No, O Messenger of God," he replied.

The Prophet encouraged him to relate what he had done so that he could find out the way to seek God's forgiveness. He said that he used to make a living by stealing the shrouds from the dead bodies and then reselling them. In his neighborhood, a young lady was about to die from an illness. Knowing her time was short, she went to him and told him that she knew about his crimes. He tried to deny it, but she told him that she had seen him going to the graveyard and begged him not to dig up her grave after she died. She even offered him new shrouds from the market to sell so that he would not have to take hers. Touched by her words, he agreed and a few days later, she died. As his habit, he walked in the funeral procession and then came home. He was determined not to leave his house that night. But Satan came to him and started whispering about how much her shroud was worth. All that money was going to waste. She was dead now; she did not need it.

Finally, temptation overwhelmed him, and he hastened to the graveyard. Quickly, he dug up her body and pulled off her shroud. The full moon was illuminating her corpse. Suddenly, a new and more twisted idea came to his mind. He tried to resist it, but Satan kept whispering to him, "She is dead now." Finally, he gave in to this horrible thought and did the sinful deed.

As he was climbing out of her grave, suddenly her voice called out to him, "May God disgrace you since you have violated and humiliated me among the dead!" He fled, guilty and terrified, and began begging for forgiveness of his evil act.

Soon after telling his story to the Prophet, he left the city and went to the mountains and continued to seek forgiveness. After forty days of penitence, God sent Angel Gabriel to tell the Prophet to relate to him that God had accepted his repentance, for he had been truly sincere.

This story shows how Satan and our desires can get the better of us. Our desires can blind us and be deadly. We cannot be sure that we will never do anything "too extreme." We never know what may happen until the situation presents itself and then it may be too late! Satan has vowed to mislead all of us.

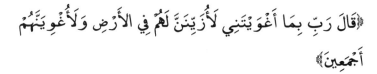

He said, "My Lord! As You have consigned me to perversity, I will surely glamorize [evil] for them on earth, and I will surely pervert them." (15:39)

Therefore, we need to prevent ourselves from getting into perilous situations before it is too late.

One way to keep ourselves from this type of harm is to abide by the Islamic prohibition of dating. It should be understood from the beginning that dating is not the same thing as spouse selection. Although dating and spouse selection do not usually go hand in hand, nonetheless, some Muslims today advocate "modernizing" Islam to make it compatible with Western customs and to allow their children to meet freely, so that they can find their own partners. However, there is no such thing as "Islamic dating," just as there is no such thing as "Islamic dancing." God has set the limits for a reason, and these limits will remain the same until the end of time, regardless of where we live, or what the day and age we are in.

Why is the Western form of dating not allowed?

To begin with, most of the time, boys and girls go out on a date to have fun, they are not searching for a life partner. The basis of dating is temporary, a passing enjoyment period, without any real form of obligation or commitment to one another. It will not stand the test of time or survive adversity; and sadly one of them will eventually get hurt.

Some people swear that they can date and not do anything wrong. They will go out and "just talk." How long can you "just talk?" A month? A year? Emotional involvement will eventually lead to physical involvement. Not only is that a sin, but you will even lose your sense of self-respect.

Boys who chase after girls to satisfy themselves are not interested in the institute of marriage. They just want to enjoy themselves. They are like wolves in human disguise and this is completely wrong. Women need to be respected, not used. If you let yourself be used, then you will regret it for the rest of your life. In addition, once you cross the line of having relationships outside of marriage, then you will find it very difficult in the future to content yourself with one partner, no matter how wonderful that person is. It will harm your future life and your marriage.

One may wonder that if "dating" is not permitted, then how Muslims are supposed to get married.

Seeking a spouse is different than seeking physical enjoyment. God has permitted the first, but prohibited the second. Islam encourages you to get to know your future spouse, but not alone. Islam does not teach us to rush into marriage. You should get to know your future partner, but through the proper means. People spend months shopping for a house or a car, so why not spend at least that long searching for a spouse? Take your time, and make sure that you are making the right decision. Visit the potential partner at their family home when others are present, and get the advice of others who know the person. Although you do not need to solemnize the marriage (*aqd*) before speaking to each other; nonetheless, you have to be careful about what subject matters you discuss. Do not transgress to inappropriate topics. Court each other respectfully in a way that your future children would admire. If you do not conduct yourselves respectfully, then your children will be the first ones to lose respect for you.

What should one look for in a spouse?

While economic security and attractiveness are good, they are not the most important qualities to look for. Beauty and money come last. The most important quality that one should seek is religious integrity (*akhlaq*). Faith alone is not enough. You need someone who believes and acts upon their beliefs. A father once asked Imam Husayn what sort of man he should marry his daughter to. The Imam replied, "Marry your daughter to a man who fears God, for if he finds fault in her, he will still treat her well because he fears God."[56] Likewise, a wife who acts on her religious integrity will keep the family intact. Keep this in mind when you are contemplating upon your partner - would this person be a great father or mother for my children?

After you are sure of his or her religious integrity, then look into the family. Genes are powerful and family habits are an integral part of a person. Some families are known for their generosity, and likewise, some families are known for their miserly; thus, a girl should ensure that a man comes from a family that is giving and not stingy. If he is used to living in a family environment where money is deliberately restricted, then he will do the same to her in marriage, even though the

---

[56] *Al-Mustadraf*, Al-Abhishi, v. 2, p. 218

tradition says, "A miserly person is distant from God, distant from the people, and distant from Paradise."[57] Finally, be watchful about your future family in-law because they will become part of your family for the rest of your life. Marriage is a unification of two families, which may even include (the challenges of) two different cultures. The other family will become your children's grandparents, aunts, and uncles. So consider them carefully and aim to find a spouse who has been raised in a decent family environment.

Aside from looking at the family, Ali b. Abi Talib also advised us not to be blinded by physical appearance, and to make sure that our future spouse is intelligent and open-minded. He advised us to avoid marrying someone unintelligent because it could be hereditary, and surely, no parent wants their child to inherit such a trait. When it comes to finding your life-long partner you have the absolute right to be selective. Also, keep in mind not be too emotional - allow wisdom to guide your decision.

No doubt, physical attraction is important. Islam does not discount it, but it should not be at the beginning of the list. You might meet someone who has an ordinary exterior, but on the inside there lies a beautiful soul. After you get to know them, you will think that they are the most beautiful person in the world. In contrast, you might meet someone who is gorgeous looking, but intolerable to love. No matter how stunning they are now, they may become the ugliest person in the world in your eyes. Nonetheless, chemistry is important. God does not want us to have a nightmare every time we see our partner's face! However, attractiveness should not be your only concern. If you find someone decent, then you will learn to love him or her for other qualities, such as honesty, nobility, commitment, and sacrifice. That is real love. Real love grows after years of staying together. Everything else beforehand is just an illusion.

---

[57] *Bihar al-Anwar*, Al-Allamah Al-Majlisi, v. 73, p. 308

Good Parenting

Chapter 9

﴿يَابُنَيَّ إِنَّهَا إِن تَكُنْ مِثْقَالَ حَبَّةٍ مِنْ خَرْدَلٍ فَتَكُنْ فِي صَخْرَةٍ أَوْ فِي السَّمَاوَاتِ أَوْ فِي الأَرْضِ يَأْتِ بِهَا اللَّهُ إِنَّ اللَّهَ لَطِيفٌ خَبِيرٌ يَابُنَيَّ أَقِمِ الصَّلاَةَ وَأْمُرْ بِالْمَعْرُوفِ وَانْهَ عَنِ الْمُنكَرِ وَاصْبِرْ عَلَى مَا أَصَابَكَ إِنَّ ذَلِكَ مِنْ عَزْمِ الأُمُورِ﴾

(Said Prophet Luqman) O my son! Even if it should be the weight of a mustard seed, and [even though] it should be in a rock, or in the heavens, or in the earth, God will produce it. Indeed God is all-attentive, all-aware. O my son! Maintain the prayer and bid what is right and forbid what is wrong, and be patient through whatever may visit you. That is indeed the steadiest of courses. (31:16-17)

PARENTS HOLD AN UNRIVALED LEVEL OF ESTEEM IN ISLAM. GOD addresses the status of parents as being second only to His. In the same chapter of the Qur'an as the above mentioned passage, God says:

﴿أَنِ اشْكُرْ لِي وَلِوَالِدَيْكَ إِلَيَّ الْمَصِيرُ﴾

Give thanks to Me and to your parents. To Me is the return. (31:14)

He teaches us that we cannot be grateful to Him without first being grateful to our parents, and that we cannot worship Him without honoring them as well.

$$﴿وَقَضَى رَبُّكَ أَلاَّ تَعْبُدُواْ إِلاَّ إِيَّاهُ وَبِالْوَالِدَيْنِ إِحْسَانًا إِمَّا يَبْلُغَنَّ عِندَكَ الْكِبَرَ أَحَدُهُمَا أَوْ كِلاَهُمَا فَلاَ تَقُل لَّهُمَآ أُفٍّ وَلاَ تَنْهَرْهُمَا وَقُل لَّهُمَا قَوْلاً كَرِيمًا﴾$$

Your Lord has decreed that you shall not worship anyone except Him, and [He has enjoined] kindness to parents. Should they reach old age at your side - one of them or both - do not say to them, "Fie!" And do not chide them, but speak to them noble words. (17:23)

If our parents are still living, then we should thank God for the opportunity to have them in our lives, for being kind to our parents is the quickest way to earn His blessings. We will regret it when we lose that opportunity.

One day, a companion of the Prophet lost his mother. Although he was an adult and still had his father, he kept weeping for his mother until people began reminding him that she had gone to Paradise. He replied that he knew she was in Paradise, but he was crying for himself because when his mother was alive he had two wide gates to Paradise open, and now one of them was closed forever. Therefore, he was mourning at the loss of an opportunity to earn God's pleasure by serving his mother.

Elsewhere, it is written that a man who committed a terrible sin asked the Prophet how he could ever be forgiven. The Prophet did not tell him to pay charity or to perform the pilgrimage, instead he asked him whether his parents were still alive. When he said that his father was alive, the Prophet instructed him to serve him for the rest of his life. As the man left, the Prophet commented that had the man's mother been alive, God would have accepted his repentance much quicker.

Abu Zayd al-Bastami, an Islamic philosopher, says that he uncovered heights of spiritual knowledge simply by serving his mother. He relates that one night he was alone with his old, ill mother. It was bitterly cold and snowing outside. In the middle of the night, she woke up and told him that she was thirsty. At first, he did not want to brave the cold weather to go outside and bring her water, but he was her only son, so he trudged out into the snow to a nearby stream and brought back some water for her. When he returned, she had fallen asleep again. He did not know what to do. On one hand, he did not want to leave the water next to her because he did not think that she would be able to find it, and on the other hand, he did not want to disturb her sleep, especially since she was ill. Finally, he decided to stand there and wait for her to wake up. He stood by her side all night long, holding the cup of water in his hand, until dawn broke and she woke up for the morning prayers. When she saw her son holding the cup of water, she prayed for him. He says that at that time, God uncovered spiritual truths in his heart, and he knew that it was a result of his mother's prayers.

That one simple act gave him so many blessings, but even so, it cannot make up for the years of trouble that mother spent raising him. It is narrated that, one day the Prophet met a man carrying his mother on his shoulders as he circled the Ka'bah. The man asked, "O Messenger of God, have I fulfilled my duty to her?" The Prophet replied, "You have not even repaid her for the pain of one contraction." Therefore carrying a parent on your back, taking them out, or bringing them medicine, can never make up for what they have done for you.

As your parents mature, so should your respect for them. No matter how old you are, your mother will always be your mother; and one should address her humbly. When you pray, pray for your parents and one of the best ways is to recite the following verse, at least once a day:

$$﴿رَّبِّ ارْحَمْهُمَا كَمَا رَبَّيَانِي صَغِيرًا﴾$$

My Lord! Have mercy on them, just as they reared me when I was a small child." (17:24)

Our parents merit our respect no matter how they have raised us. We may never understand, nor value parenthood until we become parents ourselves. Parenting is a huge responsibility.

Parents need to do their best to nurture their children into healthy adults. One of the primary responsibilities of parents, particularly fathers, is to provide for their children. According to a tradition, a man who fathers children but does not provide for them is cursed by God. Their welfare is his primary responsibility. During the time of the Prophet, one of the companions used to donate all of his wealth to the poor. When he died, he left nothing to bequeath to his children, and they went hungry. When they informed the Prophet about their situation, he replied, "Had you told me this about him earlier, then I would not have even allowed him to be buried in an Islamic cemetery."

Parents on the other hand also need to prevent themselves from going to an extreme when raising their children. Spoiling children will not prepare them for the reality and responsibilities of life. Some parents lavish their children with luxurious gifts to the point that their children exert pressure on them in order to maintain their lifestyle. Instead of being an asset to you, they become a liability. This is why another tradition says, "Your sole concern should not be your wife and children. If they are religious, then God will take care of them; and if they are not religious, then what business do you have with an adversary of God?"[58] For this reason, it is important to keep a balance, neither to over indulge, nor to disregard your children.

---

[58] *Nahjul Balaghah*, hadith 352

In addition to providing for your children physically, you also have to nurture them spiritually. You are your child's first teacher. In particular, young children will learn first from their mother.

Unfortunately, nowadays the word "mother" has become degraded. Many women bristle at being called mothers. They would rather be called a doctor, a lawyer, or a secretary - anything but a mother. However, being called a mother is one of the greatest honors. Your success today is most likely due to your mother. Had you had a neglectful mother, then your life may have been in disarray. A mother's impact on her child should not be underestimated.

It is extremely important to maintain a spiritual relationship with your children. Teach them about God and pray with them.

$$﴿يَٰٓأَيُّهَا ٱلَّذِينَ ءَامَنُوا۟ قُوٓا۟ أَنفُسَكُمْ وَأَهْلِيكُمْ نَارًا وَقُودُهَا ٱلنَّاسُ وَٱلْحِجَارَةُ...﴾$$

O you who have faith! Save yourselves and your families from a Fire whose fuel is people and stones... (66:6)

The prophets did not pray alone - they prayed with their families and children. In America, there is a beautiful saying, "A family who prays together stays together." This is very true, for if you want your family to remain united, then you need to worship together.

The best way to instruct your children is to simply be the best example you can be for them.

$$﴿وَأْمُرْ أَهْلَكَ بِٱلصَّلَوٰةِ وَٱصْطَبِرْ عَلَيْهَا﴾$$

And bid your family to prayer and be steadfast in its maintenance. (20:132)

When this verse was revealed, someone asked the Prophet, "I can barely protect myself from sins, and now God wants me to protect my wife and children as well? I cannot do that!" The Prophet replied, "It is

89

enough that you enjoin upon them what you enjoin upon yourself and forbid them from what you forbid yourself."[59] This means in simplified terms that **practice what you preach**. Sometimes as parents we think that our children are not watching us, but in fact, they are watching our every move. Children are very alert of their parents' actions, they learn mainly by them, not so much by their words. If we cheat at work, then they will cheat at school. If we behave immodestly, then they will not be chaste. Preaching without practicing will have no effect.

$$﴿ كَبُرَ مَقْتًا عِنْدَ اللَّهِ أَنْ تَقُولُوا مَا لَا تَفْعَلُونَ ﴾$$

It is greatly outrageous to God that you say that which you do not do. (61:3)

A tradition says that, "God curses those people who enjoin good but do not practice it; and He curses those people who forbid evil but do not abstain from it."[60]

There is a famous Muslim book on prayers and supplications called *Mafatih al-Jinan* (the *Keys to Paradise*). Although we have hundreds of prayer books, this one has attained a unique status due to the author's approach.

After completing it, the author, Sheikh Abbas al-Qummi, was about to publish it when he had an episteme. He said to himself that it would be useless to give it to others without first trying to perform every prayer and worship act in the book himself. So he took it back from the publisher and spent the next year praying every prayer and fasting every fast that he had written about, to make sure it was humanly possible to follow the recommendations contained in it. Only then did he submit the book for publication. This is one of the reasons that this book holds a special place; his humility is another reason.

---

[59] *Al-Kafi*, v. 5, p. 62
[60] *Bihar al-Anwar*, Al-Allamah Al-Majlisi, v. 34, p. 89

The same lesson applies to how we raise our children. If we preach to them for hours about something, but do not practice it ourselves, then our words will fall on deaf ears. However, if we model what we would like them to do, then they will learn from our example. Our actions set the standard for them more than anything else. If we are good, then they will assume the role of goodness. On the other hand, if we lie, abuse or steal, then our children will assume that those things are the norm and permitted.

Parents' responsibilities do not end with raising their children. Parents also have a vital duty to facilitate their children's marriages.

These days, this responsibility seems to be getting neglected more and more. Islam places so much importance to the institute of marriage that it equates it as fulfilling half of one's religion. However, parents seem to neglect encouraging their mature children from fulfilling this aspect of life. They set education or a career as a first priority over marriage. In fact, some parents discourage or even refuse to discuss the subject. Meanwhile, our mature youths of today are eager to get married. They are old enough to shoulder the responsibility, but some parents hinder them. If you stop or delay your children from getting married, then you will be held accountable before God, for that is one of the three primary duties of parents, which according to a tradition include: giving your child a good name, educating them, and marrying them (to good spouses).

Times have changed a lot. Our children are not being raised in the same environment as we may have lived in. When we were growing up there was a sense of innocence and morality. We lived within a generation that had a set of principled standards and limited boundaries. Today it is a different story - it seems that nothing is sacred or honored like before. Many of the innocence of our children are being lost today; and the pressure is on; it hits them from every direction - be it from the peer-pressure at school, the movies, music, and even some of the books which they read. What they watch and hear affects them tremendously. You may keep them from talking to boys or girls at home, but the moment they step out of the house, they are mingling freely. We have to fear God and keep our children from being misled by encouraging them to follow the best route, which is marriage before they go down other avenues. If one child goes astray, the entire family will suffer.

During the time of the Prophet, marriage was relatively simple. We Muslims have turned it into a nightmare. Do not say that your son does not have enough money to get married because God will provide for him in the marriage. Do not say that they have to finish college first. Some parents will never be pleased because they will keep delaying their child from marrying until their post doctorate, and by that time they will be very selective about potential partners.

A lady asked me whether women could propose to men or not. The answer is of course they can, but they should also keep in mind that there are manners and ways in how to go about it; the consultation of the parents is critical in this approach. Once, the Prophet was giving a sermon in the mosque when a Muslim lady stood in front of everyone and asked the Prophet to find her a husband. The Prophet asked the men present who wanted to marry her, and finally, a man stood. The Prophet asked him what he had to offer her as a marriage gift (*mahr*). He said he did not have anything. Then Prophet Muhammad asked him if he knew any verses of the Qur'an. He said that he knew *Surah al-Fatihah* (the Opening). The Prophet asked her whether she would agree to marry him on the condition that he would teach her *Surah al-Fatihah*. She accepted, and they were married. It was that simple, and it can be less complicating than it is even today.

Today, the gift of marriage (*mahr*) has skyrocketed way out of proportion. Men who want to marry are prevented by the high cost of the gift marriage. We have to stop overburdening our future generations and facilitate marriage for them. Marriage is not a business transaction. You are not selling your daughter. The marriage gift (*mahr*) is a symbolic gesture of love and respect; just look at the marriage gift that Ali b. Abi Talib gave to Fatima al-Zahra - it was so simple, yet theirs was the most successful marriage. Ahlul-Bayt did not demand hundreds of thousands of dollars for their daughters. We need to learn from them and then apply this into our own lives.

We also need to learn how to communicate with our children. This lack of communication is one reason why we are not hearing their voices. Often youths come to me first to discuss their personal issues, when instead they should begin with their parents. It may be normal to have a generation gap, but among the Islamic community in the West, the generation gap has become a gaping chasm. Parents and children either do not communicate well or they misunderstand each other. That is why many of them at the age of eighteen want to escape from the home. Some parents simply do not make time to talk to their children. They spend all of their time at work or on other things; although they thank God for granting them the opportunity to come to the West and make money, they do not realize that their children are slipping out of their hands.

There is a story that circulated about a boy who never saw his father. His father would leave home before he woke up and came back home after he was asleep. The son missed his father terribly. Finally, he decided to force himself to stay awake until his father came home from work. Hours passed, and he kept yawning until at last his father came through the door. As soon as he saw his father, he asked him how much he made per hour. Annoyed, his father told him he that he makes twenty-five dollars an hour. The boy then held out twenty-five dollars and asked his father to sell him an hour of his time. Just imagine how sad this is. We cannot just focus on our children's physical well-being, but then ignore them as individuals.

Fathers are not the only ones who are guilty of this. Even some mothers choose to leave their young children at a babysitter or day care so they can work even though some do not need the money. I met a mother once who earned twelve hundred dollars a month at her job. Nearly nine hundred dollars of it went to childcare and the rest of it she spent on gas. At the end of the month, she had no money left, but she kept on working. What she did not realize was that not only was she not making any money, but she was losing her children and her energy as well in the process. These early years in the lives of children can never be made up. They will be permanently affected by your actions. You have to do whatever you can to ensure that you do not miss this crucial time in their lives. What happens then will set the stage for how you interact with each other later on.

Without establishing a foundation of proper communication, both generations will stubbornly insist on following their ways. Most of the time, the older generation is entrenched in their traditions, and the younger generation is enchanted with the Western lifestyle. Many young people suffer an identity crisis. At home, they are Abdullah, and outside, they become Dave. They want to assimilate, and try to fit into society.

One day, a young man came to the mosque and told me that his name was Bob. He did not look like "Bob!" So I asked him what his real name was. He told me that it was Abbas. What is wrong with Abbas? What better name could you possibly have? We need to help our children be proud of who they are, and not at all feel ashamed. By helping them to grow up physically and spiritually sound, we will be able to instill pride in their beliefs. That way, they will be fully ready to face the challenges of society and influence in a positive way, rather than being caught up in the negative trend of it.

Events Precipitating Ashura

Chapter 10

Featured Themes:
The Prophet's Character; Major Battles; Imam Husayn; Opponents of the
Prophet: Abu Sufyan, Muawiyah, & Yazid

﴿وَمَا مُحَمَّدٌ إِلَّا رَسُولٌ قَدْ خَلَتْ مِن قَبْلِهِ الرُّسُلُ أَفَإِن مَّاتَ أَوْ قُتِلَ انقَلَبْتُمْ عَلَىٰ أَعْقَابِكُمْ وَمَن يَنقَلِبْ عَلَىٰ عَقِبَيْهِ فَلَن يَضُرَّ اللَّهَ شَيْئًا وَسَيَجْزِي اللَّهُ الشَّاكِرِينَ﴾

Muhammad is but an apostle; [other] apostles have passed before him. If he dies or is slain, will you turn back on your heels? Anyone who turns back on his heels will not harm God in any way, and God will reward the grateful ones. (3:144)

IN ORDER TO UNDERSTAND WHY IMAM HUSAYN WAS MURDERED ON THE day of Ashura, the tenth of Muharram in the year 61 AH, we need to review the history of Islam from its inception. The chain of events that led to the martyrdom of Imam Husayn did not begin a day or two before Ashura. Rather, it began a long time before that.

The first century of Islam was characterized by three important campaigns. Unlike border skirmishes, these conflicts threatened the integrity of Islam itself. The first attack was against the Prophet, the second against Ali b. Abi Talib, and the third against Imam Husayn, which ultimately led to the Battle of Ashura. Each campaign was related to the other, and each one, if not repelled, would have proven deadly to the nascent Muslim community.

The first onslaught was carried out against the Prophet by the pagans of Mecca. Threatened by the spreading fame of the Prophet and his mission, the pagans decided to end this menace to their hegemony by brutally torturing the Prophet and the early Muslims. The Prophet remained neutral for several years, but as the attacks and killings worsened, the Prophet was forced to defend his community, although that was not what he was sent for.

$$﴿وَمَا أَرْسَلْنَاكَ إِلَّا رَحْمَةً لِّلْعَالَمِينَ﴾$$

We did not send you but as a mercy to all of the nations. (21:107)

The Prophet was sent to bring mercy to humankind, not violence. However, in order to keep the mercy of the divine message alive, he had to protect the Muslims.

Even so, he never lost hope in human potential. He was the only prophet never to invoke the Lord's wrath onto his people. Prophets Noah and Jonah called upon the wrath of God onto their communities. Virtually most of the prophets cursed their people, except for Prophet Muhammad, since he was sent to bring mercy and love not chastisement. Despite all of the cruelty that his enemies subjected him to, he never mistreated them, in fact, he pardoned and forgave them.[61] As a result, even his enemies could speak no evil about him.

And indeed you possess a great character. (68:4)

The Prophet's moral standing was unfathomable. When a Jewish man came to Madinah and asked the second caliph to describe the Prophet's character, the second caliph directed him to Ali b. Abi Talib, who was sitting in the mosque. Ali b. Abi Talib rebutted the man if he

---

[61] When he recaptured Mecca, he even forgave the killer of his noble uncle, Hamzah b. Abdul Muttalib.

could put the glamour of this worldly life into words; to which the man replied that he could not. Ali b. Abi Talib asked him how he could then put the Prophet's character into words, since he was far more indescribable than this mere physical world.

$$﴿يَا أَيُّهَا النَّبِيُّ إِنَّا أَرْسَلْنَاكَ شَاهِدًا وَمُبَشِّرًا وَنَذِيرًا. وَدَاعِيًا إِلَى اللَّهِ بِإِذْنِهِ وَسِرَاجًا مُنِيرًا﴾$$

O Prophet! Indeed We have sent you as a witness, as a bearer of good news and as a warner, and a summoner to God by His permission, and as a radiant lamp. (33:45-46)

The Prophet spread light and compassion to everyone, even to his enemies, and he continues to do so today even though he is not physically in the world. His mercy reached everyone, even those who stoned him, exiled him, and persecuted him. He never said one word against them. He was truly a blessing for all of mankind.

Today, some evangelical leaders claim that the Prophet was evil. However, it is not possible to bring a single fact from history to prove this. Granted, unfortunate incidents do occur today within the Muslim world, but they are not indicative of the Prophet. People of the book make mistakes too, but that does not mean that Jesus and Moses were evil. If you study reliable history books and read the Qur'an, then you will find that nothing but compassion flowed from the Prophet's hands.

This was the man who bore the responsibility of protecting Islam against the first onslaught, led by the oligarchy of the Quraysh, and in particular Abu Sufyan - whose real name was Sakhr b. Harb. From the very beginning, he was determined to make the Prophet's life miserable and wanted to stop the spread of Islam in order to keep the status quo. What exactly was the status quo? Abu Sufyan and the enemies of the Prophet were trying to preserve Arab society precisely as it was. This was a society based on blood feuds and vengeance. The Aus and Khazraj tribes of Yathrib (Madinah today) had fought a vendetta for over a hundred years, and regularly massacred and pillaged each other. Infanticide was rampant and even one of the caliphs before accepting Islam preferred to bury his daughter alive with his own hands, rather than live the shame of having a baby girl. Poverty and decadence lived side by side; society was divided and stratified. Against all odds, and by the end of his mission, the Prophet had united these warring clans and replaced hatred with brotherhood, men and women were to be treated justly, and he had spread righteousness and humanity to such a degree that God termed the first Muslim community as:

﴿كُنتُمْ خَيْرَ أُمَّةٍ أُخْرِجَتْ لِلنَّاسِ تَأْمُرُونَ بِالْمَعْرُوفِ وَتَنْهَوْنَ عَنِ الْمُنكَرِ وَتُؤْمِنُونَ بِاللَّهِ﴾

You are the best nation [ever] brought forth for mankind: you bid what is right and forbid what is wrong, and have faith in God. (3:110)

In the new Muslim community, the Ansar in Madinah opened their houses to shelter refugees from Mecca. Former enemies sat side by side and broke bread together. Different nationalities worshiped in unison in this new religion. Bilal, an African, read the call to prayer, and Salman al-Farsi, a Persian, was referred to as one of the Prophet's family. The spirit of Islam had been realized, and fairness prevailed.

﴿وَاذْكُرُوا نِعْمَةَ اللَّهِ عَلَيْكُمْ إِذْ كُنتُمْ أَعْدَاءً فَأَلَّفَ بَيْنَ قُلُوبِكُمْ فَأَصْبَحْتُم بِنِعْمَتِهِ إِخْوَانًا﴾

And remember God's blessing upon you when you were enemies, then He brought your hearts together, so you became brothers with His blessing. (3:103)

98

The change in Arab society was so dramatic that the Roman king, seeing what had happened, summoned one of his traveling merchants to ask him how the Prophet had done it. The answer was simple. The Prophet carried out his mission with sincerity and steadfastness. He never waved from his Divine call, even for a moment. Although he had many companions, two were indispensable - his first cousin, Ali b. Abi Talib with his bravery and steadfastness; and his first wife, Khadijah b. Khuwaylid with her moral support and wealth. As a result, Muslims grew from being three to 1.3 billion today and Islam has become a world religion.

However, although dramatic, the advances that the Prophet made were fragile. Not long after his death, Islam's first civil war threatened to destroy the Muslim state. The Messenger of God had known what would happen. So before his death, he warned Ali b. Abi Talib, "O Ali, you will have to fight to preserve Islam just like you had to fight to establish it. You will fight the violators and the defectors and the seceders."[62] Just as the Prophet predicted, Ali b. Abi Talib had to fight them in three battles, which came to be known as the Battles of Jamal, Siffeen, and Nahrawan.

After the murder of the third caliph, Uthman, the people surrounded Ali b. Abi Talib's home and pressured him to take the caliphate. Once he became the legitimate caliph, Aishah, one of the wives of the Prophet, instigated a war against him. Although the Qur'an had commanded the wives of the Prophet to stay inside their homes, she rallied Talha, Zubayr and thousands of men from Madinah to Iraq to fight him. As a result, thousands of Muslims perished in the Battle of Jamal, which took place in Basra in southern Iraq. This was the battle of the "violators" that the Prophet had predicted. They violated the legitimate right of Ali b. Abi Talib as the ruler. This tragic battle was

---

[62] *Al-Kafi*, v. 5, p. 12

the first, but not the last one that the Muslims fought each other on such a grand scale.

Immediately after this battle, Muawiyah, the son of Abu Sufyan, who at that time was the governor of Syria, decided to extend his reach and invaded the territories of Iraq. Denying the legitimacy of Imam Ali, he called himself the caliph instead. His incursions led to the second confrontation at Siffeen. There, Imam Ali was forced to accept arbitration because of the loss of his supporters, his "defectors." The battle ended, but Muawiyah continued the war.

To complicate the situation further, some of Imam Ali's more fanatical fighters who disagreed with his decision to accept arbitration decided that they knew better than the Commander of the Faithful and thus seceded. They became immortalized as the Kharijites (the Seceders). Soon afterwards, they launched the Battle of Nahrawan. They proved to be pernicious opponents, for while they outwardly maintained the appearance of religiosity, they were inwardly destroying Islam.

However, Imam Ali managed to suppress them and preserve the fabric of Muslim society until he was assassinated. At that time, Muawiyah began to re-exert his hegemony, and that led to the third drastic internecine conflict within the early history of Islam - the Battle of Karbala.

In fact, this battle began long before with Muawiyah's father, Abu Sufyan's persistent attempts to obliterate Islam. Abu Sufyan had not been content with massacring the companions of the Prophet in Mecca, such as Sumayyah and Yaasir, the parents of Ammar who were the first martyrs in Islam. He and his minions had plundered the Muslims' wealth and exiled them as well. Even when they had abandoned their homeland, he still sent campaigns against them to Madinah, which resulted in the Battles of Badr, Uhud, and Ahzab. Only during the conquest of Mecca, when he was taken captive and brought before the Prophet, did Abu Sufyan agree to surrender to Islam. The

Prophet asked him, "Abu Sufyan, isn't it time for you to accept Islam?"[63] He resisted, saying that it was too difficult for him to accept Muhammad as the Prophet of God. The companions, including Umar, raised their swords. The Prophet told them to lower their weapons, but he converted, however reluctantly; in the words of Ammaar b. Yaasir, "[Bani Umayyad] surrendered to Islam rather than having accepted it."

Abu Sufyan's conversion could have been the end of his animosity towards the Prophet and Islam. The Prophet tried to win his heart (as a good will of gesture) by giving him and his tribesmen money and gifts and even position. He declared that anyone who entered Abu Sufyan's house would be granted immediate amnesty. Rather than ending his tirade against Islam, Abu Sufyan now decided to attack it from the inside. In his final days, when he had even become old and blind, Abu Sufyan gathered his relatives together and instructed them, "O my clan, take the caliphate and play with it like a toy ball. I swear that there is no Hereafter, no Paradise, and no Hell."[64]

The Prophet had all along sensed Abu Sufyan's intentions. One night, he had a terrible dream that monkeys were climbing up and down on his pulpit in Madinah. When he asked the Angel Gabriel what that dream meant, Gabriel replied that it meant the Bani Umayyad would one day seize the caliphate. In order to stave off that evil, the Prophet publicly declared that the caliphate was forbidden for Abu Sufyan and his descendants. However, it was to no avail, and they still carried out their plans. They truly were the "cursed tree" as it is described in the Holy Qur'an:

---

[63] *Bihar al-Anwar*, Al-Allamah Al-Majlisi, v. 21, p. 128
[64] *Bihar al-Anwar*, Al-Allamah Al-Majlisi, v. 31, p. 197

$$﴿وَالشَّجَرَةَ الْمَلْعُونَةَ فِي الْقُرْآنِ وَنُخَوِّفُهُمْ فَمَا يَزِيدُهُمْ إِلاَّ طُغْيَانًا كَبِيرًا﴾$$

And the tree cursed in the Qur'an. We deter them, but it only increases them in great rebellion. (17:60)

To them, the caliphate had nothing to do with the trust and responsibility of Islam; nor with upholding the message of the Prophet. It was simply an opportunity to dominate the Muslims, exploit their wealth, manipulate Islam, and remain in power. Thus Muawiyah, the son of Abu Sufyan, carried out his father's will.

As soon as he was secure in his base of power, Muawiyah b. Abu Sufyan began terrorizing the Muslims. He murdered many of the companions of the Prophet including Hijr b. Uday, Maytham al-Tammar, Rushayd al-Hajari, and Imam Hasan who was the eldest grandson of the Prophet. When Muawiyah decided to kill the grandson of the Prophet (Hasan), he sent a message to the Roman king asking him for a particularly kind of deadly poison. The king replied that his culture prohibited using that poison against human beings because of its potency. Muawiyah wrote back that he was intending to use this poison against the grandson of the Prophet who had threatened his hegemony.

Muawiyah did not only confine himself to killing the companions of the Prophet, he also ordered the prayer leaders to curse Ali b. Abi Talib, the fourth caliph, from the pulpit. He bribed others to malign the names of Ali, Fatima, Hasan, and Husayn from the pulpit. Sadly, the status of Muslim orators was determined by how well they slandered these four people. Mentioning Ali's name became such a crime that people had to refer to him as "Abu Zaynab" if they had anything to say.

Yet curiously enough, the Shia are the ones who are accused of cursing some of the companions. Nonetheless, the opinion of the Shia on the

Companions of the Prophet is the same opinion given in the Book of God. Some verses praise them, meaning the companions who did well, and others condemn them, those who went against the true teachings of Islam. Both *Surah al-Munafiqun* (the Hypocrites) and *Surah al-Tawbah* (the Repentance) condemn the evil-ones, for some of the Companions of the Prophet were hypocrites in disguise.

Therefore, the way in which the Bani Umayyad were rewriting Islam in order to serve their purpose, led Imam Husayn to give his life. He had no other choice. The masses had been blinded and had forgotten the warnings of the Prophet. Concerned primarily with their own welfare, they followed whatever their rulers decreed even when it contradicted the teachings of the Prophet. Islam was in grave danger.

The Battle of Karbala was a major turning point. There, the forces of injustice finally clashed with the forces of justice. Falsehood finally came head to head with the truth. Although that battle only lasted half a day, it has been immortalized throughout the ages. That is why we say, "every day is Ashura, and every land is Karbala." Karbala was not confined to a small area south of Baghdad; rather, Karbala is everywhere. Wherever you find an oppressive tyrant that land is Karbala, and that day is Ashura, and thus, one must rise up against oppression.

Since he was under the sole living representative of the house of the Prophet, Imam Husayn was one of the few remaining threats for the Bani Umayyad. Therefore, when Muawiyah passed away and designated his son Yazid as his successor, he left him instructions to take an oath of loyalty immediately from Imam Husayn. Needless to say, Imam Husayn refused to give allegiance to Yazid because he was even more of a dissolute than his father. He was guilty of every illicit deed mentionable. If the last survivor of the Prophet had given his hand, Islam would have come to termination.

Danger was looming over Islam when Yazid ascended the throne. People had deviated from worshipping God. Although before they were worshipping idols of stone, at the time of Muawiyah they were worshipping idols of flesh. Imam Husayn took it upon himself to save the religion. No one else could have done what he did, and as a result of his sacrifice, the third and final early threats of Islam was countered, and the message of Islam was preserved throughout the generations to come.

Islamic Revival

Chapter 11

﴿يَا أَيُّهَا الَّذِينَ آمَنُوا اسْتَعِينُوا بِالصَّبْرِ وَالصَّلَاةِ إِنَّ اللَّهَ مَعَ الصَّابِرِينَ. وَلَا تَقُولُوا لِمَنْ يُقْتَلُ فِي سَبِيلِ اللَّهِ أَمْوَاتٌ بَلْ أَحْيَاءٌ وَلَكِنْ لَا تَشْعُرُونَ. وَلَنَبْلُوَنَّكُمْ بِشَيْءٍ مِنَ الْخَوْفِ وَالْجُوعِ وَنَقْصٍ مِنَ الْأَمْوَالِ وَالْأَنْفُسِ وَالثَّمَرَاتِ وَبَشِّرِ الصَّابِرِينَ . الَّذِينَ إِذَا أَصَابَتْهُمْ مُصِيبَةٌ قَالُوا إِنَّا لِلَّهِ وَإِنَّا إِلَيْهِ رَاجِعُونَ. أُولَئِكَ عَلَيْهِمْ صَلَوَاتٌ مِنْ رَبِّهِمْ وَرَحْمَةٌ وَأُولَئِكَ هُمُ الْمُهْتَدُونَ﴾

O you who have faith! Take recourse in patience and prayer; indeed God is
with the patient. And do not call those who were slain in God's way "dead."
Rather they are living, but you are not aware. We will surely test you with a
measure of fear and hunger, and a loss of wealth, lives, and fruits; and give
good news to the patient - those who, when an affliction visits them, "Indeed we
belong to God, and to Him do we indeed return." It is they who receive the
blessings of their Lord and [His] mercy, and it is they who are the [rightly]
guided. (2:153-157)

AS THE BODIES LAY SCATTERED ON THE BATTLEFIELD ON THE AFTERNOON
of the day of Ashura, the battle seemed over. Yazid's forces appeared to
have won. Only a handful of women and children from Imam Husayn's

camp remained to cry over the martyred, and they too would soon be enslaved.

However, the day of Ashura proved much more catastrophic for the Bani Umayyad than they could have ever imagined. Rather than subsiding, the grief over Imam Husayn and his companions intensified, and it continues even more so up until today. Word of the greatest tragedy spread quickly and within a year after the battle, people began flocking to his shrine in Karbala.

Today, Imam Husayn is remembered everywhere. Onlookers often assume that we are mourning someone who was killed recently. They are shocked to learn that Imam Husayn was martyred 1,400 years ago. One thousand four hundred years - and we still keep his memory alive! In essence, remembering Husayn has kept Islam alive. Tyrants, kings, caliphs, and dictators have never been able to suppress his name, for God Himself has willed for it to be remembered.

$$﴿يُرِيدُونَ أَنْ يُطْفِئُوا نُورَ اللَّهِ بِأَفْوَاهِهِمْ وَيَأْبَى اللَّهُ إِلَّا أَنْ يُتِمَّ نُورَهُ وَلَوْ كَرِهَ الْكَافِرُونَ﴾$$

They desire to put out the light of God with their mouths, but God is intent on perfecting His light though the faithless should be averse. (9:32)

Ashura unveiled the ugly face of the Bani Umayyad. Beforehand, they had been able to disguise their animosity towards Islam. Umar b. Sa'd, the Commander-in-Chief of the Umayyad Army on the day of Ashura was able to spur on his soldiers by shouting, "O horsemen of God! Go forward! Paradise lies before you when you kill Husayn!"[65] And 30,000 men had agreed with him.

After the tragic day, rather than boast about their accomplishment, the Bani Umayyad were forced to lie about who they had captured at

---

[65] *Bihar al-Anwar*, Al-Allamah Al-Majlisi, v. 44, p. 391

Karbala - meaning that they could not disclose the fact that it was the family of the Holy Prophet. They claimed that the captives they were dragging and dishonoring from city to city (and finally to Damascus) were Romans and Persians, secessionists, and non-Muslims, who deserved to be punished for their crimes. However, soon after they arrived in Damascus, the truth came out. All that Imam Husayn's sister, Zaynab and his son, Imam Zain al-Abideen had to do was tell their story for the people to be shocked. In a sermon, Imam Zain al-Abideen began to introduce himself to the people by saying, "I am the son of Mecca, I am the son of Madinah, I am the son of Safa and Marwah, I am the son of the well of Zam Zam..." and by such a profound introduction, the people knew the gravity of what had happened in Karbala. These were no "secessionists." They came from the heart of Islam itself; they came from the heart of the Prophet himself. The martyrdom of Imam Husayn and his companions revolutionized the Muslim nation - they saw right through Bani Umayyad's facade.

The first to tumble were the killers of Imam Husayn. When they returned home, they expected accolade, instead they found scorn and shame. On the afternoon of Ashura, Umar b. Sa'd had distributed the victims' heads among the tribes as trophy. Each tribe received one head. However, Umar b. Sa'd wanted the head of Imam Husayn to reach Kufa quickly to prove his victory, so he sent it with Khiwala b. Yazid al-Asbahi. Kufa was about 15 or 20 hours from Karbala by horse, and it was already near sunset. Although he rode fast, Khiwala did not make it to Kufa until well after midnight. By that time, Ibn Ziyad (the governor of Kufa) was asleep, so he decided to go home.

He knocked on his door in anticipation. When his wife opened the door, he told her with excitement that he had great news. She asked what it was. He confided in her that he was carrying the head of the grandson of the Prophet in his bag. Immediately, she reprimanded him, "May God curse you! Is this good news? People come home with jewelry and gifts for their wives and you bring me the head of Husayn and you are proud of it?" Later that day, when Khiwala brought his prize to the governor of Kufa, even Ibn Ziyad's mother damned him. Their own families could not tolerate them anymore.

The rewards they had worked so eagerly to merit slipped right through their fingers. Umar b. Sa'd had known that what he had done was wrong. Imam Husayn was related to him through blood and that is why on the night of Ashura he hesitated to go through with having Husayn martyred. However, Yazid had promised him that if he killed Imam Husayn, he would become the governor of Ray (near modern-day Tehran). Greed for power overwhelmed him, so he shoved aside his concerns and went on with his onslaught. However, when he offered the head of Imam Husayn to Yazid to collect his reward, Yazid reproached him, "You may be stupid, but I am not stupid. I know you wavered in your resolve." Just like that, Ray fell out of his grasp. He and the others lost everything that they hoped for, in this world and in the next life.

Their lives did not last long. Shocked into revolution, the Muslims from Iraq to Madinah began revolting. Unable to enjoy his rule, Yazid abruptly lost his life. Within six years, all of the murderers of Imam Husayn had met justice. Mukhtar al-Thaqafi put Kufa under siege, and in one day, he dispensed with Umar b. Sa'd, Shimr, Khiwalah, and 280 others who had participated in the murder of Imam Husayn. Revolutions continued until the Bani Umayyad finally collapsed.

Even non-Muslims were shaken by the tragedy. As the caravan of captives traveled from Kufa to Damascus, it passed a temple inhabited by a Christian monk. The monk immediately realized that something unusual had happened, so he asked whose head was being carried on top of the spear. Since he was not a Muslim, the commanders shared their secret and told him that it was the head of the grandson of their Prophet. He reprimanded them, "Woe upon you! May God deprive you of blessings! This is how you treat the grandson of your Prophet? If Jesus had a son, we would have kept him close to us in our hearts." In

Palestine, the Christians built a famous church called the Church of the Hoof. It was built around the footprint of Jesus' donkey. Not Jesus' footprint, but that of his donkey. That was the level of respect and love that they had for the Prophet Jesus.

In contrast, the Wahhabis have been racing to obliterate the history of Islam. There are over 10,000 companions of the Prophet, including four imams buried in the cemetery of Al-Baqi in Madinah. Their headstones have been removed, no one would even know where their graves are if people did not memorize where the imams are buried. In fact, no one would even know the identities of the deceased by looking at the graves because only razor sharp rocks mark the headstones - all courtesy of the Wahhabi ideology. No one knows the name, gender, birth, or death-day of the graves. It is sad to see that even after death a human being cannot be honored by marking his name. If you attempt to recite prayers at the graves of the four imams, a guard tells you that it is religiously unlawful to "worship stones." They want to erase and eradicate every Islamic historical landmark. They see no value or reason why historical marks should be preserved. In America, next to my own home, the city has preserved a home as a historical landmark because it was the home of the first settlers in that town. People throughout the world honor its past citizens whom have cultivated, preserved, and contributed towards building their civilizations, but the Wahhabis want to desecrate the history of Islam.

Like the Wahhabis, the Bani Umayyad had tried to relegate Islam to an empty set of puritanical rituals, devoid of meaning, in order to diminish its spread. As a result, some of their soldiers came to kill Imam Husayn praying, "*qurbatan ilaa Allahi ta'aala* (we are doing this in order to seek nearness to God)" - by killing the grandson of the Prophet.

However, the massacre on Ashura uncovered the corruption that had crept into the religion. The falsehoods that the Bani Umayyad had propagated began to vanish, and the original message of Islam lay in clear view.

No one can oppose the power of truth. Many times throughout history, the ruling powers have tried to obliterate the grave of Imam Husayn. At one point, a simple man went to Karbala and walked from place to place, scooping up handfuls of dust and inhaling its fragrance, until he finally stopped and said, "This is the grave of my beloved Husayn." No one can ever suppress his grave.

If you seek happiness in this temporary life, stay with the Ahlul-Bayt. Be loyal to them, and try to serve them, especially Imam Husayn. A tradition by one of the imams says, "All of us are arks of salvation, but the ark of Husayn is the fastest." Be with him, help his cause, and teach his lessons. Although you may not consider yourself to be an orator or a writer, but if you speak about Imam Husayn, the words will come out naturally. Share his story. Tell people that this is your history, the history of Imam Husayn.

Part Two

2006 CE / 1426 AH
London, England

Our Responsibilities

Chapter 1

﴿وَالَّذِينَ هُمْ لِأَمَانَاتِهِمْ وَعَهْدِهِمْ رَاعُونَ ۞ وَالَّذِينَ هُمْ عَلَى صَلَوَاتِهِمْ يُحَافِظُونَ ۞ أُولَٰئِكَ هُمُ الْوَارِثُونَ ۞ الَّذِينَ يَرِثُونَ الْفِرْدَوْسَ هُمْ فِيهَا خَالِدُونَ﴾

And those who are keepers of their trusts and their covenant, and those who keep a guard on their prayers; these are they who are the heirs, who shall inherit the Paradise; they shall abide therein. (23:8-11)

AFTER GOD CREATED THE UNIVERSE, HE TESTED ALL OF HIS CREATIONS and offered them a profound responsibility - to be the caretakers of Earth. Most of His creations refrained from it. They all refused the responsibility except for one, and that was the human being.

﴿إِنَّا عَرَضْنَا الْأَمَانَةَ عَلَى السَّمَاوَاتِ وَالْأَرْضِ وَالْجِبَالِ فَأَبَيْنَ أَنْ يَحْمِلْنَهَا وَأَشْفَقْنَ مِنْهَا وَحَمَلَهَا الْإِنْسَانُ...﴾

Indeed We presented the Trust to the heavens and Earth and the mountains, but they refused to bear it, and were apprehensive of it; but man undertook it... (33:72)

The human being agreed to undertake this enormous responsibility, and "we" agreed that we would maintain and sustain Earth; "we" agreed that we would develop righteousness within our souls; "we" promised to establish social justice and equality upon the earth; therefore, God granted us this trust (*amanah*) to be His vicegerent on earth.

Running parallel to that responsibility, we were also given the opportunity to reach the stage of true humanity - *insaaniyah*. *Insaaniyah* (becoming true human beings) is nothing other than attaining human perfection, and since a true human being is not just flesh and blood, he must strive to fulfill this Divine challenge and reach the highest stage of human excellence.

In exchange for being God's vicegerent, and in order to assist us while on this journey and struggle, God endowed us with a tremendous ability which is the mind (*aql*). Our intellectual facility is the most important gift that God has given us, such that when God created the intellect, He told it, "By My Honor and Glory, I have not created anything more beloved to Me than you. Through you, I reward, and through you, I punish."[66]

Islam places such an emphasis on reasoning and the intellect that it is no wonder why the first verse to descend on the Prophet ordered him to "read." One of the over-arching themes of the Holy Qur'an is about reflection, meditation, contemplation, and thinking. For those who refused to use their intellect, God rebuked them, even after the fact that He had sent prophets to enlighten them, but still chose to blindly follow their traditions rather than to think for themselves.

﴿إِنَّا وَجَدْنَا آبَاءَنَا عَلَىٰ أُمَّةٍ وَإِنَّا عَلَىٰ آثَارِهِم مُّقْتَدُونَ﴾

"We found our fathers following a creed and we are indeed following in their footsteps." (43:23)

---

[66] *Al-Kafi*, v. 1, p. 10

Although the average weight of an adult brain is nearly three pounds, which is about 2% of one's total body weight, it is the most complicated system created by God. Nevertheless, how many individuals make full use of their reasoning power? Most people probably take the intellect for granted. Honestly, how many of us really challenge our thoughts, ponder on life, try to make discoveries, or find solutions to different conflicts?

$$﴿وَالَّذِينَ كَفَرُوا يَتَمَتَّعُونَ وَيَأْكُلُونَ كَمَا تَأْكُلُ الْأَنْعَامُ وَالنَّارُ مَثْوًى لَهُمْ﴾$$

As for the faithless, they enjoy and eat just like the cattle eat, and the Fire will be their [final] abode. (47:12)

Have you ever watched cattle? They spend the entire day grazing and ignore everything else around them. In many ways, some people are like that as well. Those who do not use their reasoning think that life is only about what they are going to eat, how much money they can make, and what sort of fun is in store for them. They do not reflect nor ask themselves why they are here, what purpose were they created for, or what is their objective in life is.

Today, the vast majority of Muslims world-wide follow a belief system simply because they are born into it. Their conviction is not an intellectual choice; but rather, an emotional or sentimental attachment. They are born into a Muslim family, so they are Muslim. If their family is Shia, they become Shia; if their family is Sunni, they become Sunni; if their family is Salafi, they become Salafi. They do not question what they are told. They do not even ask why they follow what they follow.

During Ali b. Abi Talib's reign as the fourth caliph, a large group of devout but ignorant worshippers called the Kharijites (Khawarij, the Seceders) fought against him. In one of his sermons, Ali b. Abi Talib explained how he felt about them saying, "Two groups tired me out:

the immoral scholars and the ignorant worshippers."[67] Although they knew better, the first group used religion for their own personal benefit and did not have the fear of God in their hearts; whereas the second group wanted to worship God but were extreme in their ways; they set out to worship God but ended up following Satan. The Kharijites fell into the second category, and in our time, a group known as the *takfiris* resembles them because they are the ones who are killing innocent Muslims in Iraq, Afghanistan, Pakistan and elsewhere. These people are ignorant and none of their acts of worship will benefit them in the least. Indeed, God instructs us to worship Him in the way which He has taught us, we are not supposed to worship Him in "our own ways." Deviating from His path will do nothing except distance us away from Him.

After equipping us with intellect (*aql*), God gave us a soul (*nafs*) to facilitate our success in fulfilling our duties as vicegerent on earth.

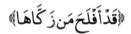

One who purifies it (the soul) is certainly felicitous. (91:9)

The soul is extremely vulnerable and volatile, and if it is not handled with extreme care then the soul can become the most deviating factor of the human being. If one can refine, polish, nurture, protect, and purify the soul then one will definitely succeed in this life.

One day, a student who had just graduated from a religious seminary asked his mentor for some advice that he could reflect on for the rest of his life. The graduate was expecting a long detailed lecture, but the scholar simply said, "My son, I have one thing to tell you, and I want you to remember this forever: do not offend (or do injustice to) the closest thing to you." The graduate asked what the closest thing to a

---

[67] *Nahjul Balaghah*

person is and the teacher replied, "Your soul." Therefore, do not offend your soul - take care of your soul - be careful and watchful over it.

Sometimes our soul seduces us.

$$﴿إِنَّ النَّفْسَ لَأَمَّارَةٌ بِالسُّوءِ﴾$$

...for the [carnal] soul indeed prompts [men] to evil... (12:53)

We do not always need Satan to lead us down the wrong path - sometimes our own soul does that. The soul can become prone to evil unless God protects it; otherwise, if we listen to the whims of our soul then we will indeed be spiritually lost.

$$﴿إِلَّا مَا رَحِمَ رَبِّي إِنَّ رَبِّي غَفُورٌ رَحِيمٌ﴾$$

...except inasmuch as my Lord has mercy. Indeed my Lord is All-Forgiving, All-Merciful. (12:53)

Prophet Muhammad explained, "The first step to committing a sin is the assent of the soul."[68]

One does not wake up in the morning and decide that they will commit a sin; rather, sinning is a gradual process and if we follow certain paths, then we will end up committing sins. For example, the Qur'an does not say "do not commit fornication," rather it says, "do not even *approach* fornication."[69] The Qur'an gives us warning signals. It is saying that at the end of that road there is a great sin, so do not even tread down that road.

Another dangerous path is improper socializing with people of the opposite gender, such as flirting. We also should pay close attention to the chatting that takes place online for hours on end. Do not say I know myself, no one can seduce me. You need to be very careful and do

---

[68] *Da'aimul Islam*, Al-Qadhi Al-Maghribi, v. 2, p. 352
[69] *Al-Qur'an*, 17:32

not even allow for that door to open - just slam it shut! However, if you have the intention of marriage and are looking for a spouse to establish a family, then search for a partner properly.

God has entrusted us with many things and one of these things is a family, not just our immediate family, but also our extended Muslim family. Your Muslim sister who walks down the street is also a part of your family, and therefore, you need to protect her as well. A tradition tells us that, "A Muslim is a brother (or sister) to another Muslim."[70] You should not lie to her, betray her, mislead her, or take advantage of her. Do not tell her that you want to get married, and then a few months later say that you were not serious. A girl should not be an easy target for you just because she is not your relative - she is part of your extended Muslim family.

Above that, we have an even bigger family, they are the human family. Ali b. Abi Talib wrote in a letter addressed to Malik al-Ashtar (his governor of Egypt) saying that, "Human beings are of two types: either your brethren in faith or your counterpart in creation."[71] Even if somebody is not a Muslim and does not want to acknowledge that we are a human family, then we as Muslims must still recognize them as family. Therefore, we need to treat each other as family and not take advantage of each other, or hurt them in any way.

Today, there are some individuals who say that they do not need to get married, they say, "We trust each other, so we do not need to have a religious contract," however what they have forgotten is that there is a third party between them. Marriage is not just an agreement between two people; rather it is a solemn covenant between three parties - the husband, the wife, and God Almighty. It is a holy contract and thus we must all fulfill our covenant.

---

[70] *Bihar al-Anwar*, Al-Allamah Al-Majlisi, v. 75, p. 39
[71] *Nahjul Balaghah*, sermon 53

﴿وَالَّذِينَ هُمْ لِأَمَانَاتِهِمْ وَعَهْدِهِمْ رَاعُونَ﴾

And those who keep their trusts and covenants. (23:8)

Among people there are some who did not honor the trusts of God, such as the Bani Umayyad. As it is has been stated, "They appropriated the wealth of the nation and enslaved the people."[72] Instead of allowing the Muslim minds to think and ponder freely, they sedated the people and silenced their intellect, and unfortunately no one could stop them. The masses were in need of a Divinely-sent leader. They needed a man like Imam Husayn to revive the corrupted and degenerated nation.

Muharram is the season of the renaissance. Not only do we mourn, but we celebrate as well. We celebrate the birth of Husayn and the rebirth of Islam. The Bani Umayyad attempted to murder Islam, the Qur'an, and the spirit of the people, and it was Imam Husayn who rose up to revive them all.

For over 1,400 years, many Christians, Jews, Buddhists, Hindus, atheists, and lost Muslims were guided to the light and glory of God through the commemorations of Imam Husayn. Think of Wahab b. Kalbi who was a Christian. A few days after he chose to embrace Islam, he gave his life for the Imam. He did not wait until he had made the pilgrimage (Hajj); he did not wait until he had been reciting his prayers for years. He was the first martyr on the side of Imam Husayn to face the enemy.

The commemorations of Imam Husayn also provide an outlet for emotional sharing and spiritual strength. When we hear about the tragedy of Ashura, we cannot hold back our tears due to the sadness of the narrative. Crying is a natural and healthy reaction for a saddened heart and is an admirable thing; it is neither appalling nor shameful.

---

[72] *Bihar al-Anwar*, Al-Allamah Al-Majlisi, v. 18, p. 126

God has informed us about many great prophets who shed tears and showed sorrow.

$$﴿إِذَا تُتْلَى عَلَيْهِمْ آيَاتُ الرَّحْمَـٰنِ خَرُّوا سُجَّدًا وَبُكِيًّا﴾$$

When the signs of the All-Beneficent were recited to them, they would fall down weeping in prostration. (19:58)

A tradition says, "A single teardrop can extinguish oceans of God's wrath." We do not need to dial 911 when we have an emergency; we have the power inside each and every one of us and we need to tap into that. Shedding tears in the middle of the night can calm and subdue God's anger and bring his mercy. When we cry for Imam Husayn, we are actually bringing ourselves closer to God and we are sympathizing with all of the prophets.

Every year in the beginning of the month of Muharram, our infallible imams would invite poets to recite the story of Imam Husayn; and when we hold gatherings every year during Muharram, we are following their practice. When we hear about Imam Husayn, we come closer to God and we return to ourselves. We reflect on how we have lived our lives, and ask what we should do to make our lives more enriching in the future.

One of the things which we need to do from the first night of Muharram is to ask ourselves whether God is really happy with us or not? Please remember that life is short; the days, if not years, are passing by very quickly. Do not say, "I do not need to pray now; I'll pray later. One day I'll read the Qur'an. One day I'll listen to my parents. One day I'll be a good Muslim." Do not say *one day*. That one day you are referring to must be today and we must try very hard to change ourselves for the better.

Islamic sources tell us that mourning for a long period of time is not recommended (*makruh*), except if one is mourning for Imam Husayn and the tragedies which he went through. Mourning for him never ends. It continues eternally. Even if we lose a loved one, it is not recommended to mourn excessively. Again, the only exception to this rule is for Imam Husayn, not so much as an individual, rather as a great cause who revived humanity.

Imam al-Mahdi, the 12th Imam who is still living and is the awaited savior of humanity says, "I will mourn for you morning and evening, and instead of tears, I will weep blood."[73]

If the imams mourn like this, then it cannot be something negative, it must be a recommended act for all of us to follow.

Prophet Muhammad said, "If a Muslim scholar dies, then the sky weeps for him for 40 days." Even if a scholar dies a natural death, the sky will still weep out of grief for his death. When the people asked the Prophet how the sky weeps, he said that during sunrise and sunset a distinctive redness will appear. If this is something which holds true for an ordinary scholar, just imagine how the sky would be if an infallible Imam was brutally murdered along with 72 of his closest family and followers?

---

[73] *Ziyarah Al-Nahiya Al-Muqaddasa*

The Threat of Radicalism
Chapter 2

﴿وَمَنْ أَحْسَنُ قَوْلاً مِمَّنْ دَعَا إِلَى اللَّهِ وَعَمِلَ صَالِحًا وَقَالَ إِنَّنِي مِنَ الْمُسْلِمِينَ﴾

Who has a better call than him who summons to God and acts righteously and says, "Indeed I am one of the muslims." (41:33)

TODAY, ISLAM IS FACING A FORMIDABLE CHALLENGE; HOWEVER, THE danger is not only external, it is also internal. Our ummah (Muslim nation) is suffering from internal bleeding as the teachings of "extremism" and "fanaticism" has infiltrated the Islamic thought. A few over-zealous and puritanical Muslims have grossly misunderstood the Qur'an, and such people through their misunderstanding of the Qur'an, have acted heinously and put the entire world in danger. Their results have been seen in London, Madrid, New York City, Baghdad and other regions. A select few have turned Islam into a religion that seems to glorify violence and fear, thus making people afraid of Islam and Muslims.

How did this happen?

Despite the current propaganda against Muslims, Islam is not a militant religion. In fact, not only is Islam a religion of peace, but the Prophet and the twelve imams - the successors of Prophet Muhammad

- were all peaceful individuals. Even when the enemy forces of the Bani Umayyad mobilized around Imam Husayn in Karbala, his companions urged him to attack the enemies but he refused saying, "I hate to be the one who starts a war." He was never a warmonger or an instigator. Up until the last moment of his life, the Imam attempted to make peace with Umar b. Sa'd, the leader of the Umayyad army. He even held a private meeting with him in his tent, but it became quite clear to him that Umar b. Sa'd did not want to accept any solution except for war.

Imam Husayn learned his peaceful methods through the tradition (Sunnah) carried forth from his grandfather Prophet Muhammad. When the Prophet came home dripping with blood after his enemies had thrown stones at him, his wife Khadijah asked him, "O Messenger of God, why don't you invoke the curse of God upon them?" To this innocent question, he replied, "I was not sent as a curse. I was sent as a mercy to mankind."[74]

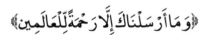

We did not send you but as a mercy to all of the nations. (21:107)

The Prophet was not a militant minded person, and although he had to lead the Muslims in defensive battles, he preferred and inclined more to peaceful solutions.

Today, a small number of fanatical "Muslims" have deviated from the Prophet's tradition and have threatened the world.

What is their rationale?

They argue that we are living in a world inherently hostile to Islam and religion in general; they argue that we live in a world dominated by modern secularism in which Islam has been reduced to mere rituals in which the spirit of Islam has disappeared, and therefore they feel that they need to fight to revive Islam and return it to its "past glory."

---

[74] *Al-Ghadir*, Allamah Al-Amini, v. 8, p. 252

However, this is a completely fallacious argument. Perhaps some of the points are correct, in that we live in a predominately secular world and the spirit of religion is starting to fade, however the conclusion and the manner in which they are carrying out their message is warped.

During the time of Ali b. Abi Talib's caliphate, the Kharijites used to chant, "There is no authority except with God!" in order to reject Imam Ali's leadership and authority. The Kharijites were not chanting their slogan to praise God and they knew that Ali b. Abi Talib never denied the true authority of God, but they were chanting it to bring down Imam Ali, thus their intent was malicious.

The *takfiris* do the same thing today. In particular, the *takfiris* will brand you as an infidel (*kafir*) *if* you disagree with their ideology. If you do not believe in everything that they say then you become an apostate, a heretic, and a rejecter in their eyes - even if you say, "There is no God but God, and Muhammad is the Prophet of God." Even if they find you in the heart of Mecca praying five times a day, they will still label you an infidel, and once you are an infidel your blood is lawful - this is exactly what is happening today in the region.

Unfortunately, the *takfiri* movement is spreading. What started out as a phenomenon contained to the Middle East has now reached the shores of Europe and America.

I was in Seattle, Washington visiting a mosque in which I gave a brief speech about the necessity of Muslim unity. After I finished a man came up to me and objected saying, "Unity is very important, but there is one group that we cannot unite with." I asked who that was and he said, *"The Shia."* I pointed out that I was Shia to which he replied that he knew that, and thus he could never be united with me. I asked him why, to which his blatant reply was that we (the Shia) have a different Qur'an. When I told him that we do not have a different Qur'an and that the Qur'an I use was printed in Saudi Arabia, he insisted that I was lying and asked me to leave the mosque. This incident did not occur in some far off or impoverished country - it happened in America!

However, this problem is not limited only to the Muslims as every religion has its own violent fanatics. There are Jews who gun down worshippers in holy places; Christians who bomb abortion clinics and people of other faiths who commit other atrocious acts. Nevertheless, what makes Muslims different is that we end up paying the price of the actions of a select few disconcerted people. Not all of the Jews are ostracized because of the actions of a few Jews; not all Christians are branded evil because of a few Christian terrorists; however, all Muslims bear the burden of the sins of a few wicked people.

It must be understood though that the bombing and killing of innocent people is explicitly against the teachings of Islam and murder is actually an assault on the entire human race.

﴿مِنْ أَجْلِ ذَٰلِكَ كَتَبْنَا عَلَىٰ بَنِي إِسْرَائِيلَ أَنَّهُ مَنْ قَتَلَ نَفْسًا بِغَيْرِ نَفْسٍ أَوْ فَسَادٍ فِي الْأَرْضِ فَكَأَنَّمَا قَتَلَ النَّاسَ جَمِيعًا وَمَنْ أَحْيَاهَا فَكَأَنَّمَا أَحْيَا النَّاسَ جَمِيعًا﴾

That is why We decreed for the Children of Israel that whoever kills a soul, without [its being guilty of] manslaughter or corruption on the earth, is as though he has killed all of mankind, and whoever saves a life it is as though he has saved all of mankind. (5:32)

﴿وَمَن يَقْتُلْ مُؤْمِنًا مُّتَعَمِّدًا فَجَزَاؤُهُ جَهَنَّمُ خَالِدًا فِيهَا وَغَضِبَ اللَّهُ عَلَيْهِ وَلَعَنَهُ وَأَعَدَّ لَهُ عَذَابًا عَظِيمًا﴾

Should anyone kill a believer intentionally, his requital shall be Hell, to remain in it [forever]; God will be wrathful at him and curse him and He will prepare for him a great punishment. (4:93)

The Qur'an is very adamant about taking the life of innocent people. Whoever kills another person unjustly will be deprived of God's mercy. He will never be forgiven and will suffer eternal torment and bear the wrath of God. In fact, Prophet Muhammad said, "The destruction of the cosmos is less painful to God than the blood of a single person who is slain unjustly."[75] This is what the essence of Islam is, yet we hear about "Islamic fundamentalism" every day.

It is worth noting that fundamentalism is not an inherently Islamic term. It was coined in the early 20th century America by strict Protestants who wanted to distinguish themselves from the more liberal Christians. They wanted to go back to the basics of religion, so they called themselves "fundamentalists." Thus, the negative connotations which go with the term "fundamentalism" have nothing to do with Islam.

With that said, do we as Muslims have "fundamentalism" as part of our belief system?

Indeed we do.

Fundamentalism or *usuliyyah* means going back to the basics - the basics of Islam, the teachings of the Qur'an and the ways of Prophet Muhammad. Islamic fundamentalism calls for openness, religious tolerance, diversity, forgiveness, respect for human life and dignity.

For example, we see the fundamentals of Islam in its early history when a delegation of Christians came from Najran (in the southern part of the Arabian Peninsula) to meet with the Prophet for the first time. When they arrived, he opened the mosque for them, which he had built with his own hands.

Islam is not anti-Christianity; Islam is not anti-Judaism; Islam is not anti-humanity.

---

[75] *Mustadrak*, v. 18, p. 209

﴿قُلْ يَا أَهْلَ الْكِتَابِ تَعَالَوْا إِلَى كَلِمَةٍ سَوَاءٍ بَيْنَنَا وَبَيْنَكُمْ
أَلَّا نَعْبُدَ إِلَّا اللَّهَ وَلَا نُشْرِكَ بِهِ شَيْئًا وَلَا يَتَّخِذَ بَعْضُنَا بَعْضًا أَرْبَابًا
مِّن دُونِ اللَّهِ فَإِن تَوَلَّوْا فَقُولُوا اشْهَدُوا بِأَنَّا مُسْلِمُونَ﴾

*Say, "O People of the Book! Come to a word common between us and you: that
we will worship no one but God, and that we will not ascribe any partner to
Him, and that we will not take each other as lords besides God." But if they
turn away, (then) say, "Be witnesses that we are muslims (those who submit)."
(3:64)*

﴿لَّا يَنْهَاكُمُ اللَّهُ عَنِ الَّذِينَ لَمْ يُقَاتِلُوكُمْ فِي الدِّينِ وَلَمْ يُخْرِجُوكُم
مِّن دِيَارِكُمْ أَن تَبَرُّوهُمْ وَتُقْسِطُوا إِلَيْهِمْ إِنَّ اللَّهَ يُحِبُّ الْمُقْسِطِينَ﴾

*God does not forbid you in regards to those who did not make war against you
on account of religion and did not expel you from your homes, that you deal
with them with kindness and justice. Indeed God loves the just ones. (60:8)*

Kindness and justice are the main characteristics of Islam, and right
from the beginning, Islam called for mutual understanding between
Muslims and other human beings.

In sharp contrast, Christian history reveals that until few centuries
ago, one of their slogans was "killing non-Christians pleases God."

Although the West considers itself the source of religious tolerance,
the fact is that religious tolerance only entered Western thought
recently, and in fact, one of the main aims of the early American
Christian missionaries was to convert the ingenious natives to
Christianity.

Anyone who equates "Islamic fundamentalism" with "terrorism" has
misunderstood the true teachings of the Prophet. Unfortunately,
however, there are some who have misunderstood this concept.

﴿وَمَامُحَمَّدٌ إِلَّا رَسُولٌ قَدْ خَلَتْ مِن قَبْلِهِ الرُّسُلُ أَفَإِن مَّاتَ أَوْ قُتِلَ انْقَلَبْتُمْ عَلَى أَعْقَابِكُمْ وَمَن يَنقَلِبْ عَلَى عَقِبَيْهِ فَلَن يَضُرَّ اللَّهَ شَيْئًاوَسَيَجْزِي اللَّهُ الشَّاكِرِينَ﴾

Muhammad is but an apostle; [other] apostles have passed before him. If he dies or is slain, will you then turn back on your heels? Anyone who turns back on his heels will not harm God in any way, and God will reward the grateful ones. (3:144)

The Prophet had foretold that by the time the last Imam reappears, Islam will have become so tainted that when he (the Imam) brings back the authentic Islam, people will say that he is bringing about a new religion.

Part of what we are witnessing today is that tainted "fundamentalism" - violence, intolerance, and hatred. Although this trend has never reflected in the majority of Muslims, it did begin early on during the time of the Prophet. Muslim history teaches how a select few (not the Prophet or his true companions or relatives) began a campaign of intolerance and rejection.

One prime example is this: Why do Muslims gather to remember Imam Husayn? Why was he murdered? What excuse did they have for killing the grandson of the Prophet when many of them saw the Prophet with their own eyes holding Husayn and saying, "Husayn is from me, and I am from Husayn. May God love one who loves Husayn." How did the situation deteriorate to such a point that he had no one to help him except for 72 relatives and companions? What happened to the Muslim ummah?

When some people discuss the tragic events of Ashura, they say, "Both sides were with God. Husayn was with God and Yazid was with God, and God will judge between them." Sadly enough, some Muslims actually believe this. When you try to discuss and critique the history

129

of Islam after the Prophet's death, they object saying, "Don't do this! You are not allowed to do this!" Why aren't we allowed to do that? What possible reason is there not to become aware about our own history? What are we afraid of? Those who do not know their own history are doomed to repeat it. We need to know who was right and who was wrong so we can avoid making the same mistakes in the future. God does not want the believers to be naïve, and therefore, we need to understand why we are doing what we are doing.

$$﴿وَلَا تَرْكَنُوٓاْ إِلَى الَّذِينَ ظَلَمُواْ فَتَمَسَّكُمُ النَّارُ وَمَا لَكُم مِّن دُونِ اللَّهِ مِنْ أَوْلِيَآءَ ثُمَّ لَا تُنصَرُونَ﴾$$

And do not incline toward the wrongdoers; lest the Fire should touch you, and you will not have any friend besides God, then you will not be helped. (11:113)

God wants us to follow the truth with our eyes wide open.

It has been related that in Paradise we will be graded according to our understanding of the faith; it is through the intellect that God will reward or punish us. Imam Husayn said, "Good (*ma'rouf*) is in proportion to understanding (*ma'rifah*)."[76] The more confident you are in what you do, the higher you will ascend in Paradise. Paradise is not a one-story building; rather, God has fashioned it with many levels because people will be put into different grades according to their level of understanding.

In the early period of Islam, after the time of the Prophet, a few prominent Muslims continued to intensify their campaign of bigotry and bloodshed until it reached the peak during the time of Muawiyah b. Abi Sufyan.

---

[76] *Bihar al-Anwar*, Al-Allamah Al-Majlisi, v. 44, p. 196

$$﴿قَالَ مَا مَنَعَكَ أَلَّا تَسْجُدَ إِذْ أَمَرْتُكَ قَالَ أَنَا خَيْرٌ مِّنْهُ خَلَقْتَنِي مِنْ$$

$$نَّارٍ وَخَلَقْتَهُ مِن طِينٍ﴾$$

Said He, "What prevented you from prostrating when I commanded you?" "I am better than him," he said. "You created me from fire and You created him from clay." (7:12)

Islam forbids discrimination, nepotism, and favoritism of any kind, and although the Prophet spent a great deal of his ministry abolishing racial prejudice and discrimination amongst the early Muslim community, at the onslaught of his reign, Muawiyah divided the Muslims into Arabs and non-Arabs (*mawali*).

Even though the non-Arabs were Muslims, they were treated as non-Muslims, and thus, had to pay extra taxes to the government which ended up in Muawiyah's pocket. Muawiyah inclined to free the state and society of some of the noblest companions of the Prophet, thus many of the companions of the Prophet were tortured, imprisoned, and executed. Even Imam Ali did not escape the persecution. Just mentioning the name of Ali was enough to bring down an official punishment upon someone; no one during Muawiyah's rule dared utter his name. If they wanted to refer to Ali, they had to call him "Abu Zaynab," despite the fact that the Prophet declared, "O Ali! You are with the truth, and the truth revolves around you wherever you go."[77]

Every Friday, which is the holiest day in Islam, the Friday preacher would mount the pulpit and curse Ali, Fatima, Hasan, and Husayn. What did these holy personalities do to merit this treatment?

In a tradition noted by Al-Bukhari, it says, "God is happy with whoever makes Fatima happy and angry with whoever makes her angry."[78]

---

[77] *Al-Amalee*, p. 150
[78] *Al-Ghadir*, v. 7, p. 191

Fatima al-Zahra was a pure and honorable woman, but the preachers would still deliver cursing words toward her and her children while the masses held their tongues and called Muawiyah, "Amir al-Mumineen (the Commander of the Believers)," even though this was a title which was exclusive for Imam Ali b. Abi Talib.

That was the first wave of extremism.

The second wave of extremism began 700 years ago with Ahmad b. Taymiyyah al-Harrani al-Hanbali. He wrote a book (*Minhaj al-Sunnah*) to defame the Ahlul-Bayt. Contrary to the vast majority of Muslim scholars, he asserts that God has a physical body (*tajseem*) and that some people can see Him! Even worse, he degrades the status of the Prophet and claims that Abu Hurayrah came to the Prophet and said, "I want you to pray for God to guide my mother." Thus the Prophet raised his hands and prayed for her. God guided her and she became a good Muslim. Abu Hurayrah returned to the Prophet and said, "I want you to pray for God to guide my clan." Thus the Prophet raised his hands and prayed for his clan. God guided them and they became good Muslims. Finally, he says that the Prophet then prayed for his own mother, Aminah b. Wahhab, but the Prophet said, "I asked God to let me pray for my mother, but God refused!"

Isn't it very odd that the Prophet can pray for Abu Hurayrah's mother, but God would not allow the Prophet to mention a prayer for his own mother?

Ibn Taymiyyah is the mastermind of Islamic extremism, and strangely enough, he continues to be a model that inspires so many extremists even up until today. The title of one of his thesis says it all, *A License to Kill the Rejecters (Jawazu Qital al-Rafidhah)*. In this book, he applauds the Kharijites for assassinating Imam Ali and refers to the Shia as "rejecters," since they rejected the leadership of the first three caliphs. Furthermore, he asserts that the blood of the Shia is lawful since they are not Muslims; thus, in his opinion, even killing them is permitted.

Unfortunately, his influence persists in the sectarian violence that plagues Muslim and non-Muslim countries.

About 300 years ago, another man rose up in Najd, Arabia by the name of Muhammad b. Abd al-Wahhab al-Najdi, he is the founder of the modern-day Wahhabism. Inspired by Ibn Taymiyyah, he continued his tradition and declared that whoever did not accept his personal ideas of Islam was a non-Muslim - an infidel (*kafir*) or a rejecter. That word is ascribed to every person they deem as unconventional to their ideology. The Prophet himself said that no one has the right to call a person who declares the profession of faith (*La ilaha illallah Muhammadan rasulullah*) as an infidel and he said that, "Whoever calls another Muslim a disbeliever has himself disbelieved."[79]

Despite the Prophet's warning, the Wahhabi movement considers everyone (including Muslims) who does not follow their ideology as an infidel.

After Muhammad b. Abd al-Wahhab published his treatise, his own brother, Sulayman b. Abd al-Wahhab wrote another treatise refuting it. Hundreds of Muslim scholars, of all persuasions, joined Sulayman in countering Muhammad b. Abd al-Wahhab's ideas.

In fact, Muhammad b. Abd al-Wahhab caused a giant schism in Islam, and just like his predecessor Ibn Taymiyyah, he denigrated the status of the Prophet. One day while giving a speech, Ibn Abd al-Wahhab raised his cane and insulted the Prophet by proclaiming, "My cane is much more useful than Muhammad because today Muhammad is dead and useless while I can use my cane."[80]

Until today, the Wahhabis continue to fight to keep the teachings and moral guidance of the Ahlul-Bayt away from the masses. They do not recognize them, let alone mention them. When a Muslim visits the

---

[79] *A'yan Al-Shia*, Sayed Muhsin Al-Ameen v. 1, p. 37
[80] *Shuhada'ul Fadheelah*, Ibn al-Wahhab, p.288

holy lands of Mecca and Madinah, the first thing that the Wahhabi establishment does is inundate them with literature attacking the Shia Islam. They know that millions of people are on their way to visit the Mosque of the Prophet and the cemetery of Al-Baqi and so they attempt to brainwash the people into believing that it is polytheism (*shirk*) to pay your respect to the deceased, despite the fact that the Prophet said, "Whoever performs Hajj and does not visit me, he did a disservice to me."[81]

It is these immaculate beings who lead us to the true understanding of the Qur'an and the hadith, and this is why the legacy of the Prophet was two-fold, "I am leaving behind two weighty things: the book of God and my progeny." We are doomed to failure if we hold to only one of them and leave the other.

God himself asserts in the Qur'an that some of His verses are indistinct (*mutashabihat*) and that is why we need someone to explain them to us. However, He Himself chose the interpreters; He did not leave that choice to us.

In order to understand the true message of the Noble Qur'an, we need the Ahlul-Bayt, for they are the speaking Qur'an, and that is why the Prophet told Imam Ali, "Whoever loves my Ahlul-Bayt has grasped hold of the firmest handhold."[82]

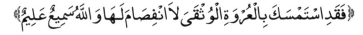

...has held fast to the firmest handle for which there is no breaking; and God is All-Hearing, All-Knowing. (2:256)

Unfortunately, the *takfiris* and the anti-Ahlul-Bayt groups blindly disregard the duty to take care of the progeny of the Prophet, and much

---

[81] *Al-Hidayah*, Sheikh Al-Sadooq, p. 67

[82] *Manaqib Al Abi Talib*, Ibn Shahrashoob, v. 2, p. 274

worse than this is that they seek to destroy their credibility and even silence their followers.

People often love the friends and family of a person whom they love and respect, and it is for this reason that I do not understand how someone can say that they love someone but do not love his immediate family. How can they attack the family of the Prophet when God instructed the Prophet to say to the people:

$$﴿قُل لَّا أَسْأَلُكُمْ عَلَيْهِ أَجْرًا إِلَّا الْمَوَدَّةَ فِي الْقُرْبَى﴾$$

Say, "I do not ask from you any reward for it (for the conveyance of the message of Islam) except the affection for [my] relatives." (42:23)

Sahih Al-Bukhari narrates how the Prophet emphasized the position of the Ahlul-Bayt to him, "Some Muslims asked, 'O Messenger of God, we know how to greet you; but teach us how to send prayers upon you.'"

The Prophet replied, "Say, O God! bless Muhammad and the family of Muhammad, as You have blessed Abraham and the family of Abraham; verily, You are Praiseworthy and Honorable (*Allahumma, salli ala Muhammadin wa Aali Muhammad kama sallayta ala Ibraheema wa Aali Ibraheem innaka Hameedun Majeed*)."

Then he added, "Do not send me an incomplete praise."

They asked, "O Messenger of God, what is an 'incomplete praise'?"

He replied, "When you send prayers upon me and omit my family."[83]

Almost 80 years ago, the Wahhabis destroyed the holy shrines in the Al-Baqi Cemetery.[84] Since the cemetery is only a few hundred meters

---

[83] *Al-Sawa'iq Al-Muhriqa*, Ibn Hajar, p. 87

[84] Starting in 1924, Abd al Aziz b. Saud began his occupation of the Hejaz (present day Saudi Arabia; named after the family that rules over the country) and he began his campaign to demolish the Islamic monuments, holy places, tombs and mausoleums, including the birth place of the Prophet, gravesite of Lady Khadijah, clearing the gravesites of the martyrs

from the Mosque of the Prophet, one will instantly notice a sharp contrast. On one side, you see the glorious Mosque of the Prophet bustling with visitors, well kept and well lit. Across the way, just on the other side of the marble floor, you will see a dark, deserted, and forbidden cemetery. If you inquire as to who is resting in that cemetery, they will say 10,000 companions of the Prophet, but they will make no mention of the four infallible imams - the direct descendents of the Prophet- who are also buried there. Their graves are unmarked and partitioned off. They do not even allow you to approach their graves, let alone offer your respect to them.

Another contrast observed in Madinah, visitors are allowed to pay their respect and offer their prayers at the gravesites of Abu Bakr and Umar b. al-Khattab. At the Great Mosque of the Prophet, two signs flank the resting place of the Prophet. One reads, "Greet the Prophet here," and the other reads, "Greet Abu Bakr and Umar, may God be pleased with them, here." They put up signs so that you know where to pay your respect. However, if you want to stand by the grave of the grandsons of the Prophet they accuse you of heresy. It is heresy to say, "Peace be upon you, O Son of the Messenger of God."

The opponents of the Ahul-Bayt thought that by demolishing the cemetery of Al-Baqi they would destroy the love for the Ahlul-Bayt in the hearts of the people, however they were dead wrong!

One should question, what brings millions of people around the world to gather at the local mosques, *hussayniyyahs* (Islamic centers), and homes during the season of Muharram? They gather only for the love of God, His Apostle, and the Ahlul-Bayt.

While the shrines are very important, it is not paramount to us whether or not the physical shrines are present or not because the love

---

of the Battle of Uhud, demolishing the gravestones of the four Imams in Al-Baqi Cemetary, and many other places.

for the Ahlul-Bayt runs through our veins and we are always with them. A tradition says that even if you are with a small stone in this life then you will be joined with it on the Day of Judgment, and therefore, whoever associates with the Ahlul-Bayt in this world, they will definitely be with them in the next life.

Gender Equality

﴿وَالْمُؤْمِنُونَ وَالْمُؤْمِنَاتُ بَعْضُهُمْ أَوْلِيَآءُ بَعْضٍ يَأْمُرُونَ بِالْمَعْرُوفِ وَيَنْهَوْنَ عَنِ الْمُنكَرِ وَيُقِيمُونَ الصَّلاةَ وَيُؤْتُونَ الزَّكَاةَ وَيُطِيعُونَ اللَّهَ وَرَسُولَهُ أُوْلَئِكَ سَيَرْحَمُهُمُ اللَّهُ إِنَّ اللَّهَ عَزِيزٌ حَكِيمٌ﴾

But the faithful men and women are comrades of one another: they bid what is right and forbid what is wrong and maintain the prayer, give the charity, and obey God and His Apostle. It is they to whom God will soon grant His mercy. Indeed God is All-Mighty, All-Wise. (9:71)

GOD CREATED MEN AND WOMEN EQUAL - BUT NOT IDENTICAL. GOD DID not create Eve out of the remnants of Adam. She was not a by-product of his creation; rather they were both created at the same time, from the same substance and the same matter. They were made to complement each other, and this is why the Prophet referred to women as the "siblings" of men. This means that both genders are part of each other and they are equal in creation. God says most eloquently about the relationship between women and men in the Holy Qur'an:

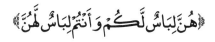

They are a garment for you and you are a garment for them. (2:187)

Our clothing protects us from the outside bad elements, adorns us, covers up our defects, and gives us status. By describing men and women as garments of each other, God is showing mankind how having a spouse protects and beautifies us and helps us to recognize our value. Just as our clothes provide shelter for us, as well as protection, warmth, comfort, and accompanies us throughout our lives, our spouses should also provide the same qualities for us. This is why God uses the example of a garment because men and women are necessary and complimentary to each other.

Nowhere in the Holy Qur'an or in the tradition of the Prophet will you find the notion that one gender is superior to the other. The good of society - not men or women is emphasized. Nonetheless, one may question then what is it meant in the following verse:

$$﴿ٱلرِّجَالُ قَوَّامُونَ عَلَى ٱلنِّسَآءِ بِمَا فَضَّلَ ٱللَّهُ بَعْضَهُمْ عَلَىٰ بَعْضٍ وَبِمَآ أَنفَقُوا مِنْ أَمْوَالِهِمْ﴾$$

Men are the maintainers of women (qawamun ala an-nisa) because God has made some of them to excel others and because they spend out of their property. (4:34)

Qawamun does not mean "superiority" of the male over the female; nor does it imply that God prefers men to women. It means that men are supposed to bear an extra degree of responsibility towards their family in regards to their maintenance.

Some people use such verses to show that Islam discriminates against women; however to combat these arguments, we must learn and comprehend certain basic facts about men and women in the Qur'an and compare them to what other major faiths hold, so that we are able to answer concerns from other people in regards to the issue of gender equality.

First and foremost, the Qur'an describes men and women as being created equal. The Old Testament maintains that God created the man first and then created the woman from his rib. Furthermore, it forewarns that the nature of women is warped because she was made from a crooked piece. In Islam the first verse of *Surah al-Nisa* (the Women) disproves this notion:

$$﴿يَا أَيُّهَا النَّاسُ اتَّقُوا رَبَّكُمُ الَّذِي خَلَقَكُم مِّن نَّفْسٍ وَاحِدَةٍ وَخَلَقَ مِنْهَا زَوْجَهَا وَبَثَّ مِنْهُمَا رِجَالاً كَثِيرًا وَنِسَاءً﴾$$

O mankind! Be wary of your Lord who created you from a single soul, and created its mate from it, and from the two of them, scattered numerous men and women. (4:1)

Therefore, no gender can claim superiority over the other. Spirituality is devoid of gender or race. "Verily, God does not look at your faces or features but He looks at your hearts."[85] He will judge us according to our intentions and conduct, not our gender or race.

The Qur'an also holds men and women at the same moral standard, and treats them as a pair. In contrast, some other religions assign the burden of moral responsibility towards the women, such that they describe Eve as the temptress. They teach that Satan approached her first, and after he corrupted her weak spirit, then she went to her husband and did Satan's job for him. However, the Qur'an teaches otherwise. It puts the responsibility for what happened on Adam and simply says, "Adam disobeyed his Lord."[86] Nowhere does it suggest that Eve herself was to blame for misleading Adam, or that women throughout the ages have to bear the divine perpetual curse and punishment of childbirth for her error. Other religions teach that the Divine gift of having children is actually a primordial curse, and in

---

[85] *Mustadrak*, v. 11, p. 264
[86] *Al-Qur'an*, 20:121

order to prevent women from committing more mischief, men must dominate them and guard themselves against women's guiles. However, in Islam the Prophet promised a renewal on life when a woman gives birth. A woman is forgiven for all of her past sins when she delivers a child into this world. Pregnancy and delivery is viewed with compassion, forgiveness, and love - not retribution.

Islam also asserts that no society can function without the active participation of women. If a society marginalizes women, it will not prosper, for surely women must play an integral role in society. Take the example of Prophet Muhammad, his mission would have never succeeded had it not been for his wife Khadijah for she was inseparable from his life and mission; she supported him emotionally, spiritually, and financially. For 29 years, the Prophet lived with Khadijah, and had no other wives except for her, and when she died, the Prophet continued to remember and love her. One of his later wives asked him, "O Messenger of God, do you still feel sad about losing Khadijah? God has given you many other younger and prettier wives." The Prophet replied that God did not replace Khadijah with a better wife. He said, "She believed in me when others disbelieved in me, trusted me when others rejected me, provided for me when others denied me, and she showered her wealth on Islam when others withheld their help from me."[87] Khadijah was a very unique lady. When she first married the Prophet, she was the richest woman in Mecca, but when she passed away, she could not even afford a shroud for herself. She offered all of her wealth in the way of Islam to the point that the Prophet had to shroud her dead body with his own robe. This was pure nobility and loyalty. This is why scholars say "Islam would not have risen without the courage of Ali and the wealth of Khadijah."[88]

With examples such as these, how can anyone claim that women have no role in Islamic society?

---

[87] *Sahih Al-Bukhari*, v. 4, p. 231
[88] *Shajarat Tooba*, Sheikh Al-Hairi, v. 2, p. 233

The Holy Qur'an provided women with remarkable rights at a time when they were only considered as mere property. Islam gave women rights and options that they did not have in previous times.

During the time of the Prophet, girls were considered a liability to the family, and infanticide of a female baby was unfortunately witnessed, to the extent where they would bury them alive. Islam adamantly denounced such a practice.

The Prophet also taught that women need to be educated; and he reiterated that, "Seeking knowledge is a duty for every Muslim man and woman."[89] One day, a group of women complained to the Prophet that they could not learn from him because men always surrounded him. He responded by designating a day specifically for teaching women. Education is a religious obligation that should not be neglected.

Islam also gave women the right to own their own property and dispose of it freely without the involvement of a male guardian.

Similarly, it gave them the absolute right to accept or refuse marriage offers. In Islam, parents must ask their daughters before promising them in marriage to someone else. Even the Prophet, "who has a greater claim on the faithful than they have on themselves"[90] went to ask his daughter Fatima if she wished to marry Imam Ali. When Imam Ali came to ask for Fatima's hand, he told him that he had to obtain Fatima's permission first. This is a lesson for all parents, particularly in some cultures who give away their daughters without asking them first, for that is an un-Islamic practice. No father can accept a marriage proposal on his daughter's behalf without first getting her approval in the matter.

---

[89] *Al-Kafi*, v. 1, p. 30
[90] *Al-Qur'an*, 33:6

Islam also gave women the right to vote by granting them the right to pay allegiance (*bayah*) on their own behalf.

﴿يَا أَيُّهَا النَّبِيُّ إِذَا جَاءَكَ الْمُؤْمِنَاتُ يُبَايِعْنَكَ عَلَى أَن لَّا يُشْرِكْنَ بِاللَّهِ شَيْئًا وَلَا يَسْرِقْنَ وَلَا يَزْنِينَ وَلَا يَقْتُلْنَ أَوْلَادَهُنَّ وَلَا يَأْتِينَ بِبُهْتَانٍ يَفْتَرِينَهُ بَيْنَ أَيْدِيهِنَّ وَأَرْجُلِهِنَّ وَلَا يَعْصِينَكَ فِي مَعْرُوفٍ فَبَايِعْهُنَّ وَاسْتَغْفِرْ لَهُنَّ اللَّهَ إِنَّ اللَّهَ غَفُورٌ رَّحِيمٌ﴾

O Prophet! when believing women come to you giving you a pledge that they will not associate aught with God, and will not steal, and will not commit fornication, and will not kill their children, and will not bring a calumny which they have forged of themselves, and will not disobey you in what is good, then accept their pledge, and ask forgiveness for them from God; surely God is Forgiving, Merciful. (60:12)

Paying allegiance at that time is akin to voting today. Islam extended suffrage to women long before Western democracy existed. If today women are denied the right to vote in certain Muslim countries, that does not mean that Islam does not give them the right to vote because denying them the right to vote does not come from the teachings of the Qur'an. Rather, women have the right to participate fully in politics.

Women also have the right to economic contribution. No career is closed to women unless it threatens her dignity, or her Islamic obligations cannot be upheld.

After discussing women, we come to the subject of marriage. God created everything in the universe in pairs, including human beings.

﴿وَمِن كُلِّ شَيْءٍ خَلَقْنَا زَوْجَيْنِ لَعَلَّكُمْ تَذَكَّرُونَ﴾

And of everything We have created pairs that you may be mindful. (51:49)

144

$$\text{﴿سُبْحَانَ الَّذِي خَلَقَ الْأَزْوَاجَ كُلَّهَا مِمَّا تُنبِتُ الْأَرْضُ وَمِنْ أَنفُسِهِمْ وَمِمَّا لَا يَعْلَمُونَ﴾}$$

Glory be to Him Who created pairs of all things, of what the earth grows, and of their kind and of what they do not know. (36:36)

Marriage is a necessity, not just a luxury. A woman once came to the 6th Imam, as-Sadiq and said to him, "I have decided to remain single my entire life." He asked her why, and she said it was so that she can be closer to God if she stayed untouched. The Imam replied that if it was purer to remain single then his grandmother Lady Fatima al-Zahra would have been the first woman never to marry. God created us to get married and to have a family. Human beings are gregarious creatures, they are not meant to live a hermetic life. We need the interaction, acceptance, love, communication, and companionship of our spouses. We need to share our lives and experiences, to grow, to protect, and to better ourselves with our partners and families.

In a family, the role of the mother is not just to tidy the home and prepare the meals. Her role is very critical, even more so than that of the father. She must provide spiritual nourishment for the family and stand as a model of proper and moral conduct for her children to live by. Children should find love, tenderness, and compassion within the heart of a mother. Without these important qualities, we as human beings will miss out on the most important ingredients to make this world a better place to live in.

Despite its importance, respect, and admiration for the institute of motherhood, at present it has significantly diminished. Women are distancing themselves from being called a "mother," and find it degrading. However, being called a mother is an honor and every mother should take pride in being a mother; for they are the ones who nurture and foster successful leaders, innovators, scientists, physicians; and even grown men became good husbands and fathers because of

145

their mothers. Mothers bear a giant responsibility and it is the great mothers who produce great children and future leaders.

Similarly, look at the people who went down the wrong path. If the cases are deeply analyzed, then one will find that those people came from troubled homes; many of them were deprived of love and compassion from their mothers. The first few years in a child's life are very critical for their development. It is worth reconsidering to serve others in an office while your children are deprived of your love and tenderness, for once gone, those priceless years will never come back.

The mother's role in a family is central. If you do not want to chase your future children through the streets or in the police stations, then find a good woman to marry; one who will make a great mother, one who will nurture and sustain your children out of her love and belief. If you want to get married, then look at your prospective wife as being the mother of your children.

Search for a woman with faith and commitment. A wife needs to be educated in Islam in order for her to raise the children rightfully. Otherwise, do not expect your children to mature properly. A mother is the child's first teacher; children will open their eyes and heart to her first.

Most of the youth who attend the mosque and listen to the Islamic sermons do so because of their mothers. Mothers warmly remind and request their children to stay close to God. They constantly want to feed their children with the spirit of Islam because they know it is the only protection and savior both in this world and in the next.

A man was once asked why he loved Imam Ali so much. He said that 30 years ago his mother blended the love of Ali b. Abi Talib into his milk. Mothers do not just give children physical food; they also give them the food of life, love, and spirituality.

Raising one child who believes in God is better than raising many children without faith; hence, we have to prepare our daughters for the great task that is awaiting them. Becoming a good mother does not happen overnight, it begins way before she becomes a mother - she must especially pay attention to what she says, does and how she behaves. When God decreed that the Prophet would have a daughter called Fatima who would be unmatched with other women in the world, he sent the Angel Gabriel to inform the Prophet that God, the Exalted greets him and instructs him to abstain from his wife for 40 days. After 40 days, He sent exceptional food for the Prophet from Heaven and then commanded that he should approach his wife. Therefore, we can see that food has an enormous effect. Prepare your body and your mind so that you can be a good mother.

Although Islam maintains that men and women have equal status, we have to address the fact that unfortunately gender discrimination still exists amongst Muslims even today. Many Muslim women feel marginalized and alienated, and even in the West we see gender discrimination between Muslims. Most of the time, our sisters play a secondary role in the Islamic community. Increasingly, they are complaining about their seclusion in the mosques. Regrettably, the Muslim community is not the perfect equal opportunity community. While the Qur'an maintains that believing men and women are guardians of each other, in practice, Muslim women are marginalized. Everywhere, men enter and sit in the best area of the mosque and have exclusive access to the speakers. Nowadays, we have relegated women to the dark corners of the mosque or secluded them to cramped, isolated rooms. They are not permitted to come into the main hall to listen, engage, and feel the spiritual fellowship of faithful believers. During the time of the Prophet, women used to sit in the Prophet's mosque and question him while he was speaking. They were free to question him wherever they wanted, even inside the mosque. They participated fully in public debate. Of course, the Islamic hijab and moral etiquettes have to be observed to the fullest in such circumstances.

Why is it that we have few female Muslim speakers, writers, professors, or activists? Who is to blame? Is it the men or the women, or both of them? We have exceptional male preachers, but believe me, bring one woman to deliver a dynamic lecture and she will put the best of the male speakers aside. Every Islamic program should include sessions that are run by the sisters for the sisters. We need to encourage women and provide them with the opportunity to speak, and they too should also make an effort to come forward.

One time, after the death of the Prophet, Umar b. al-Khattab announced that he was going to set a limit for the amount of a woman's *mahr* (marriage gift), a lady stood up in front of the crowd and objected, "Are you doing that, or is it God?" He replied, "A woman said the right and Umar erred."[91] She questioned him openly. We need female activists and speakers. Muslim men cannot always be the ones defending the rights of Muslim women. I cannot stand up in a Western university and talk about the rights of women in Islam. They will tell me that I am a man and that my wife or daughter should speak for themselves. Women need to take up this responsibility.

Next, there is the issue of hijab. And this does not only apply to the women. Although we usually limit the discussion of hijab to women, it applies to both men and women. A man's hijab begins in the heart, as well as his appearance.

$$﴿قُل لِّلْمُؤْمِنِينَ يَغُضُّوا مِنْ أَبْصَارِهِمْ وَيَحْفَظُوا فُرُوجَهُمْ ذَٰلِكَ أَزْكَىٰ لَهُمْ إِنَّ اللَّهَ خَبِيرٌ بِمَا يَصْنَعُونَ﴾$$

Say to the believing men that they cast down their looks and guard their private parts; that is purer for them; surely God is Aware of what they do. (24:30)

Men have to be especially careful in society, and should not bring about a sin by staring at the opposite gender. Imam Ali was sitting with some men when a beautiful woman passed by. They all began to stare at her. He told them not to stare because their eyes were being covetous and she was a woman like their wives. Hence, Islam instructs men (as well as women) to lower their gaze - meaning that they should not entertain their thoughts with sinful images when they look at a woman. Many problems begin with the first sinful glance. They become an arrow from the arrows of Satan. He whispers in your ears and tells you this is an attractive woman, don't miss out. God created this beauty for you to look at. The Prophet said that if you cast your eyes down from this artificial beauty, then God will reveal to you the real beauty which is the mysteries of the universe. However, one cannot have both. If you want to experience the beauty of God, then you have to have self-restraint, and self-restraint begins with the eyes. Even if you marry the most beautiful woman in the world and you have wandering eyes, you will still want to stare at other women. It will become a habit and will affect your family life tomorrow; therefore, we must learn to control our glances.

We live in a society where your look proclaims your identity. You are what you reveal. Whether you like it or not, society will judge you by your appearance. One's hairstyle, clothing, jewelry, and body piercing speak volumes on the type of person that one is. When you are young, you do not realize the future consequence of the choices that you make now, but they will affect you. Your body is not a canvas for dot-to-dot tattoos or a puncture board filled with numerous holes to dangle your jewelry. You have been gifted with an incredible body, shaped and created by God, therefore one must not abuse this magnificent work of art with one's own design. Besides, these add-on "attractions" are not really doing you any justice. Brothers, do not think that morally decent, intelligent, and aspiring sisters will ever give you the time of day if your hair is color-spiked, arms are painted with tattoos, jewelry is clicking all over your body, or your pants are dangling - they laugh at such guys.

Your value is not in your hairstyle, but it is in your heart. It is in your personality and attitude, not your outer appearance. If you want to touch the heart of a girl, do it through your honesty, sincerity, kindness, intelligence, faith, and manners. Do not say that you pray and fast, but your hairstyle is not important because it is. You have to look like those who are humble, sincere, people of faith, not those who are on the wrong path. Your appearance screams out to the world what you represent.

Similarly for sisters, hijab is an honorable way to live by. In the West, they call it a "veil," but hijab is not a veil. The term "veiling" has a very negative connotation. It somehow implies that you have no identity and no presence in the society. However, introducing the phrase "hijab" into the English language will give Muslim women an honorable identity.

Hijab is a privilege, not a curse. You may not realize it now, but when you are mature and become a mother you will then understand how important it truly is.

Islam always sides with those who are vulnerable or who have the propensity to be taken advantage; therefore, Islam puts the barrier of hijab from the advancements of men. Hijab protects you from the dangers around you, therefore do not underestimate it. It forces men to focus on your interior character, not your exterior physique. It directs them to focus on your values and personality, not at your looks. A man who is only attracted to your face, hair, or body is in reality disrespecting you. He has no respect for your intelligence, honor, or the beauty that is inside of your heart. Your inner beauty is unparalleled and unmatched. Through it, you can create miracles in this life. Anyone can make themselves beautiful on the outside. Anyone can have cosmetic surgery, but the inner beauty is what is important and that cannot be forged or made up beautified.

True hijab begins in the heart. Spiritual hijab is much more important than the physical hijab. The physical hijab is just a piece of cloth. Hijab begins with how you carry yourself. If your behavior is an un-Islamic one, then being covered from head to toe will not help. You have to resemble Lady Fatima al-Zahra and Lady Zaynab al-Kubra. They are our real role models. Do not be taken in by the women on the magazine covers, for they are not our real role models in life.

One day, the Prophet asked, "My daughter Fatima, what is the best thing for a woman?" Although she was still young, she replied, "The best thing is for a strange man not to see her and for her not to see a strange man."[92] The theme behind this message is that Islam does not want any circumstances to arise that could jeopardize the chastity of a woman. Chastity is one of the noblest traits for a woman. Thus, live by the sentiments of Fatima al-Zahra - for she is our true role model.

Unfortunately, for some Muslim women in America, hijab has become somewhat of a fashion and social trend. An emphasis is placed on the social aspect of hijab, but the spiritual aspect is forgotten. It is disheartening to see hijab lose its spiritual value the way that God had intended it in the Qur'an:

$$
\text{﴿يَا أَيُّهَا النَّبِيُّ قُلْ لِّأَزْوَاجِكَ وَبَنَاتِكَ وَنِسَاءِ الْمُؤْمِنِينَ يُدْنِينَ عَلَيْهِنَّ مِنْ جَلَابِيبِهِنَّ ذَلِكَ أَدْنَى أَنْ يُعْرَفْنَ فَلَا يُؤْذَيْنَ وَكَانَ اللَّهُ غَفُورًا رَّحِيمًا﴾}
$$

O Prophet! say to your wives and your daughters and the women of the believers that they let down upon them their over-garments; this will be more proper, that they may be known, and thus they will not be given trouble; and God is Forgiving, Merciful. (33:59)

---

[92] *Mustadrak*, v. 14, p. 183

Certainly, God wants us to be beautiful, but for who? Certainly, not for men who are outsiders, for they are not worthy of our attention. They want to take advantage of a woman's body and then discard them. They will not even have the courtesy to return your phone calls or ask about you. Some men are merciless, and thus women have to guard themselves. One cannot expect that a stranger will look out for your best interest. A woman complained that once she goes out with Muslim men they are no longer interested in her after the first date. Perhaps she was being too accommodating. When a woman is too generous with herself, then men will lose interest in them. God Himself tells women to be on their guard from the men and not to be too complaisant with them:

﴿يَا نِسَاءَ النَّبِيِّ لَسْتُنَّ كَأَحَدٍ مِّنَ النِّسَاءِ إِنِ اتَّقَيْتُنَّ فَلَا تَخْضَعْنَ بِالْقَوْلِ فَيَطْمَعَ الَّذِي فِي قَلْبِهِ مَرَضٌ وَ قُلْنَ قَوْلًا مَّعْرُوفًا﴾

O wives of the Prophet! You are not like any of the other women; If you will be on your guard, then be not soft in (your) speech, lest he in whose heart is a disease yearn; and speak a good word. (33:32)

We must follow Lady Zaynab, the partner of Imam Husayn in his sacrifice. Everyone agrees that if it were not for Zaynab's stand in the aftermath of Ashura, then Imam Husayn's message would have been silenced. She was the one who made all of us, and millions of others worldwide, commemorate the martyrdom of Imam Husayn.

Journey of Life

﴿مِنْهَا خَلَقْنَاكُمْ وَفِيهَا نُعِيدُكُمْ وَمِنْهَا نُخْرِجُكُمْ تَارَةً أُخْرَى﴾

From it We created you and into it We shall send you back and from it will We raise you a second time. (20:55)

WHEN WE PLAN FOR THE VACATION OF A "LIFETIME," WE PREPARE ourselves for it way in advance. Our main reason to take a vacation is to relax and have fun. Certainly, no one invests in a vacation that is going to be chaotic or disturbing. We want a destination that is peaceful and scenic; and we plan our retreats with a step-by-step itinerary. We research the places of interest and read about the featured attractions. We pack for the weather accordingly and take the necessary precautions. We check over our list and then anticipate the arrival of our great trip. Islam tells us that we should plan in the same way for our final destination in the Hereafter.

Although the Qur'an and the traditions mention what we will experience in the next world, most of what will happen at the moment of death and the life after death still remains a mystery to us, yet this journey is imminent. Whether we are rich or poor, young or old, educated or illiterate, we will all be compelled to undertake this journey. We need to understand that whatever awaits us there depends on what we do here, in our present lives. The Prophet explained that two options await us at death, "Either the grave will be a garden from the gardens of Paradise or it will be a hole from the pits of Hell."[93] Which way we want to go depends upon us, and our actions in this world.

Despite the fact that the Prophet witnessed horrific battles and the torturing of his companions, he still claimed that, "I have not seen anything more terrifying than what will happen in the grave."[94] God gave him the ability to hear and see clearly the events of the grave. When we look at a gravesite, we see nothing but dirt and a deep hole. However, a day will come when the veil will be lifted from our eyes and we will see the reality of the grave. We will see what the Prophet saw, but then at that time it will be too late.

Our true mother is the earth. "O son of Adam!" the earth is narrated as saying every day, "You are stepping on my back, but soon you will reside in my womb."[95] Our brief life span pales in comparison to the age of Earth, which scientists place, along with the solar system, at about 4.9 billion years. They date the universe itself to be between 15 to 20 billion years, and theorize that space and matter came into being by a sudden expansion of an infinitesimal singularity, known as the "Big Bang theory."

$$﴿أَوَلَمْ يَرَ الَّذِينَ كَفَرُوا أَنَّ السَّمَاوَاتِ وَالْأَرْضَ كَانَتَا رَتْقًا$$

$$فَفَتَقْنَاهُمَا وَجَعَلْنَا مِنَ الْمَاءِ كُلَّ شَيْءٍ حَيٍّ أَفَلَا يُؤْمِنُونَ﴾$$

Do not the Unbelievers see that the heavens and the earth were joined together (as one unit of creation), before we clove them asunder? We made from water every living thing. Will they not then believe? (21:30)

---

[93] *Al-Kafi*, v. 3, p. 242
[94] *Mizan Al-Hikmah*, v. 3, p. 2478
[95] *Al-Kafi*, v. 3, p. 241

Perhaps this verse refers to that primal explosion after which most of the galaxies were formed, including our home galaxy. Our planet is the only one known so far to support life, and this is our home.

We can approximate with reasonable precision how long the universe has been in existence. Scientist have even forewarned that life on Earth and our solar system will one day come to an end. However, no one can give the precise number of years of our lives; some people may live to be over 100 years old and some may only live for a few hours. A skeptic person once asked the Prophet when the final Hour (Day of Judgment) would come. Instead of answering his question, the Prophet asked him, "And what have you done to get ready for it?" It does not matter when the Hour will come. It could come in a million years or it could come tomorrow. What matters is whether you are prepared for it or not.

Do not assume that you have forever just because you are young. A young vibrant man had just finished medical school and for his graduation he was planning a ski trip. Just before he left, he told his mother that he was looking forward to the vacation because he had worked so hard at school and accomplished his goal in becoming a doctor. On his way driving through the mountains he had a terrible car accident and died instantly. He was at the prime of his life, he had labored in his studies and graduated medical school, his future looked prosperous, he was going to be saving the lives of others, but within a second he was gone. Death put an end to everything. Therefore, we never know what will happen to us.

God tells us beforehand to prepare ourselves for death. He even gives us two combined instructions to follow that would assist us when we are buried and alone in the grave:

﴿إِنَّ الَّذِينَ قَالُوا رَبُّنَا اللَّهُ ثُمَّ اسْتَقَامُوا تَتَنَزَّلُ عَلَيْهِمُ الْمَلَائِكَةُ أَلَّا تَخَافُوا وَلَا تَحْزَنُوا وَأَبْشِرُوا بِالْجَنَّةِ الَّتِي كُنْتُمْ تُوعَدُونَ﴾

As for those who say, "Our Lord is God," and then pursue steadfastly the right way - the angels descend on them (from time to time and say): "Fear you not! (they suggest), nor grieve! but receive the Glad Tidings of the Garden (of Bliss), that which you were promised!" (41:30)

First, we need to have solid belief in God "as for those who say, 'Our Lord is God', followed by "pursue steadfastly the right way," meaning that we not only have to believe in God, but we also have to adhere to all of His commandments. Hence, belief alone will not save you; it must be matched with practice.

﴿وَالْعَصْرِ إِنَّ الْإِنسَانَ لَفِي خُسْرٍ إِلَّا الَّذِينَ آمَنُوا وَعَمِلُوا الصَّالِحَاتِ وَتَوَاصَوْا بِالْحَقِّ وَتَوَاصَوْا بِالصَّبْرِ﴾

I swear by the time, most surely man is in loss, except those who believe and do good, and enjoin on each other truth, and enjoin on each other patience. (103:1-3)

The Prophet advised, "A Muslim is someone whose hand and tongue other Muslims are safe from."[96] Your faith reflects in how you treat others around you. Putting pictures of Mecca and Madinah on your walls does not make you a good Muslim. Growing a long beard or reciting the *tasbeeh* (prayer beads) does not give one certainty. However, treating people with good manners (*akhlaq*) is.

﴿وَمَا هَـٰذِهِ الْحَيَاةُ الدُّنْيَا إِلَّا لَهْوٌ وَلَعِبٌ وَإِنَّ الدَّارَ الْآخِرَةَ لَهِيَ الْحَيَوَانُ لَوْ كَانُوا يَعْلَمُونَ﴾

And the life of this world is nothing but a sport and a play; and as for the next abode, that most surely is the life - did they but know! (29:64)

---

[96] *Al-Kafi*, v. 2, p. 234

We have been highly advised to visit the cemetery, for it is the world's largest museum. It teaches us about our reality. Witness the burial of a person and remember that one day the same thing will be done to you.

If your parents have passed, make a special effort to visit their graves, for they are waiting for you. God will forgive the sins of whoever visits his parents' graves. Visit the graves of your loved ones, for they are thirsty for a few verses of the Qur'an to be recited and dedicated to them. The Prophet said, "If someone sits by his brother's grave and recites the Qur'an, then the deceased will feel solace and delight."[97] Even if the gravesite is in another country, still recite verses from the Qur'an on their behalf, and the reward of it will reach them wherever they are. We all know someone who has left this world, so while we are alive, we should try and dedicate some verses to ease their souls, and hopefully, when we pass away someone will ease our souls with a few verses. It is interesting to note that in the last *takbeer* of *Salat al-Mayyit* (prayer for the deceased) we say, "We will not remain after you except for a short time."

The Prophet has given us a slight depiction of the grave. We will no longer have any connection with the outer world. No one will be able to hear us or help us there; it will be dark and constrictive. From time to time, we will hear the moans of the other deceased people. The angels will come and question us, and we will not be able to find any way out of their questioning except by speaking the truth. Only once in a while will a kind believer who is still among the living ones send us a gift by reciting the Qur'an or prayers on our behalf.

Nonetheless, there is hope; we can act now to illuminate the darkness in our graves. "*Tahajud* (the Night Prayer) will become a light in our graves," the Prophet assured. We will all desperately need that light. The Prophet also said, "No soul knows what delight for the eyes is

---

[97] *Bihar al-Anwar*, Al-Allamah Al-Majlisi, v. 79, p. 64

hidden in *Tahajud*,"[98] and Imam as-Sadiq told us that God has specified His reward for every good act, except for *Tahajud*. Even in this life every prayer has innumerable benefits. You will never know unless you experience it. God has told the Prophet that one of the ways to ascend to true spiritual heights is through *Tahajud* prayer.

$$ ﴿وَمِنَ اللَّيْلِ فَتَهَجَّدْ بِهِ نَافِلَةً لَّكَ عَسَى أَن يَبْعَثَكَ رَبُّكَ مَقَامًا مَّحْمُودًا﴾ $$

And during a part of the night, pray Tahajud [optional mid-night prayers] (which is) beyond what is incumbent upon you; maybe your Lord will raise you to a position of great glory. (17:79)

If you do not already perform it, then make a sincere effort, for it takes just half an hour to say these prayers. If one can spend all night watching a sporting match or movies then one should be able to perform the *Tahajud*. We are young and energetic now, and we may not have the time or energy when we get older. One will see that when we perform that prayer, our lives will change for the best in many different areas.

Salat al-Wahsha[99] also sends light into the grave. When your loved one passes away, it is recommended to pray *Salat al-Wahsha* for them on the first night after their burial, for that is the time when the deceased one is in a great trial. This prayer offers a form of assurance, calmness, and ease for the dead person. Reciting this prayer will help them adjust to

---

[98] See translation of *Al-Qur'an*, 32:17

[99] *Salat al-Wahsha* is a prayer that is performed for the deceased person on the first night of burial: It has two *rakahs*. In the first, recite *Surah al-Fatihah* and *ayat al-Kursi* (from "*Allahuu laa ilaaha illa huwa...*" to "*... hum fihaa khaalidun*"). In the second, recite *Surah al-Fatihah* and *Surah al-Qadr* ten times. When you have finished the *salat*, say, "*Allahumma salli ala Muhammadin wa ali Muhammad wabath thawabaha ila qabri* _____ (and mention here the name of the deceased and his or her father's name)."

the grave because this transition is not an easy one. Not only do they have to get used to being in a confined space, but the angels, Munkar and Nakeer will immediately come to question them. Only genuine believers will be able to greet the angels as "Mubashir"[100] and "Bashir"[101] instead of Munkar and Nakeer.

In order to help the deceased one at the moment of death, we recite the *talqeen* for them before they are buried; once when they are dying and then once before they are put in the grave. We sit by their head at their deathbed and remind them to say, "There is no god but God, Muhammad is the Prophet of God, Ali is the guardian of God (*La ilaaha illa Allah, Muhammadun Rasulullah, Aliyan waliullah*)." Our last words before we leave this world should be professing the faith (*shahadah*), for the Prophet has said, "Whoever's last words are *la ilaaha illa Allah* will enter into Paradise." Many people try to utter these words at the moment of death but are not able to due to some circumstances. We beg God for that opportunity to be amongst those who recite it before we die.

Just before we bury the dead, we repeat the *talqeen* again. We say to them, "*Isma, ifham, ya fulan ibne fulan, idha ja akaal malikanal muqarraban mabuthayni min qiballahi taala...*" (See index for full text)

The angels will come right after the burial and there will be no respite. The first thing that they will ask the person is, "Who is your Lord? Who is your Prophet? Who is your Imam? What is your book? What is your faith? What is your *qiblah* (direction of prayer)?" Do not fear them, rather reply to them by saying, "God is my Lord, Muhammad is my Prophet, Ali is my Imam," and mention the names of the eleven imams after him, "Islam is my religion, the Qur'an is my book, and the Ka'bah is my *qiblah*."

---

[100] "Bearer of good news"
[101] "Glad tidings"

Do not think that you can lie, or make up the right answers. If you do not follow the Prophet here (in your lifetime) it will be impossible to pretend that you do when you are put into your grave.

It is narrated that when the Prophet buried Fatima bint Asad, the mother of Imam Ali, who was also the Prophet's aunt and foster mother, in Al-Baqi Cemetery, he went down into her grave and lay beside her body for a few moments before covering her with his robe and then climbing out again. When his companions asked why he did that, he replied:

> One day, I was telling her about death, about the sadness and the fear of the grave. She said, "I cannot bear that!" I told her not to worry. I decided that I would lie beside her body for a little while and cover her with my robe to take away some of the fear.
>
> When I listened to the angels questioning her, she answered the questions: "Who is your Lord? Who is your Prophet? What is your Book? What is your faith?" Then she was silent when they asked, "Who is your Imam?" So I told her to say, "Your son, your son Ali." She replied, "My son Ali."[102]

Although she had passed away during the time of the Prophet, before Imam Ali had succeeded him as the Imam, she was still asked about who was her Imam, even though it was her own son.

After the angels are finished with the person, then they will face the torment of the grave, about which the Prophet says, "Only a few survive the torment of the grave." It will begin with the squeezing. Your sins will be squeezed out of your body with pressure proportional to the level of your misdeeds. The vast majority of people are unable to bear this torment, but they will have no choice. The crushing of the

---

[102] *Bihar al-Anwar*, Al-Allamah Al-Majlisi, v. 35, p. 76

grave threatens all of us. We want to think that we will be safe in the next world, but only God knows. When one of the companions of the Prophet, Sa'd b. Ma'adh was fatally wounded in the Battle of Uhud, he survived until he returned to Madinah. There he passed away and the Prophet buried him in Al-Baqi Cemetery. As the Prophet was burying him, his mother said warmly, "Congratulations Sa'd, you have attained Paradise." The Prophet turned to her and cautioned, "Wait, Um Sa'd, do not put it on God to grant him Paradise yet. Right now, his grave is crushing the joints of his bones."[103]

The Prophet could see what she could not see. Commentators believe that Sa'd did not treat his family well and the punishment in the grave was in line with what the Prophet had said that, "Most of the punishment of the grave will be for a man's bad temper." If you disrespect your mother, father, husband, wife, or children, then be aware of the torment of the grave. If you do not appreciate what they do, or you go home and raise your voice at your mother or wife for not having the food ready - as if she is your servant - then you are increasing your punishment in the grave. Be extremely careful of how you treat others. You may not see the repercussions here, but you will definitely have to face them there.

In addition, those who take their prayers lightly will also have to endure the crushing of the grave. The Prophet says, "If a person takes his prayers lightly, his grave will be completely dark. He will have to endure the squeezing of the grave."

All of the prayers are important, but God emphasizes the morning prayers in the Qur'an:

﴿أَقِمِ الصَّلَاةَ لِدُلُوكِ الشَّمْسِ إِلَى غَسَقِ اللَّيْلِ وَقُرْآنَ الْفَجْرِ إِنَّ قُرْآنَ الْفَجْرِ كَانَ مَشْهُودًا﴾

---

[103] *Mustadrak*, v. 1, p. 269

Keep up prayer from the declining of the sun until the darkness of the night and the morning recitation; surely the morning recitation is witnessed. (17:78)

Do not ever miss the morning prayers. If someone told you they had a delicious breakfast ready for you at dawn or a special gift waiting for you, then you would be right there in anticipation of it. You have to wake up for the prayer and stand before God, for He pays special attention to these prayers.

Other people have no problem saying the morning prayers, but when the time comes for the noon or afternoon prayers they are careless about it because they are eating their lunch, watching TV, or chatting, and then five minutes before sunset they remember they forgot to pray. This is what the Prophet meant by "taking the prayers lightly." Taking your prayers lightly is dangerous just as Imam as-Sadiq warned the believers that, "Our intercession on the Day of Judgment will not reach those people who take their prayers lightly."[104]

Take care of your prayers and pay special attention to them. Make sure that you are doing *wudhu* (ablution) properly, and that you are saying your prayers correctly, and perform them on time.

﴿إِنَّ الصَّلَاةَ كَانَتْ عَلَى الْمُؤْمِنِينَ كِتَابًا مَوْقُوتًا﴾

Surely prayer is a timed ordinance for the believers. (4:103)

Read *Surah al-Muminoon* (the Believers), and see how God describes the believers in that chapter, He begins and ends His description with the importance that they give to their prayers:

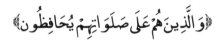

﴿وَالَّذِينَ هُمْ عَلَى صَلَوَاتِهِمْ يُحَافِظُونَ﴾

And those who keep a guard on their prayers. (23:9)

---

[104] *Bihar al-Anwar*, Al-Allamah Al-Majlisi, v. 79, p. 227

Recognizing that the quickest way to God is through the prayers, believers make their daily prayers a priority. No matter how successful they may be, they know that they always need God. We need Him at school; we need Him at home; we need Him at work; we need Him when we are single; we need Him when we are married; we need Him when we have children. Therefore, we must always be with Him. God says that if you take one step towards Him, He will come running towards you. He has promised this, but He needs to see the first gesture come from you, "And You do not conceal Yourself from Your creation, except that their deeds hide them from You."[105]

Have no doubt that God is always there. If you look hard enough, you will see Him. A man once asked Imam Ali, "Have you seen your Lord?" Imam Ali replied, "Would I worship a Lord that I could not see?"[106] One cannot see God with their physical eyes, but we see Him with the vision of (our) hearts. The souls of the prophets and the imams are pure. They could see God, Paradise, Hell, and the life after death with their inner eyes. We limit ourselves, and thus we draw a curtain between God and ourselves. When we stand before Him, what do we think about? Are our hearts and minds with Him, or do they wander somewhere else?

Although, mistreating the family and taking prayers lightly increase the pressure in the grave; nonetheless, there is hope and mercy from the torments of the grave.

$$﴿يَوْمَ لَا يَنْفَعُ مَالٌ وَلَا بَنُونَ. إِلَّا مَنْ أَتَى اللَّهَ بِقَلْبٍ سَلِيمٍ﴾$$

The day on which property will not avail, nor sons except him who comes to God with a heart free (from evil). (26:88-89)

The Prophet left for us some ways to help us from the punishment in the grave.

---

[105] *Dua Abu Hamzah al-Thumali*
[106] *Al-Kafi*, v. 1, p. 195

First, he instructed that God would lessen the torment for one who performs a special prayer of two units (*rakah*) regularly on Thursday nights. In each unit (*rakah*), after Surah al-Fatiha (the Opening), recite Surah al-Qadr (the Destiny) 15 times. It takes no more than about 15 minutes to recite it.

The second thing is to perform Hajj. The Prophet said, "Pilgrims are divided into several groups. The best ones are forgiven of all of their past and future sins, and the punishment of the grave is lifted from them." Try to go for Hajj. Even if you are students, try to save your money. You do not need to buy new clothes for every occasion. Your value is in your heart and mind, not in your clothes. Do not put off the Hajj until you get older. Would you send someone on vacation to Disneyland in a wheelchair? Of course not! Hajj too needs vitality, energy, youth, and minds that are eager to search and inquire. You will never enjoy its richness at an old age. Enjoy Hajj while you are still young, and when you can walk on your own two feet and appreciate the meaning of the rituals. If you go for the first time when you are in your seventies or eighties, then you will be confused and worried because you do not know what you are doing or why you are performing those acts. Most importantly, you need God beside you now - during your youthful age - when you are beginning to map out your future. You need Him next to you guiding you through your life. By going for Hajj you are renewing your commitment to Him. You are in essence saying that you need Him to help you get into that good university, pass those heavy exams, secure a good job, find the best wife or husband, and raise a prosperous family. By the time you are old it is too late to ask for these things.

People view Hajj as a way to repent for their past sins. After accumulating a lifetime of mistakes, they then go for Hajj. That is not how it should be. Hajj is supposed to immunize us against committing sins. When you gaze at the Ka'bah and millions of people who are circling it, then you will be forced to ask yourself why you were created. What is your goal in life? The Prophet advised, "Those who are in the graves wish they could exchange the world and everything that is in it for just one Hajj."[107] The effect of it is inconceivable so try to go. Say, "Oh God, I don't have the money now, but I am going to start saving money from today, and if You so will, next year I will perform my Hajj." Transform your life through going for Hajj.

---

[107] *Man La Yahdharahul Faqih*, Sheikh Al-Sadooq, v. 2, p. 228

Family Values

Chapter 5

﴿يَا أَيُّهَا النَّاسُ اتَّقُوا رَبَّكُمُ الَّذِي خَلَقَكُم مِّن نَّفْسٍ وَاحِدَةٍ وَخَلَقَ مِنْهَا زَوْجَهَا وَبَثَّ مِنْهُمَا رِجَالًا كَثِيرًا وَنِسَاءً وَاتَّقُوا اللَّهَ الَّذِي تَسَاءَلُونَ بِهِ وَالْأَرْحَامَ إِنَّ اللَّهَ كَانَ عَلَيْكُمْ رَقِيبًا﴾

O mankind! Be wary of your Lord who created you from a single soul, and created its mate from it, and from the two of them, scattered numerous men and women. Be wary of God, in whose Name you adjure one another, and the wombs. Indeed God is watchful over you. (4:1)

THERE IS NOTHING MORE DEARER TO GOD THAN THE INSTITUTE OF marriage, so if you want to please God, then you must get married. In the eyes of God, marriage is one of the most honorable acts, and family is the most sacrosanct institution. Families form the building blocks of a sound society; and when families prosper then society prospers as well and vice versa. Virtually everyone agrees that the family structure today, in particular to, but not exclusive to the West, is definitely breaking down.

The ideal Muslim family is one that provides love, security, respect, and happiness. Love and compassion form the essence of the Islamic family. A Muslim home should be the place where one seeks shelter, recognition, and refuge from the chaotic world that we live in. The

Muslim home is not built on material possession. It is not about the area which one lives in or the type of car that one drives. Rather, it is about caring, sharing, forgiveness, compassion, and sacrifice.

$$\text{﴿وَمِنْ آيَاتِهِ أَنْ خَلَقَ لَكُم مِّنْ أَنفُسِكُمْ أَزْوَاجًا لِّتَسْكُنُوا إِلَيْهَا وَجَعَلَ بَيْنَكُم مَّوَدَّةً وَرَحْمَةً إِنَّ فِي ذَلِكَ لَآيَاتٍ لِّقَوْمٍ يَتَفَكَّرُونَ﴾}$$

And among His signs is that He created for you mates from your own selves that you may take comfort in them, and He ordained affection and mercy between you. There are indeed signs in that for a people who reflect. (30:21)

However, for some people, the family has unfortunately become a danger zone. Statistically speaking, people nowadays are much more likely to be physically and emotionally abused by their own relatives than by strangers. In the world's most modern democracy, namely the United States, researchers say that a woman is beaten by her husband or partner every 12 seconds. Who knows what the statistics are for the Islamic world. The home, which should be a safe haven, in some cases has become a source of pain and danger.

In past years, several generations used to live together under one roof. Ask your father or grandfather how many family members lived with them. They all learned how to get along. Today, two individuals cannot even live under the same roof; and if they do live together, then more often than not, they live emotionally distant lives from one another; they are physically united but spiritually and emotionally away. As a result, the divorce rate has reached 50% or even higher in some countries.

Divorce is not just a problem in the west; in fact, divorce trend cuts across all sectors. It is even on the rise in Muslim countries as well.

Why has this become the case today? What is leading to so many separations in the world?

Sociologists blame lack of education, lack of responsibility, ethnicity, poverty, feminism, and more.

Traditionally, and Islamically, men are viewed as the breadwinners, but today, women all over the world work, and sometimes they even earn more money than their husbands do. If the duty of a husband is merely to bring home money, then what does a woman need a man for? Thus, some women question why they should get married. Is not money the number one reason why a man postpones marriage? Mostly everyone thinks that marriage is contingent on money. However, this is not what God has said - He bases marriage on something completely different.

If only we were to deeply reflect on the spirit of marriage then perhaps we would not see such a rise in the divorce rate around the world.

In verse 30:21, God describes marriage as a source of emotional and psychological shelter, not financial support. You do not need someone to cook for you or to give you a credit card. You need a spouse to grow with morally, emotionally, spiritually, socially, and intellectually. This is why marriage is very vital; and why the Prophet said, "Marriage is from my tradition (Sunnah), and whoever turns away from my Sunnah is not from me."[108] Thus we see that marriage is not optional; it is not a luxury; rather it is a necessity. One will never progress in life, nor reach full potential if one remains single. One will never be at peace. It is not about money; but rather, it is about being a true human.

The divorce factors that sociologists mention may or may not play a role, but one factor they generally neglect to mention, and in my opinion is the real cause of the upswing in divorce is the moral decline in society - specifically, promiscuity. We are surrounded by it

---

[108] *Bihar al-Anwar*, Al-Allamah Al-Majlisi, v. 22, p. 180

everywhere. Everyday men and women are interacting in close proximity with others, either at work or at school. All of their energy, communication, contribution, and sense of humor are spent with their co-workers or classmates. By the time they return home, they are too exhausted to spend time with their spouse or family. Half the time, they do not even have the time to talk to each other at home. If they do have time, what usually happens? One watches TV and the other is on the phone or the Internet. They communicate with everyone else except with one another. Someone once told me that when his wife calls, he will talk to her for a maximum of 60 seconds, but if any other female friend calls he will talk to her for at least 60 minutes. What kind of marriage is this? Unfortunately, however this is the social reality that we are living in.

Some people get married out of convenience. They treat marriage as a bed and breakfast. One wife confided that she wished her husband would treat the home as a "bed and breakfast" because he looks at it as a *bread* and breakfast - she only saw him when there was food on the table; he hardly came home at night. Setting aside the humor, such problems do exist and they are very serious. If the husband does not come home at night or stays out very late, then this is a serious problem. A marriage like this will not last.

Everyone suffers from a divorce - the couple, the children, the extended family, and the society at large. Even if the marriage is horrible, divorce is still a traumatic experience. Sadly, the children pay the highest price. They say that in the United States, over a million children every year are involved in a new divorce. Today, 25% of American children live in a single parent family because of divorce.

The percentage of children born to unwed parents, especially teenagers is also on the rise. Some schools have had to provide a nursery room to accommodate the number of teenage mothers. The odd thing is that there are no fathers to show for it. The fathers are absent - they have abandoned the babies and their mothers. Would another male figure, such as a boyfriend or stepfather ever compensate for the role of the biological father?

Even worse in the U.S. is that about one million teenagers get abortions every year and this number is on the rise. Abortion is forbidden in Islam, for it is murder. However, there are rare exceptions, such as when the life of a mother is at risk and others.

The Prophet was once asked, "O Messenger of God, tell me the best way to remain safe from committing sins." He replied, "Before you decide to do something, think about its consequences." At that moment, everything may seem good. Maybe you erred and got intoxicated, or went dancing, or watched an adult movie. Satan is always present and he whispers into your ears; he pushes you to do what he wants, but you need to then stop and ask yourself, how will you feel tomorrow? Will you be happy with yourself about what you did? Will you be ashamed? If so, you must control yourself. Always think about the future. A few reckless moments can destroy your life forever.

It should be noted that children of absentee parents do not necessarily come from a single parent home. Some fathers are physically present at home, but are emotionally absent from their children. They neglect to nurture and foster the emotional aspects of their offspring. Even worse, some fathers are not even physically present because they spend their time traveling or living somewhere else. Some men get married without recognizing the immense responsibility of married life. They father several children, but do not nurture them emotionally or spiritually. This is a major problem, for parental neglect will scar children forever. Children need both parents to raise them rightfully.

﴿يَا أَيُّهَا الَّذِينَ آمَنُوا قُوا أَنفُسَكُمْ وَأَهْلِيكُمْ نَارًا وَقُودُهَا النَّاسُ وَالْحِجَارَةُ﴾

> *O you who have faith! Save yourselves and your families from a Fire whose fuel is people and stones. (66:6)*

Look at the example of the prophets. Prophet Abraham prayed to God:

$$﴿رَبِّ اجْعَلْنِي مُقِيمَ الصَّلَاةِ وَمِن ذُرِّيَّتِي رَبَّنَا وَتَقَبَّلْ دُعَاءِ﴾$$

> *Lord! Make me a maintainer of the prayer, and my descendants [too]. Our Lord, accept my supplication. (14:40)*

He did not want to worship God alone. He wanted his children to stand with him. The ideal Muslim family stays together in this life and in the next. This life is too short; and if you cannot unify your family together here, then how will you keep them together there?

Supporting your family financially is not enough. An increasing number of Muslim mothers complain that their husbands ignore the family. A wife does not only need the husband's money, especially today. They need love and attention from their husband. She wants a soul mate, not a fancy house. An expensive mansion will not provide any good if the people inside the home are unhappy. One builds a home with love and affection - not by remodeling it.

Society today encourages divorce by presenting it as the primary solution to marital problems. When spouses quarrel, someone suggests divorce. We must avoid this habit! When one argues, and keep in mind that *everyone* argues, do not bring up the issue of divorce as a scapegoat. Take a step back; do not rush into divorce. Divorce should be the last option, not the first, especially if there are children involved. Marriage is a test and no one ever said that it would be easy. No one ever said that life is easy. Try to find solutions to your problems. Encourage and observe patience and try to work out your problems. Your children will learn from you how to try to resolve life's difficulties. This is your struggle (*jihad*). No one wants to suffer the feelings of desperation, remorse, guilt, low self-esteem, loneliness, depression, and rejection that come with divorce. There is a reason why divorce is the most hated of all of the lawful actions in Islam. Try to hold your marriage together for the sake of God.

$$﴿قُلْ إِنَّ صَلَاتِي وَنُسُكِي وَمَحْيَايَ وَمَمَاتِي لِلَّهِ رَبِّ الْعَالَمِينَ﴾$$

Say, "Indeed my prayer and my worship, my life and my death are for the sake of God, Lord of all the worlds." (6:162)

It is true that sometimes divorce is unavoidable. Although hated, divorce is permissible because God does not want people to suffer unbearably. He made marriage to be a blessing, not a curse. Islamic law does not force two people to stay together if they feel that there is absolutely no love or compassion, or feel despair that their relationship will never improve. Without harmony or unity, marriage is a failure. If you are suffering in your marriage, God knows about it. He does not want you to suffer, but He did not intend for people to rush into a hasty divorce either. Take time for reconciliation and forgiveness. The door to divorce will always be open later as a last resort if need be.

$$﴿وَإِنْ خِفْتُمْ شِقَاقَ بَيْنِهِمَا فَابْعَثُوا حَكَمًا مِّنْ أَهْلِهِ وَحَكَمًا مِّنْ$$
$$أَهْلِهَا إِن يُرِيدَا إِصْلَاحًا يُوَفِّقِ اللَّهُ بَيْنَهُمَا إِنَّ اللَّهَ كَانَ عَلِيمًا$$
$$خَبِيرًا﴾$$

And if you fear a split between the two of them, then appoint an arbiter from his relatives and an arbiter from her relatives. If they desire reconcilement, God shall reconcile them. Indeed God is All-Knowing, All-Aware. (4:35)

It is mandatory for husbands and wives to seek arbitration, whether through family members, friends, scholars, professionals, or other sincere people before initiating divorce. If you are having problems with your marriage and cannot seem to resolve your issues, then ask for help. If you and your partner are sincere, then God will bring you back together. He is the One who puts love and harmony between peoples' hearts. We cannot do that ourselves. The closer you become to God, the closer you will become to your spouse. The more your faith will grow, the better your relationship will be.

Marriage is extremely important, but while maintaining a strong marriage be sure that you do not neglect other family ties.

$$﴿وَاتَّقُواْ اللَّهَ الَّذِي تَسَاءَلُونَ بِهِ وَالأَرْحَامَ إِنَّ اللَّهَ كَانَ عَلَيْكُمْ رَقِيبًا﴾$$

Be wary of God, in whose Name you adjure one another, and the wombs. Indeed God is watchful over you. (4:1)

The Arabic word, *'arhaam'* are your kinsmen, your family, and your relatives; and the closest relatives that you have are your parents.

$$﴿وَقَضَى رَبُّكَ أَلاَّ تَعْبُدُواْ إِلاَّ إِيَّاهُ وَبِالْوَالِدَيْنِ إِحْسَانًا إِمَّا يَبْلُغَنَّ عِندَكَ الْكِبَرَ أَحَدُهُمَا أَوْ كِلاَهُمَا فَلاَ تَقُل لَّهُمَآ أُفٍّ وَلاَ تَنْهَرْهُمَا وَقُل لَّهُمَا قَوْلاً كَرِيمًا﴾$$

Your Lord has decreed that you shall not worship anyone except Him, and [He has enjoined] kindness to parents. Should they reach old age at your side - one of them or both - do not say to them, "Fie!" And do not chide them, but speak to them noble words. (17:23)

God has made your parents' pleasure tantamount to His pleasure. Once a man asked the Prophet, "What is my father's right upon me?" He replied, "His right is that you respect and obey him as long as he lives," given of course, that he is obeying God. If he wants you to attend a wedding reception, where unlawful (*haram*) activities are taking place, then gently tell him that you love him and respect him, but you cannot go there because your Creator has forbidden this. Otherwise, try to do what he wants as long as it does not violate the commands of God.

﴿وَوَصَّيْنَا الْإِنسَانَ بِوَالِدَيْهِ حُسْنًا وَإِن جَاهَدَاكَ لِتُشْرِكَ بِي مَا
لَيْسَ لَكَ بِهِ عِلْمٌ فَلَا تُطِعْهُمَا إِلَيَّ مَرْجِعُكُمْ فَأُنَبِّئُكُم بِمَا
كُنتُمْ تَعْمَلُونَ﴾

We have enjoined man to be good to his parents. But if they urge you to ascribe to Me as a partner that of which you have no knowledge, then do not obey them. To Me will be your return, whereat I will inform you concerning that which you used to do. (29:8)

Next, the man asked what his mother's right upon him was. The Prophet replied, "Oh-no, there is no answer."[109] Even if you serve her for twenty-four hours a day, seven days a week, 365 days a year for the rest of your life, you will not have paid her back for one day in her womb. This is your mother's right upon you.

One is very fortunate if their parents are still alive. Ask those who have lost them. Take care of them while you have them; respect them; be a good son or daughter; and be humble before them. Be the jewel of your family. No matter how much wealthier or smarter you are than your mother or father, you would not be here without them. God wanted them to be the cause of your existence, and they deserve the utmost of respect.

"Maintaining family ties purifies the wealth, extends one's lifespan, repels tragedies, and eases the judgment of one's deeds,"[110] is according to a Muslim tradition. Staying connected with your immediate and extended family brings you many blessings. It brings you love and respect in the community. Everyone likes to see people who are close with their families. If you have a difficult relationship with your parents, then go to them today and try to set things right with them.

---

[109] *Mustadrak Al-Wasael*, v. 15, p. 182

[110] *Al-Kafi*, v. 2, p. 156

Even if they are in the wrong, take the first step and be the one who is generous and forgiving.

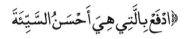

Repel ill [conduct] with that which is the best. (23:96)

Forgiveness and reconciliation are the way of the prophets. Humility does not mean defeat, rather it is an honor. Go back to your parents and tell them, "I am at your service. I am your son (or daughter); I belong to you. I want to make up for the wrongs I did and to respect you."

The story of Imam Husayn and his companion touches our hearts so much, in part because of their family loyalty. Even under severe hardships, they demonstrated unwavering fealty to their relatives. We cannot help but to be moved by how Abbas refused to drink water before his brother, or how Qasim insisted on defending his uncle. Their examples are etched in our hearts, and we should try to imitate and cultivate their actions into our own lives.

Imam of our Time

Chapter 6

﴿إِنَّمَا وَلِيُّكُمُ اللَّهُ وَرَسُولُهُ وَالَّذِينَ آمَنُوا الَّذِينَ يُقِيمُونَ الصَّلَاةَوَيُؤْتُونَ الزَّكَاةَوَهُمْرَاكِعُونَ﴾

Your guardian is only God, His Apostle, and the faithful who maintain the prayer and give the zakat while bowing down [in the state of ruku]. (5:55)

THE DOCTRINE OF *IMAMAH* (OR *KHALIFAH*; LEADERSHIP/SUCCESSOR) holds paramount importance in Islamic theology. Without the belief in *Imamah*, faith will be incomplete and salvation will remain impossible. Numerous Sunni and Shia narrators, including Ahmad b. Hanbal transmit the following tradition, "Whoever dies without recognizing the leader (imam) of his time dies the death of paganism (*jahiliyyah*)."[111] Succession to the Prophet is closely linked to the canon of monotheism (*tawhid*) because obeying the Prophet[112] is obeying the higher order of God. Thus, in order for faith to be complete, *Imamah* is necessary.

Our relationship with our imam does not exist only in this sphere of life he will be our imam on the Day of Reckoning as well.

---

[111] *Al-Kafi*, v. 1, p. 376

[112] *Al-Qur'an*, 4:59: "O you who have faith! Obey God and obey the Apostle and those vested with authority among you. And if you dispute concerning anything, refer it to God and the Apostle, if you have faith in God and the Last Day. That is better and more favorable in outcome."

﴿يَوْمَ نَدْعُوا كُلَّ أُنَاسٍ بِإِمَامِهِمْ فَمَنْ أُوتِيَ كِتَابَهُ بِيَمِينِهِ فَأُوْلَـٰئِكَ يَقْرَؤُونَ كِتَابَهُمْ وَلَا يُظْلَمُونَ فَتِيلًا﴾

That day We will summon every group of people with their imam, then whoever is given his book in his right hand - they will read it, and they will not be wronged so much as a single date-thread. (17:71)

When the Prophet conveyed this verse (*ayah*), he explained that on the Day of Judgment people will line up behind the person who they sincerely followed in this world. Those who truly followed Prophet Moses will line up behind him; those who truly followed Prophet Jesus will line up behind him; and those who truly followed Prophet Muhammad will line up behind him. Similarly, those who deep down, followed the tyrants will line up behind them as well. People will be compelled to join whoever inspired them in this transient life. The curtains of hypocrisy will be cast aside on that day; everyone will be forced to admit the bare truth, even against themselves. Therefore, if you have hope of joining God's true leaders then you first need to know who they are.

Whoever questions the necessity of following God's leader should know that God intimately links obedience to Himself with the obedience to His chosen leaders.

﴿يَا أَيُّهَا الَّذِينَ آمَنُوا أَطِيعُوا اللَّهَ وَأَطِيعُوا الرَّسُولَ وَأُولِي الْأَمْرِ مِنكُمْ فَإِن تَنَازَعْتُمْ فِي شَيْءٍ فَرُدُّوهُ إِلَى اللَّهِ وَالرَّسُولِ إِن كُنتُمْ تُؤْمِنُونَ بِاللَّهِ وَالْيَوْمِ الْآخِرِ ذَلِكَ خَيْرٌ وَأَحْسَنُ تَأْوِيلًا﴾

O you who have faith! Obey God and obey the Apostle and those vested with authority among you. And if you dispute concerning anything, then refer it to God and the Apostle, if you have faith in God and the Last Day. That is better and more favorable in outcome. (4:59)

If you choose to ignore the leader that God has chosen for you then you are disregarding the command of God. He instructed us to approach Him through His gate; for surely not all roads lead to God. He has set out the path to reach Him, and that trail lies in obeying His Messenger, and his true successors.

$$ \text{﴿مَنْ يُطِعِ الرَّسُولَ فَقَدْ أَطَاعَ اللَّهَ وَمَن تَوَلَّىٰ فَمَا أَرْسَلْنَاكَ عَلَيْهِمْ حَفِيظًا﴾} $$

Whoever obeys the Apostle certainly obeys God; and as for those who turn their backs [on you], We have not sent you to keep watch over them. (4:80)

Without *Imamate*, the road to monotheism (*tawhid*) is lost. For this reason, God declared, "We have completed your religion for you," only after the Prophet had given the final incontestable declaration at Ghadir Khum that Imam Ali was to succeed him. Although he had mentioned this succession many times before, but at Ghadir Khum the masses gave public allegiance to Imam Ali and this was 70 days before the Prophet left this world. He had established the prayers, the fast, and the Hajj, but before ensuring the leadership (*khalifah*), Islam was still incomplete until this final revelation:

$$ \text{﴿الْيَوْمَ أَكْمَلْتُ لَكُمْ دِينَكُمْ وَأَتْمَمْتُ عَلَيْكُمْ نِعْمَتِي وَرَضِيتُ لَكُمُ الْإِسْلَامَ دِينًا﴾} $$

Today I have perfected your religion for you, and I have completed My blessing upon you, and I have approved Islam as your religion. (5:3)

People cannot choose their imam. God chooses the imam. The leadership (*Imamate*) did not begin with Imam Ali. God appointed many leaders throughout history, in each case saying, "He made (*ja'ala*) this person an imam."

﴾يَادَاوُودُ إِنَّا جَعَلْنَاكَ خَلِيفَةً فِي الْأَرْضِ﴾

"O David! Indeed We have made you a vicegerent on the earth." (38:26)

﴾وَجَعَلْنَاهُمْ أَئِمَّةً يَهْدُونَ بِأَمْرِنَا وَأَوْحَيْنَا إِلَيْهِمْ فِعْلَ الْخَيْرَاتِ وَإِقَامَ الصَّلَاةِ وَإِيتَاءِ الزَّكَاةِ وَكَانُوا لَنَا عَابِدِينَ﴾

We made them imams, guiding by Our command, and We revealed to them the performance of good deeds, the maintenance of prayers, and the giving of zakat, and they used to worship Us. (21:73)

It is up to God to decide who He wants to appoint to rule on the earth. He delegates His authority to whomsoever He wills, and we have no option in this matter.

﴾وَرَبُّكَ يَخْلُقُ مَا يَشَاءُ وَيَخْتَارُ مَا كَانَ لَهُمُ الْخِيَرَةُ﴾

Your Lord creates whatever He wishes and chooses. They have no choice. (28:68)

The imams were not selected to be imams during their lifetime any more than the prophets were chosen to be prophets after they were born. They were born into that position; they were predestined. According to the Prophet, the position of himself and Ali with God went back before the creation of man, when he and Ali were "two lights between the hands of God even before the creation of Adam."[113]

﴾وَإِذْ قَالَ رَبُّكَ لِلْمَلَائِكَةِ إِنِّي جَاعِلٌ فِي الْأَرْضِ خَلِيفَةً﴾

When your Lord said to the angels, "Indeed I am going to set a vicegerent on earth." (2:30)

---

[113] *Shatharat Al-Thahab*, v. 7, p. 270

Khalifah holds two meanings here, one is general and the other is specific. In general, khalifah here refers to humanity as a whole, since God created all human beings to carry out His will on earth. However, specifically speaking, khalifah also refers to an imam chosen by God. This imam must declare the will of God; and no one can do this except for him. If anyone else tries, then they will err.

Many Muslims are confused about who should lead them. Many assume that whoever sits on the Prophet's pulpit or leads the prayers at the Sacred Mosque represents Islam; however, this is definitely not the case. Representing God's ordination is no easy task. The most prominent person is not necessarily the best guided. Fame or political power plays no part. People should scrutinize a leader to determine whether or not he is the right person to lead. One should do this not only for the chosen Imam whom we follow (Imam Mahdi), but even for the temporal leaders. Learn from Imam Ali's words in the Battle of Jamal when a confused man came to him in the heat of the combat and asked, "O Amir al-Mumineen, I am shocked because so many companions of the Prophet, like Talha, Zubayr, and the wife of the Prophet are fighting us. Should we be fighting them?"

Ali b. Abi Talib gave a superb response, "You must know that right and wrong cannot be identified by personalities. Know and acquaint yourself with what is right, then you will recognize who is right; know and acquaint yourself with what is wrong, then you will recognize who is wrong."[114] Truth stands independent of falsehood. Thus, we must apply the *truth* onto people to find out who they truly are.

Nonetheless, in order to find who the imam is of our time, one must inquire from the experts of religious sciences - the scholars. They are able to provide you with the necessary guidelines and directions.

The seat of *Imamah* is not hinged on whether or not the imam is active and leading the masses, or if he is patiently waiting. Many prophets

---

[114] *Faydh Al-Qadeer Sharh Al-Jami' Al-Sagheer*, Al-Manawi, v. 1, p. 28

were exiled from their homelands, unable to preach their message, thus did that make them any less of a prophet? Of course not.

The primary requirements for any Islamic leader are founded on two heavy principles - justice and righteousness.

﴿الَّذِينَ إِن مَّكَّنَّاهُمْ فِي الْأَرْضِ أَقَامُوا الصَّلَاةَ وَ آتَوُا الزَّكَاةَ وَأَمَرُوا ابِالْمَعْرُوفِ وَنَهَوْاعَنِ الْمُنكَرِ وَلِلَّهِ عَاقِبَةُ الْأُمُورِ﴾

Those who, if We granted them power in the land - maintain the prayer, give the zakat, and bid what is right and forbid what is wrong. And with God rests the outcome of all matters. (22:41)

﴿لَقَدْ أَرْسَلْنَا رُسُلَنَا بِالْبَيِّنَاتِ وَأَنزَلْنَا مَعَهُمُ الْكِتَابَ وَالْمِيزَانَ لِيَقُومَ النَّاسُ بِالْقِسْطِ﴾

Certainly We sent Our apostles with manifest proofs, and We sent down with them the Book and the Balance, so that mankind may maintain justice. (57:25)

﴿يَا دَاوُودُ إِنَّا جَعَلْنَاكَ خَلِيفَةً فِي الْأَرْضِ فَاحْكُم بَيْنَ النَّاسِ بِالْحَقِّ وَلَا تَتَّبِعِ الْهَوَى فَيُضِلَّكَ عَن سَبِيلِ اللَّهِ إِنَّ الَّذِينَ يَضِلُّونَ عَن سَبِيلِ اللَّهِ لَهُمْ عَذَابٌ شَدِيدٌ بِمَا نَسُوا يَوْمَ الْحِسَابِ﴾

"O David! Indeed We have made you a vicegerent on the earth. So judge between the people with justice, and do not follow the lower desires, or they will lead you astray from the way of God. Indeed those who stray away from the way of God - there is a severe punishment for them because of their forgetting the Day of Reckoning." (38:26)

Leadership in short is piety and justice. Imam Ali advised his chief justice on the fundamentals of ruling:

Do not sit turned towards one party or another, nor face one party or another, nor look at one of them more than another, so that your relative realizes that you will not favor him, and your enemy realizes that you will not discriminate against him.

If only Muslim judiciaries would heed to the advice given by Imam Ali; under Imam Ali's rule, there was neither favoritism nor nepotism. Whether someone had personally offended him or favored him, Imam Ali was impartial. No one can deny the justice of Ali, even his enemies. After his death, one of his companions, Dhirar b. Dhamrah al-Kanani was summoned unwillingly by Muawiyah and asked to describe Imam Ali. Although, to no avail, he tried to be excused from the task, he then commenced a long, moving eulogy, part of which read, "The strong did not intimidate him, and the weak did not despair of his justice."[115] No one in history could ever blackmail Imam Ali; the disenfranchised found justice in his court.

One must really question - where is this justice in the Muslim countries today?

Islamically, a leader must be the servant of his people. Imam Ali neither rested during the day nor the night. When his aides advised him to take a break he replied, "If I sleep during the day, I neglect my responsibilities; and if I sleep during the night, I neglect my soul."[116] All of his time was spent for the people. Unlike today's leaders, he had no guards or entourage and his home was modest. Oftentimes, when he walked through the streets, people had no idea that he was the leader of the Muslim ummah.

Contrast how he ruled with today's political leaders. While Imam Ali walked humbly through the streets, today's rulers live entirely in

---

[115] *Bihar al-Anwar*, Al-Allamah Al-Majlisi, v. 33, p. 275
[116] *Tareekh Dimashq*, Ibn Asakir, v. 44, p. 273

seclusion. You only see them in the newspaper or on the television. Many contemporary rulers rule for power's sake and maintain their hegemony through bribery, intimidation, and corruption. What is the difference between them and Muawiyah? This is why the entire world is going forward while the Muslims are going backward because of their political and economic corruption.

We need to follow the advice that Imam Ali gave to his governor, Malik al-Ashtar, "Let the people feel your mercy and kindness towards them, for they fall into two groups: either they are your brothers in religion or your partners in creation."[117]

All Muslims agree that Imam al-Mahdi will reappear at the end of time. Sunni scholars maintain that he has not been born yet, while the Shia believe that he is already born and is still living. Points to note, whenever the Prophet spoke of Imam Mahdi, he used the phrase "will reappear (*sa-yazhar*)," not "will be born." One famous Sunni tradition transmitter, Muhammad b. Yusuf al-Kanji al-Shafi, compiled 1,000 hadiths about the reappearance (and not the birth) of Imam Mahdi in his book, *Al-Bayan fi Akhbar-i-Sahib-iz-Zaman*. Some of these traditions also appear in *Al-Bukhari*. In one famous tradition, the Prophet asked his companions, "What will it be like for you when the Messiah, the son of Mariam, descends upon you and your Imam is (already) among you?"[118]

Our Imam is already alive and exists in the world. He is an integral part of our lives whether we accept or reject him. We need to build our relationship with him. We need to remind ourselves that we have a leader. We need to try and catch his attention by remembering him.

Make the prayer for his reappearance, "*allahumma kun li-waliyyika al-hujjat ibnil Hasan,*" part of your lives.

---

[117] *Nahjul Balaghah*, "Commandments of Imam Ali to Malik al-Ashtar"
[118] *Sahih al-Bukhari; Musnad Ahmad*, v. 2, p. 272

اَللّٰهُمَّ كُنْ لِوَلِيِّكَ الْحُجَّةِ بْنِ الْحَسَنِ، صَلَوَاتُكَ عَلَيْهِ وَ عَلَى آبَائِهِ، فِي هٰذِهِ السَّاعَةِ وَ فِي كُلِّ سَاعَةٍ، وَلِيًّا وَ حَافِظاً وَ قَائِداً وَ نَاصِراً وَ دَلِيلاً وَ عَيْناً حَتّى تُسْكِنَهُ أَرْضَكَ طَوْعاً وَ تُمَتِّعَهُ فِيهَا طَوِيلاً

O' God, be for Your deputy, al-Hujjah ibnil Hasan, may Your Blessings be upon him and his forefathers, now and at all times, the Master, Protector, Guide, Helper, Proof and Guard until he resides peacefully on Your earth and let him enjoy (the blessings of this life) for a long time.

God is All-Merciful, and He would never leave us without guidance. He has assured us, repeatedly, in the Holy Qur'an that creation (*khalq*) comes hand in hand with guidance (*hidayah*). It is for this reason that God would not leave the world empty-handed without a representative guiding the people toward salvation. The words are there, in the Qur'an, but one has to read deeply in order to understand the message:

﴿سَبِّحِ اسْمَ رَبِّكَ الْأَعْلَى. الَّذِي خَلَقَ فَسَوَّى. وَ الَّذِي قَدَّرَ فَهَدَى﴾

Celebrate the Name of your Lord, the Most Exalted, Who created and proportioned, who determined and guided... (87:1-3)

﴿قَالَ فَمَن رَّبُّكُمَا يَا مُوسَى. قَالَ رَبُّنَا الَّذِي أَعْطَى كُلَّ شَيْءٍ خَلْقَهُ ثُمَّ هَدَى﴾

He said, "Who is your Lord, Moses?" He said, "Our Lord is He who gave everything its creation and then guided it." (20:49-50)

﴿أَلَمْ نَجْعَل لَّهُ عَيْنَيْنِ. وَ لِسَاناً وَ شَفَتَيْنِ. وَ هَدَيْنَاهُ النَّجْدَيْنِ﴾

Have We not made for him two eyes, a tongue, and two lips, and shown him the two paths [of good and evil]? (90:8-10)

Prophet Abraham put guidance before the other basic necessities, such as food and water. Prophet Abraham explained:

$$\text{﴿الَّذِي خَلَقَنِي فَهُوَ يَهْدِينِ. وَالَّذِي هُوَ يُطْعِمُنِي وَيَسْقِينِ. وَإِذَا مَرِضْتُ فَهُوَ يَشْفِينِ﴾}$$

Who created me, it is He who guides me, and provides me with food and drink, and when I get sick, it is He who cures me. (26:78-80)

In reality, guidance far outweighs creation. God did not create us as mere physical shells; rather He created our bodies only for our souls. Unfortunately, how many people display exquisite physiques but rotten consciences?

$$\text{﴿أَمْ تَحْسَبُ أَنَّ أَكْثَرَهُمْ يَسْمَعُونَ أَوْ يَعْقِلُونَ إِنْ هُمْ إِلَّا كَالْأَنْعَامِ بَلْ هُمْ أَضَلُّ سَبِيلًا﴾}$$

Do you suppose that most of them listen or apply reason? They are just like cattle; rather they are further astray from the way. (25:44)

At the beginning of time, when only four people lived on earth (Adam, Eve, Cain, and Abel), God appointed one of them as a divine guide. Now that we have surpassed 6 billion people, would He leave us without the guidance of a divinely appointed leader?

Muslims are not the only people who agree that they need guidance. Do parents send their children to school so that they can be taught and guided by someone who is not a professional in the field of teaching? Children can read books. They have eyes, ears and brains. Nevertheless, they need a guide to give them instructions, clarity, and a direction in life. Not only do young children need a guide, but even graduate students require assistance. True that there are millions of books, but we also need someone to show us the way. Every day, even the most independent people submit to their need for guidance. Why then, when it comes to religion, do some people reject this basic principle?

Once, I was sitting next to a Muslim cleric (*sheikh*) at an Islamic conference in America. A man asked him whether Imam Mahdi existed or not and he said no. The man asked him why, and he said because no one has ever seen Imam Mahdi. I asked the cleric (*sheikh*) if he had seen God or the Prophet, and he said that of course he had not. He had not seen God, the Prophet, Heaven, or Hell, but he still believed in them. Part of one's faith is to believe in the unseen. We believe that the Qur'an is the Word of God, therefore we believe that whatever this Book says is true. Since the Qur'an tells us about Muhammad, we believe that Muhammad existed. Since the Qur'an tells us about Jesus, we believe that Jesus existed. Although no one has seen them for over a thousand years, we know and accept that they are not fiction. It is the same with Imam Mahdi. Since we trust the Prophet, we believe in what he said. He told us that the Imam is said to be among us; thus, he is alive and living amongst us.

We need prophets and the imams to guide us and that is why our Imam still lives amongst us today. Of course, believing that he has been alive for 1,200 years is another story. If we read that Prophet Noah lived for 1,600 years, of which 950 he spent preaching the message, and that Prophet Jesus is still alive, then it is not hard to believe that our Imam could continue to thrive after so many years. We know that miracles and unusual occurrences happen by the will of God, so why is it hard to believe in this?

﴿وَقَوْلِهِمْ إِنَّا قَتَلْنَا الْمَسِيحَ عِيسَى ابْنَ مَرْيَمَ رَسُولَ اللهِ وَمَا قَتَلُوهُ وَمَا صَلَبُوهُ وَلَـٰكِن شُبِّهَ لَهُمْ وَإِنَّ الَّذِينَ اخْتَلَفُوا فِيهِ لَفِي شَكٍّ مِّنْهُ مَا لَهُم بِهِ مِنْ عِلْمٍ إِلَّا اتِّبَاعَ الظَّنِّ وَمَا قَتَلُوهُ يَقِينًا﴾

And for their saying, "We killed the Messiah, Jesus son of Mary, the apostle of God" - though they did not kill him, nor did they crucify him, but so it was made to appear to them. Indeed those who differ concerning him are surely in doubt about him: they do not have any knowledge of that beyond following conjectures, and certainly they did not kill him. (4:157)

One may subsequently question that when will the Imam return? He will return when God wills it for him to reappear. God will determine him to return when we have demonstrated our willingness to accept and help him in his mission to establish peace and justice in the world. We are the ones who contribute to this decision to some extent:

$$\text{﴿ذَٰلِكَ بِأَنَّ ٱللَّهَ لَمْ يَكُ مُغَيِّرًا نِّعْمَةً أَنْعَمَهَا عَلَىٰ قَوْمٍ حَتَّىٰ يُغَيِّرُوا۟ مَا بِأَنفُسِهِمْ وَأَنَّ ٱللَّهَ سَمِيعٌ عَلِيمٌ﴾}$$

That is because God never changes a blessing that He has bestowed on a people unless they change what is in their own souls, and God is All-Hearing, All-Knowing. (8:53)

God is waiting for us, He is patient, but He is outside of time. However, are we ready to receive the Imam? Will we accept the ultimate justice that he will enforce? What if he comes to your house today? Would he be happy with what he sees - the posters, the movies, the music, your family, your friends, your clothes, or your life? Are we encouraging him to come back or are we pushing him away? The Imam is here and can see what we do by the power given to him by God. God can make him appear on earth in the fraction of a second or He can wait for millions of years until we are ready to receive him. We have to prepare ourselves for his return.

Preparation does not just come in the form of a supplication (*dua*). *Dua* is invaluable, but even more so are our deeds and actions. We must transform ourselves. The nights of Muharram are one of the best opportunities for us to do that. They are only ten nights; but they give us a chance to pledge to God and Imam al-Zaman that we will be their servants. We will change ourselves to be better for them. We will conduct ourselves in such a way that we will be proud to stand before our Imam. We will make him happy with us, until he is able to return to earth.

We need to look at the immortal examples of the companions of Imam Husayn to learn what the Imam wants from us. They were peerless among the other human beings. Although they knew that they would die, they never wavered; and they were honored to exchange their souls for God's satisfaction. They knew what they were in for, but they were determined to stay with the Imam until the end of their lives.

﴿إِنَّ اللَّهَ اشْتَرَى مِنَ الْمُؤْمِنِينَ أَنفُسَهُمْ وَأَمْوَالَهُم بِأَنَّ لَهُمُ الجَنَّةَ يُقَاتِلُونَ فِي سَبِيلِ اللَّهِ فَيَقْتُلُونَ وَيُقْتَلُونَ وَعْدًا عَلَيْهِ حَقًّا فِي التَّوْرَاةِ وَالإِنجِيلِ وَالْقُرْآنِ وَمَنْ أَوْفَى بِعَهْدِهِ مِنَ اللَّهِ فَاسْتَبْشِرُوا بِبَيْعِكُمُ الَّذِي بَايَعْتُم بِهِ وَذَلِكَ هُوَ الْفَوْزُ الْعَظِيمُ﴾

Indeed God has bought from the faithful their souls and their possessions for Paradise to be theirs: they fight in the way of God, they kill, and are killed. A promise binding upon Him in the Torah and the Evangel and the Qur'an. And who is truer to his promise than God? So rejoice in the bargain that you have made with Him, and that is the greatest success. (9:111)

Challenges Facing the Youth

Chapter 7

Featured Themes
Generation Gap; Parents; Education; Friends; Smoking

﴿أَلْحَمْدُ لِلَّهِ الَّذِي وَهَبَ لِي عَلَى الْكِبَرِ إِسْمَاعِيلَ وَإِسْحَاقَ إِنَّ
رَبِّي لَسَمِيعُ الدُّعَاءِ﴾

"All praise belongs to God, who despite [my] old age, gave me Ishmael and Isaac. Indeed my Lord hears all of the supplications." (14:39)

LIFE IS FULL OF CHALLENGES. EACH GENERATION AND EVERY COMMUNITY has been faced with trials and tribulations and our life is no different, in fact, even the prophets and the imams faced severe trials, some even more so than any of us.

﴿أَحَسِبَ النَّاسُ أَن يُتْرَكُوا أَن يَقُولُوا آمَنَّا وَهُمْ لَا يُفْتَنُونَ. وَلَقَدْ
فَتَنَّا الَّذِينَ مِن قَبْلِهِمْ فَلَيَعْلَمَنَّ اللَّهُ الَّذِينَ صَدَقُوا وَلَيَعْلَمَنَّ
الْكَاذِبِينَ﴾

Do the people suppose that they will be let off because they say, "We have faith," and they will not be tested? Certainly We tested those who were before them. So God shall surely ascertain those who are truthful, and He shall surely ascertain the liars. (29:2-3)

$$\text{﴿إِنَّا خَلَقْنَا الْإِنسَانَ مِن نُّطْفَةٍ أَمْشَاجٍ نَّبْتَلِيهِ فَجَعَلْنَاهُ سَمِيعًا بَصِيرًا﴾}$$

Indeed We created man from the drop of a mixed (amshaji) fluid such that We may test him. So We made him endowed with hearing and sight. (76:2)

Some people pass the test, however others fail. We have been created to succeed and the word *amshaji* ("mixed") in this verse refers to this fact. Keeping the biological meaning aside, the word *amshaji* in this verse refers to the constant struggle between right and wrong that goes on within us. We were created to undergo such a test and try to become victorious.

In addition to the trials of this life, those growing up in the West have to face their own unique challenges. Today, many young people find it difficult to relate to their immediate family, and while the "generation gap" has always existed, it has become an increasing problem for Muslims in the West, since it is not only two generations, but also two different cultures living under the same roof. If one is born to parents who immigrated, or came to the West at an early age, then chances are that he or she has developed an outlook on life that is quite different from that of their parents.

It is tempting to flout this cultural conflict by insisting that "my way is the only way," however this is not a proper Islamic solution. Today, family members need to find common ground. We cannot just resign from our family responsibilities and spend all of our time outside of the house, expecting to be taken care of by our parents. We need to contribute towards the family in whatever way possible, however most importantly we need to be appreciative of our parents and the many sacrifices that they have made.

Just go and ask the elders of a community how the first wave of Muslim immigrants came, settled and began a new life in the West.

They were poor and alone. Back then, no one even knew what Islam was. Society ostracized them. Nevertheless, they overcame the obstacles and flourished. Those early Muslim immigrants went to universities, built successful businesses and established mosques. In summary, they built the foundations and the structures that we benefit from today.

Unfortunately, many children do not appreciate what their parents have done for them because their parents spoil them. We are not saying to parents that they should throw their children out on the streets; however, be aware that the more children are spoiled, the more they will take everything for granted - food, money, shelter, and yes, even love. Usually, children who are pampered and spoiled turn out to be irresponsible and immature adults with no understanding on how to cope with the various challenges that life entails. As parents, our duty is not only to provide the material requirements for our children, but also, to prepare them to live an independent adulthood.

A family needs to be filled with cooperation and mutual respect for one another otherwise it is not a real family; and within this structure, the youth especially need to be careful about how they treat their parents. In the Qur'an, God places kindness to the parents tantamount to obedience to Him:

$$﴿وَقَضَىٰ رَبُّكَ أَلَّا تَعْبُدُوٓا۟ إِلَّآ إِيَّاهُ وَبِالْوَالِدَيْنِ إِحْسَٰنًا إِمَّا يَبْلُغَنَّ عِندَكَ الْكِبَرَ أَحَدُهُمَآ أَوْ كِلَاهُمَا فَلَا تَقُل لَّهُمَآ أُفٍّ وَلَا تَنْهَرْهُمَا وَقُل لَّهُمَا قَوْلًا كَرِيمًا﴾$$

Your Lord has decreed that you shall not worship anyone except Him, and [He has enjoined] kindness to parents. Should they reach old age at your side - one of them or both - do not say to them, 'Fie!' And do not chide them, but speak to them noble words. (17:23)

Similarly, there is a hadith *al-Qudsi* tradition which says, "By My glory and honor and exalted position, I swear that if My servant carried out all of the deeds of each of the prophets (ever sent), but was undutiful to his parents and then came to Me on the Day of Judgment, I would never accept any good deed from him!"[119]

Be extremely conscious about your attitude at home and be careful of what you say to your parents because to become a good person begins with being good to your parents. If you are not good to your parents, then you will not be a good friend, husband, wife, or parent. Try to be the jewel of your family and seek to be an integral part at home

As a youth, one must be particular not to waste time on insignificant or unproductive things because time is very precious. Imam Ali advised us by saying, "O mankind! You consist of a few numbered days. Every passing day takes something from your existence."[120] Therefore, make the most of what you are given. In the Qur'an, God swears by the Time:

$$﴿وَالْعَصْرِ. إِنَّ الْإِنسَانَ لَفِي خُسْرٍ. إِلَّا الَّذِينَ آمَنُوا وَعَمِلُوا الصَّالِحَاتِ وَتَوَاصَوْا بِالْحَقِّ وَتَوَاصَوْا بِالصَّبْرِ﴾$$

By (the token of) Time! Indeed man is at a loss, except those who have faith and do righteous deeds, and enjoin one another to [follow] the truth, and enjoin one another to patience. (103:1-3)

One of the most important things which the youth need to focus on is the amount of time that they spend sleeping. It is very crucial that one does not spend too much time sleeping. If you need eight hours of sleep, then do not sleep for nine because a tradition says that, "God hates His servant who oversleeps."[121]

[119] *Jami' Al-Sa'adaat*, Al-Naraqi, v. 2, p. 202
[120] *Mizan al-Hikmah*, v. 3, p. 2112
[121] *Al-Kafi*, v. 5, p. 84

﴾وَجَعَلْنَا اللَّيْلَ لِبَاسًا. وَجَعَلْنَا النَّهَارَ مَعَاشًا﴿

And We made the night a covering, and We made the day for livelihood.
(78:10-11)

God did not create us to stay up all night and then sleep during the day; rather, He made the night for us to sleep, and the day for us to work.

We need to begin our day early with the obligatory morning prayer. After that, we should try to recite the morning supplication (*Dua al-Sabah*). If we are not already in the habit of reciting it regularly, then we need to start reciting it right away after the morning prayer. Learn to appreciate how Imam Ali established his relationship with his Lord, "My God, if mercy from Thee does not begin with fair success for me, then who can take me to Thee upon the evident path?"[122] If we are feeling self-conscience or depressed, then without a doubt, such a prayer will strengthen us - just try it for a few days and you will see and feel the results.

Another area that we need to focus on is school. Despite being a good student, school brings another set of problems. Some parents are concerned about the future of their children. They are worried that sometimes, their children start college with a lot of diligence and enthusiasm, but after a while, they lose interest and ultimately drop out. What we have to know is that knowledge is vital and just being "religious" is not enough, for religion and knowledge go hand in hand. Prophet Muhammad said, "I prefer the virtue of knowledge to the virtue of worship."[123] The broader our understanding is of the world, the closer we will become to God. Thus advanced schooling is critical and our children should be encouraged to finish college.

---

[122] *Du'a Al-Sabah*, Imam Ali
[123] *Al-Khisaal*, Sheikh Al-Sadooq, p. 4

One day the Prophet came to the mosque and saw two groups of people, one was praying and engaged in acts of worship, while the other group was learning and discussing knowledge. He said both groups were doing good things, but he preferred the latter - we need to emulate the Prophet and study the different aspects of life.

Imam as-Sadiq knew the importance of knowledge so much so that he said, "Sometimes I wish I could physically discipline my disciples to make them study."

Without a doubt, the more we know the more valuable we will be. There is a tradition which says, "If mankind knew what lies in seeking knowledge, then they would have chased after it, even if they had to swim the oceans and risk their lives."

We are living in the West where higher education is readily available. Believe me that thousands of people in the Middle East would love to pursue higher education, but for many different reasons, they simply cannot do so. When we recently established a private university in Karbala (the first one to open since the removal of Saddam) thousands of people flocked to the gates to register, however we had to turn some of them back because there was not enough room for all of them. Therefore, do not take this opportunity for granted; God did not bring you to the West to go to nightclubs or hang out in the cafés. Use this golden opportunity to study.

I know that many youth are eager to leave their families and go off to college abroad at age seventeen or eighteen, but as much as possible, if one can stay at home with their parents and go to school near the home, even if they have to commute, it would be better. It will not only be easier for you, but it will also be easier on them.

We all need the guidance and foundation of our parents, whether we are a boy or a girl; especially in the younger years of our lives. We may not realize it today, but only our parents can provide us with things that others simply cannot.

During the time of Prophet Muhammad, a man wanted to go away to study, however his parents had no one else but him to rely on and they were very much attached to him. This man asked the Prophet what to do and the Prophet said, "Go back to them. By the One between Whose hands the soul of Muhammad lies, spending one day and one night with them to make them happy is better than spending a year fighting in the way of God."

In addition to this important issue, we must also be very careful about who our friends are. Some friends will have a positive influence on us and others can be negative; and parents often cannot protect a child from the influence of a bad friend. No matter how much we feel that our friends are not influencing us, the reality is that they are indeed exerting pressure upon us - we just may not see it happen immediately. We have to find good friends who will help us grow into righteous people, for surely wrong friends can destroy our lives.

Another issue to keep in mind is that having boyfriends and girlfriends causes many problems. There are good reasons to explain why these things are unlawful (haram) in Islam. When relationships fail, many young people end up in depression, while others even contemplate suicide. Remember that just because a relationship does not work out, it is not the end of the world. One might think that a person that he or she has met and has spent some time with is the best person on earth, but this is just an illusion; God has other plans for you. As we say in *Dua al-Iftitah*, "Perhaps what You kept from me is better for me in Your knowledge for the long run." Thus, only God knows - we do not know the future.

We must also realize that a boyfriend-girlfriend relationship is most likely not going to last; it is usually temporary. Such temporary relationships are usually not based on a realistic or lifetime intention. When a boy and girl start going out, they are not thinking about a permanent commitment, and therefore instead of such relationships, we must start thinking about long term commitment which is marriage and not having a boyfriend or girlfriend. One must not think that you are not old enough to get married; if one is mature, then they can handle married life. Thus, do not waste time with such temporary relationships for they will only bring harm.

In summary, we need to protect ourselves and our souls from bad friends and unlawful (haram) relationships.

Another issue which we need to keep in mind is that: even though we are young and our bodies are at their peak, we still have to protect our health. Today, smoking *shishah* (the water pipe/*argeelah*) has become a popular fad in our community and the society as a whole. Aside from the many health related side-effects, smoking *shishah* signifies a rebellious counter culture. You do not find people smoking *shishah* at academic institutes or in the mosque. Without a doubt, the type of people who are out there smoking it in public will not be a good influence upon you. You may be a good person, but if you sit and smoke with such people, they will definitely lead you the wrong way.

Smoking cigarettes also destroys the body. Unfortunately, 30% of adults worldwide smoke; Americans spend billions of dollars every year purchasing various tobacco products. If only this money was put to better use such as for hospitals and schools.

Unfortunately, many teens start smoking to prove that they are stylish or independent and do not think about the consequences on their health, intellect, lives, or pocketbook.

Sadly, from this "innocent" starting point, some youth then begin to experiment with drugs to escape their problems, and worse - the "experiment" becomes an addiction. In reality, taking drugs will not solve your problems because after the rush fades, people feel worse than if they just tried to deal with the problem - it is a never-ending, vicious cycle of grief, and this will eventually lead to one being enslaved to the addiction. Therefore, do not try drugs even once; we have been created for much greater things in this world. As well, many, if not all of the drugs are addictive even after one use, therefore we need to be strong when our friends ask us to try something harmful - we have to just say NO! Initially, a friend may even offer the drugs free of charge the first couple of times, but once someone is hooked, you will need to come up with the money yourself. It is not farfetched to say that drug addicts eventually have to resort to desperate measures such as stealing and prostitution in order to get money for their next fix.

Drugs can also have profound effects on the psychological, biological, and intellectual anatomy. The body can become highly addictive on drugs to the extent that the user needs it in order to function in their daily routine. You can often tell immediately when you talk to someone who takes drugs because they act differently; they show signs of paranoia and hallucination; and their I.Q. is permanently affected because the use of drugs destroys brain cells. Everything about drugs is harmful.

We have something much better than drugs, something which does not harm or destroy you, and will actually help you in all the times of your life - and that treasure is Islam. We need to turn towards God when we are depressed or confused; we need to pray to Him; we need to read the Qur'an; and in all honesty, we need to tell God, "You created me and sustained me. Now I need Your help. You are the only One who will save me!" Do not resort to other means, for surely God will help you, and Imam Husayn and the other members of the Ahlul-Bayt will help you through the permission of God.

Marriage
Chapter 8

﴿وَالَّذِينَ يَقُولُونَ رَبَّنَا هَبْ لَنَا مِنْ أَزْوَاجِنَا وَذُرِّيَّاتِنَا قُرَّةَ أَعْيُنٍ وَاجْعَلْنَا لِلْمُتَّقِينَ إِمَامًا﴾

And those who say, "Our Lord! Grant us comfort in our spouses and our descendants, and give us the grace to lead the righteous." (25:74-75)

ONE OF THE GREATEST BLESSINGS THAT GOD HAS GIVEN TO HUMANITY IS the institution of marriage. Marriage is considered to be one of God's greatest signs.

﴿وَمِنْ آيَاتِهِ أَنْ خَلَقَ لَكُم مِّنْ أَنفُسِكُمْ أَزْوَاجًا لِّتَسْكُنُوا إِلَيْهَا وَجَعَلَ بَيْنَكُم مَّوَدَّةً وَرَحْمَةً إِنَّ فِي ذَلِكَ لَآيَاتٍ لِّقَوْمٍ يَتَفَكَّرُونَ﴾

And among His signs is that He created for you mates from your own selves that you may take comfort in them, and He ordained affection and mercy between you. There are indeed signs in that for a people who reflect. (30:21)

God's intention for marriage is so that people may find tranquility, love, and protection. It is intended as a blessing, but unfortunately for some people, marriage has become a curse. The institution of marriage as a whole is suffering because people do not recognize its value and its purpose. Stripped of its sanctity, it is has become relegated to mere amusement, taken lightly, or as an act to fulfill. We as Muslims need to restore it to its rightful place.

Young Muslims in the West have tremendous difficulty finding the right spouse because they are in a quagmire. The Eastern and Western cultures present them with two varying choices - either as an arranged marriage or an independent dating. On one side lies the traditional family values and ways, but on the other hand, an exclusive individual choice. Islam advocates neither, but maintains that there must be a balance between the two. Islam does not advocate blind marriage where the man or the woman knows nothing about each other; and at the same time, it does not tolerate an open, independent "dating" system. Everyone, male and female, has the right to decide what he or she wants in a spouse; but at the same time, they must safeguard their moral integrity.

Three elements of spouse selection are crucial for its success: one must inquire about the family, consult with one's parents or family, and the element of prayer. To neglect or underestimate anyone of these may hamper your chances in finding the best spouse.

One needs to take enough time when choosing a partner for life, but it is not necessary to take an entire lifetime deciding. Start looking for a husband or wife early on. Marriage is a lifetime commitment and one cannot change one's mind afterwards. It is not something that one can easily undo by a divorce. Your life and youthfulness will have been lost. Therefore, a person must be very selective and careful when seeking a partner for life; and the person you want to marry should be scrutinized. One must also keep in mind that you will never find a person who will fit *every* criterion on your list.

A man once made a list of the top five most important things that he wanted in a wife; the list consisted of beauty, wealth, intelligence, culinary skills, and able to bear children. Absent from the list were the most important qualities - was she capable of loving, being patient in adversity, holding firm to one's faith, displaying honesty and trustworthiness?

One should not marry someone in a rush just because one is desperate or lonely; nor should one's hormones be the driving force. If you marry blindly, your marriage will be on rocky footing from the very beginning.

Along the same line of thought, one must involve their families. If one is in love, it will be extremely difficult for one to see their partner objectively. According to Imam Ali, love blinds a person. Your family, particularly your parents, may see that person differently than you do. No matter how old you are, they can help you. They have more experience in life and with people than you do. They are able to see things that you may not be able to.

Ask your parents to help you find the right partner, and then request them to help you have an Islamic wedding. You do not want to curse your marriage by solemnizing it in a way that incurs the wrath of God just to please other people or to follow the culture. We all know what happens at most weddings; music, dancing, unclad attire, unlawful mixed gatherings, and some even drink alcohol. Marriage pleases God more than anything else does, but we must make sure that our actions do not turn His face away from our wedding.

While one is seeking the right partner, one must continuously ask God for help. Ask Him to guide you to the right person and make you certain about them. Marriage is the most important and critical decision you will make in your entire life. We all need His guidance. Unfortunately, some of us approach God about marriage in the wrong way. Instead of asking Him to show us the person that He knows would be best for us to marry, we tell Him who we like and ask Him to bring us together. Do not tell God what to do. He knows better than us and He wants the best for us. A person whom we like might make our lives miserable in the end.

﴿وَيَدْعُ الْإِنْسَانُ بِالشَّرِّ دُعَاءَهُ بِالْخَيْرِ وَ كَانَ الْإِنْسَانُ عَجُولاً﴾

Man prays for ill as [avidly as] he prays for good, and man is overhasty. (17:11)

Although one should look for many qualities in a spouse, the foremost is faith.

﴿قُلْ إِنَّ صَلَاتِي وَنُسُكِي وَمَحْيَايَ وَمَمَاتِي لِلَّهِ رَبِّ الْعَالَمِينَ﴾

Say, "Indeed my prayer and my worship, my life and my death are for the sake of God, Lord of all of the worlds." (6:162)

Faith does not just mean being a Muslim or praying. It is much deeper than this. One should be able to see the effects of faith on a person's life. A person with true faith has good morals, a positive outlook on life, and the best character. Rituals, such as prayers are only a physical manifestation because true prayers curtail evil acts.

﴿إِنَّ الصَّلَاةَ تَنْهَى عَنِ الْفَحْشَاءِ وَالْمُنكَرِ وَلَذِكْرُ اللَّهِ أَكْبَرُ وَاللَّهُ يَعْلَمُ مَا تَصْنَعُونَ﴾

Indeed the prayer prevents indecencies and wrongs, and the remembrance of God is surely greater. And God knows whatever [deeds] you do. (29:45)

Shared faith will hold a marriage together. A man once asked Imam Husayn to advise him on whom to marry his only daughter to. The Imam said, "Give her to someone who has deep faith because if he loves her, he will cherish her; and if he does not love her, then he will at least not wrong her." Faith is irreplaceable.

After faith, the next most important thing is responsibility and sacrifice. One needs to find someone who is responsible, mature, and committed to marital life and family values. The essence of marriage is responsibility and sacrificing oneself for their spouse and children.

Once you get married, you will be sharing the same room, house, food, car, and the same goals with that person for the rest of your life. That person will become your family, and you will become part of their life. One has to be ready to accept them completely. You cannot change your mind afterwards. One has to be fully prepared for the commitment.

Some men get married but then they do not spend time with their wives. They spend most of their time with their friends. A woman complained that every day when she came home from work she found her husband and his friends sitting in the living room smoking the *arghilah* (water pipe) and watching TV until two or three in the morning. The home should be a place to regain one's strength; it is supposed to be a place to find comfort and ease. This woman could not even walk freely through some parts of her home because of her husband's inconvenience. Her husband was violating the sanctity of the home. One must be committed to one's family first and foremost.

Marriage is not just about having a physical relationship. The Prophet did not obligate us to marry by saying, "marriage is my tradition, and whoever turns away from my tradition is not from me" just for this aspect. Marriage is as emotional shelter. A wife needs love, attention, compassion, happiness, and care. These qualities are what count the most for a wife. The Prophet warned us that, "May the mercy of God be away from the man who does not take care of his family."[124]

Compatibility is also vital. Two people with different mentalities, intellect, aspirations, or pecuniary upbringing cannot be united. They will not understand or appreciate each other. Although they may be

---

[124] *Al-Kafi*, v. 4, p. 12

physically present with each other, but emotionally they will be distant. Incompatibility in a marriage will cause a lot of suffering. This is why we have family conflicts and such a high divorce rate.

There are a few simple things that can make one's marriage happier. The Prophet said, "When a man tells his wife 'I love you' it never leaves her heart."[125] Many men complain that their wives do not care about them and do not pay attention to them. You cannot blame a wife who turns away from her husband when the husband is not involved in her life or does not interact with her. In this aspect, you have no one to blame but yourself because if you neglect her, she will then spend her time and energy on other things instead of you. If you do not care to ask her how her day went, or care to have a simple or deep conversation with her, nor offer your support or understanding, or find ways to assist her then do not be surprised of her distance from you. The Prophet said, "May the mercy of God not be on the man who goes home and thinks only of satisfying his own physical desire without thinking about his wife."

What if one is already married? How can one sustain their marriage and minimize the conflict between spouses?

Does love expire?

Yes it does.

Does it have a refill?

It also does.

How do we keep our marital life alive?

The most important element in keeping a husband and wife together is *taqwa* or consciousness of God. Before even thinking about your partner, think of God. He is always present in our lives. He is the third party between us. A solemnized and sacred Muslim marriage exists

---

[125] *Al-Kafi*, v. 5, p. 569

only because God is partnered in it. The closer one is to God, the happier and more solid your marriage will be. "The more a worshipper increases in faith, the more one will love their spouse,"[126] says a tradition.

Build a strong family. Have a family that can stand with you before God on the Day of Judgment. Have a family that will make the Prophet happy. The Prophet said, "There is no intercessor for a woman before her Lord better than the satisfaction of her husband."[127] A religious person puts his family first. There is a tradition that says, "A believer eats whatever his family likes, and a disbeliever makes his family eat whatever he himself likes."[128] So try to put your family's desires before your own desires.

Humility and forgiveness are the best manifestation of faith. Be humble, especially towards your own family; and forgive and care for them. Do not hold grudges for past mistakes. Even in the best of marriages, spouses may often hurt each other, but one has to forgive and move on. The Prophet says, "The closest one to me on the Day of Judgment will be the person who was the best with his family."[129]

---

[126] *Bihar al-Anwar*, Al-Allamah Al-Majlisi, v. 100, p. 228
[127] *Mizan Al-Hikmah*, v. 2, p. 1184
[128] *Al-Kafi*, v. 4, p. 12
[129] *Bihar al-Anwar*, Al-Allamah Al-Majlisi, v. 68, p. 387

Healthy Parenting

Chapter 9

﴿وَوَصَّىٰ بِهَا إِبْرَاهِيمُ بَنِيهِ وَيَعْقُوبُ يَا بَنِيَّ إِنَّ اللَّهَ اصْطَفَىٰ
لَكُمُ الدِّينَ فَلَا تَمُوتُنَّ إِلَّا وَأَنْتُم مُّسْلِمُونَ﴾

Abraham enjoined this [creed] upon his children, and [so did] Jacob, [saying],
"My children! God has indeed chosen this religion for you; so never die except
as submitters (muslims)." (2:132)

IT IS CRUCIAL THAT WHEN DISCUSSING FAMILY MATTERS BOTH THE
parents and children must be addressed. According to Islam, parents
and children have mutual responsibilities towards each other. While
we remind children to respect their parents, we also have to remind
parents to take care of their children. No sacrifice can be one-sided
only. For a family to remain stable, parents and children need to work
together and acknowledge their mutual duties and responsibilities.

If you neglect your children, then you will fail your duty as a parent.
Even if you care for them but do not raise them on Islamic ethics and
morals, then you will not have fulfilled your duty to God as a parent.
Both parents and children must hold fast to the Islamic values.

Parents need to ask themselves, what does my child need from me?
First and foremost, parents need to establish a close friendship with
their children. Secondly, parents need to set an example of a good role

model for their children. Thirdly, parents have to prepare their children for the future. All of these are equally important.

Fostering true friendship with your children preserves the family. It keeps your children with you, not against you. We all know that the generation gap between parents and children is incessantly widening. Parents need to try to close this gap by developing a close friendship with their offspring. When someone asks your child who is your best friend, they should say, "my mom" or "my dad." Children should be able to confide in their parents, and not feel like they have to go to others for anything. Parents need to be there emotionally and intellectually for their children, not just financially.

In order to strengthen the relationship with your children, one needs to be open and honest with them, while maintaining the honor and respect of a parent. Children need to respect their parents, but at the same time, the respect should not act an emotional barrier. If your children are afraid to talk to you, how will you know what they are doing or going through? If you do not speak to them, how will you be able to help them? Spend time with your children, for they are a gift from God. He did not give us these gifts just to feed them; we need to instill values into their hearts, and make them into true human beings.

In particular, fathers need to spend quality time with their children. Designate a day just for your kids. Leave aside your business and other concerns to be with them. Take them to the mosque, both, the sons and the daughters. Take them to Hajj and umrah,[130] or camping, skiing, or to other places where they can enjoy themselves. Wouldn't you rather that they went to the mall, movies, or sporting events with you instead of someone else? Take them with you when you travel. Let them feel like you are really their friend. This is how you can keep them close to you. We cannot monitor everything that they do. We do not have cameras to keep track of everything that they do at home, at

---

[130] The smaller pilgrimage to Mekkah

school, in the car, and so forth. However, we can monitor them in another way, and that is by reaching out to their hearts so that they tell us what is on their minds. Do not make them confide in someone else who might mislead them or take advantage of their weakness.

If your child is trying to attain faith, then encourage and support them, even if you may not be practicing it much. It was most disheartening to hear a story about a young girl who lived in a Muslim country and asked her father to take her to umrah as a high school graduation present, but her father refused, not because it was too expensive, but because he said she was too young. Imagine, 18 years old and he says she was too young for umrah. Instead of encouraging her to make umrah and forge a connection with God and her religion, he offered her $6,000 for plastic surgery! This was a Muslim man. What kind of message did he give his daughter? How do you think she feels being told by her own father that her entire self-worth is in her body? If she turns against him, then he has no one to blame but himself. He is a person who brought evil and destruction to his family. Instead of leading her closer to God, he sent her in the opposite way. We are responsible not only for our own misery, but also for the misery we may cause towards others.

When you talk to your children, use modern language. Take a contemporary approach to discussing religious or social issues. They need to relate that you understand the world that they are living in. Do not use violence or harsh words and try not to be too imposing or domineering. Do not threaten them, instead encourage them. Do not be a dictator with them. Many children are terrified of talking to their fathers and they ask others instead to speak to them. Parents need to make time for their children, talk to them, and be there for them. How many people come to the West to make money but lose their children? A man I know became temporarily unemployed when he left a very lucrative job to live next to an Islamic school. I asked him why he did that. He said that although it is not easy to find another job, but if you lose your kids, it is not easy to bring them back to the teachings of Islam. Islamic values must outweigh a few dollars.

Next, be a role model; be the best example for them. They will follow what you do rather than what you say, so show them Islam in action.

$$﴿يَا أَيُّهَا الَّذِينَ آمَنُوا لِمَ تَقُولُونَ مَا لَا تَفْعَلُونَ﴾$$

O you who have faith! Why do you say that what you do not do? (61:2)

You cannot fool your children. They are smart and they learn from what you do. Even if they do not see everything that you do, they will still sense it and harbor those feelings. Enjoin good by doing what is right and your family will follow you. It is said that God has cursed those who enjoin good to others but do not practice it themselves and forbid others to do evil but commit evil themselves. The world has enough hypocrites. When your children see you do the right thing, then they will feel confident that they can trust you. If they see you lie, cheat, or steal then what will happen to them? They will resent you for the rest of their lives and one day your family situation will explode. They will run away, not because of what happened today, but as a result of what happened in the past. Let us bring them back to Islam through practicing Islam and implementing our beliefs.

Finally, you have to prepare them for the future. Empower their faith by strengthening their relationship with the Qur'an, to Islam, to Prophet Muhammad and the Ahlul-Bayt. Instill the love of the Ahlul-Bayt into their hearts and minds while they are still young. You have to strengthen this connection. In the West, our youth know more about singers and musicians than they do about their own religious leaders and imams. It is very important to connect them to the Ahlul-Bayt. Make them akin to people like the daughter of Abul Aswad al-Duwali, who was one of the disciples of Imam Ali in Kufa. Their family was very poor and could barely afford bread. One day, Abul Aswad al-Duwali came home, and found to his surprise, his young daughter eating honey. Astonished, he asked her where she got it from. She told him that a nice man had come to their house and given it to them. After asking around, he discovered that Muawiyah had sent them the honey. Bending down to his daughter, he said, "I know you are hungry, and you have never had anything sweet before, but what you are eating is poisonous. It has come from Muawiyah, and Muawiyah wants to take the love of Imam Ali away from your heart. Is that what you want?" Immediately she said, "No, of course not!" She forced herself to throw up all of the honey. Despite her young age, she told her father that nothing could take away the love of Imam Ali from the blood that flowed through her veins. This is what we need to teach our children, and ingrain within them.

In addition to faith, your children need to be educated. Always encourage them to learn. Instead of buying them new clothes for special occasions, buy them books, but not just any books, rather ethical books that they can learn from. Support them by paying for their tuition. Make school an enjoyable experience for them; and do not criticize them for their shortfalls at school. Rather, continue to praise them for their hard work and accomplishments.

Finally, when they are old enough to shoulder the responsibilities of marriage, then persuade them to get married. They need you to encourage and help them find a good partner. Do not tell them they are not old enough. Many young men and women need and want to get married, but some parents object by saying that they are too young. You must have faith in your children. If they say that they are ready for marriage then let them prove it and help them to get married. There is nothing wrong with helping them financially. Some parents say that they first need to stand on their own two feet, but what they are often waiting for is for them to make a fortune first. God promises us in the Qur'an that if we marry sincerely, He will provide for us, and His promise is true. If you make them wait to get married until you think that they have enough money, then you are denying God's word. You have to trust in Him, and place your full reliance on Him alone.

$$﴿وَأَنكِحُوا الْأَيَامَى مِنكُمْ وَالصَّالِحِينَ مِنْ عِبَادِكُمْ وَإِمَائِكُمْ إِن يَكُونُوا فُقَرَاءَ يُغْنِهِمُ اللَّهُ مِنْ فَضْلِهِ وَاللَّهُ وَاسِعٌ عَلِيمٌ﴾$$

Marry off those who are single among you and the upright among your male and your female. If they are poor, then God will enrich them out of His grace, and God is All-Bounteous, All-Knowing. (24:32)

Sometimes, suitors come to a father to propose marriage for his daughter, but the father refuses them and does not even inform his daughter of the prospective suitor because in his mind his daughter is still young, even if she is over 25. At this age, she is not young; she knows enough and is more than ready to be a wife and a mother.

Challenge your children to show you that they appreciate the meaning of marriage and family, and then when they prove themselves support them.

The best way to protect the family and community against promiscuity and corruption is to encourage the youth to get married at a young age, provided that they respect the value of married life. Thus encourage them, for this is part of a parent's responsibility.

The points mentioned above are just some of the responsibilities that parents have towards their children. Children also have responsibilities towards their parents. Although there are plenty of obligations that they have towards their parent, three take precedence. First, respect for your parents, for they deserve it. They cared for you and raised you in the best way that they could. You can never repay them for what they did. The least that you can do is to acknowledge what they have done for you.

Respect comes in different forms. God says in the Qur'an:

$$﴿وَاخْفِضْ لَهُمَا جَنَاحَ الذُّلِّ مِنَ الرَّحْمَةِ وَقُل رَّبِّ ارْحَمْهُمَا كَمَا رَبَّيَانِي صَغِيرًا﴾$$

Lower the wing of humility to them, out of mercy, and say, "My Lord! Have mercy on them, just as they reared me when I was [a] small [child]!" (17:24)

Address your parents kindly and humbly, for you are the dearest person to them. You are their best friend and companion. It is all right to humor and joke with them, but never forego the respect and dignity that they represent as parents. The Prophet said, "Whoever looks at his parents mercifully receives the reward of a complete Hajj for every glance."[131] One of his companions asked that if he looks at his mother or father 500 times a day, would he receive the reward of 500 Hajjs. The Prophet replied yes. He further said that, "When a child looks at a parent, it is worship." This is one kind of respect.

Another form of respect is obedience. One must obey their parents as long as what they say is in accordance with God. Listen to them and obey them. Do well to them and help them whenever you are able to.

Secondly, strive to be a righteous son or daughter. If you do, then you will continue helping them even after they have left this world. The Prophet taught us not to limit our kindness to our parents only during their lifetime. Rather, he taught us to respect them even after they have departed from this world. Someone asked him how we can do this? He replied, "If you are a righteous son or daughter, then whenever you do something good, part of that *thawab* (credit) will go to your parents in their grave." He also said, "When a man dies, all of the opportunities for good deeds are cut off except for three things."[132] One of those three is a righteous son or daughter. Another tradition says that when a

---

[131] *Bihar al-Anwar*, Al-Allamah Al-Majlisi, v. 71, p. 73

[132] *Sharh Usual Al-Kafi*, Al-Mazandarani, v. 6, p. 137

person dies, he leaves inheritance to two groups: his family and God. His money and his property go to his relatives, but his righteous children are bequeathed to God. That is God's share of the inheritance.

There are four types of children. One helps his parents only in this world, either physically or financially, but he has no faith. He will be of no use in the after-life (*akhirah*). Then there is the one who neither helps his parents in this world, nor in the after-life, and this is the worst kind of a child. The third benefits them only in the after-life. However, the fourth, which is the best type, is the one who helps them in this life and in the next. Try to make yourself the fourth kind.

Third, give sound advice to your parents. Even though you are much younger than they are, you can still assist them. As children, we have to ensure that when our parents leave this world, they embark on a safe and easy journey (*aqibat al-khayr*), not to an evil end. Parents are not infallible, and thus they are not immune to making mistakes. If you see something wrong in the family, approach them gently. However, do not embarrass or insult them, but speak to them carefully, respectfully, and in an honorable way and advise them that what they are doing is not correct. Reassure them that you are telling them this because you love them, just like Prophet Abraham did when he advised Azar.

Be careful of the language that you use with them. Never use harsh words even if you are angry. If you are upset, and the whispers of Satan are telling you to go home and yell at your parents, do not go home until you calm down. Do not take out your anger on your poor mother who carried you for nine months, fed you, changed your diapers, and never complained. Your mother suffered a lot to give birth to you, but as soon as you were born, the first thing she did was kiss you. That is enough to prove that your mother loves and cares much about you.

If your parents are restricting your freedom, then it is because they are concerned about you. Freedom is not being able to go wherever you want or do whatever you want. Real freedom is to be able to restrain yourself from your desires. If you have the willpower to say no to yourself to do bad, then you are free. Imam Ali says that the most powerful ruler is the one who can control his own soul, not his kingdom or the army. That is a person who has true power. Sometimes parents have to say no to their children because they want to protect them. You will realize this when you yourself become a father or mother. When you turn 40 or 50 years old, and if you father is still alive, you will then kiss his hand and thank him for keeping you from doing what you wanted to or going to the places that you desired to go to. You will understand why he did what he did.

Try to continue going to religious sessions. They will protect and enlighten you. They will show you the way. Do not limit yourself to just the ten nights of Muharram. Do not think that once Ashura is over your faith is complete and you do not need to go anymore to the Islamic centers. You have to go at least once a week. That is why God ordained the Friday prayer and said that one should try and attend them.

$$﴿يَاأَيُّهَاالَّذِينَ آمَنُوا إِذَا نُودِي لِلصَّلَاةِ مِن يَوْمِ الْجُمُعَةِ فَاسْعَوْا إِلَى ذِكْرِ اللَّهِ وَذَرُوا الْبَيْعَ ذَلِكُمْ خَيْرٌ لَّكُمْ إِن كُنتُمْ تَعْلَمُونَ﴾$$

O you who have faith! When the call is made for prayer on Friday, hurry towards the remembrance of God, and leave all business. That is better for you, should you know. (62:9)

If you are not intoxicated with wealth or worldly gain then you will realize that going to the Friday prayer will benefit you a lot. They will energize you for the whole week. If you can go to the Friday prayer, then go to a place that takes you to God. Go to a religious center that leads you to the right path - the path of God, the Messenger of God, and the Ahlul-Bayt. That is the right path. So go at least once a week when you are able to.

Some of you say that you listen to lectures on the Internet, this is good, but the Internet is not enough. You have to be present in a session physically. One day, a blind man came to the Prophet and said, "I want to go to the mosque to pray but I have no one to guide me." The Prophet told him, "Tie a rope between your house and the mosque and use that rope to guide you to the mosque." The Prophet did not tell the blind man just to pray at home, instead he encouraged him to come to the mosque even if he had to tie a rope to the mosque to find it.

The mosque is not just a place of worship. It is also an environment where one can strengthen their relationship with fellow brothers and sisters in faith, especially in a country where we are the minority. Everyone can empower and comfort each other.

﴿إِلاَّ الَّذِينَ آمَنُوا وَعَمِلُوا الصَّالِحَاتِ وَتَوَاصَوْا بِالْحَقِّ وَتَوَاصَوْا بِالصَّبْرِ﴾

Except those who have faith and do righteous deeds, and enjoin one another to [follow] the truth, and enjoin one another to patience. (103:3)

Try to help the mosque as well, in any which way possible; whether intellectually, physically, or financially. They need everyone's assistance; and without the help, the mosque may not have a future. If you appreciate what they are doing, then contribute towards it. Giving money or time is an investment; it will not go to waste. In fact, you benefit most from it because parting with your money cleanses the soul.

﴿خُذْ مِنْ أَمْوَالِهِمْ صَدَقَةً تُطَهِّرُهُمْ وَتُزَكِّيهِم بِهَا وَصَلِّ عَلَيْهِمْ إِنَّ صَلاَتَكَ سَكَنٌ لَّهُمْ وَاللَّهُ سَمِيعٌ عَلِيمٌ﴾

Take charity from their possessions to cleanse them and purify them thereby, and bless them. Indeed your blessing is a comfort for them, and God is All-Hearing, All-Knowing. (9:103)

Once you give your money to God, you are showing your real generosity. So help these institutions when you can, whenever they have a fundraiser or even when they put the small donation box in front of you, help them. Perhaps someone else may donate more, but when you give money yourself, you are showing them a token of respect and acknowledging that you appreciate their services.

As mentioned before, none of us are infallible. Some sins are major, but there are some sins which are "minor," and we sometimes overlook them. However, God warns us not to underestimate any sin. A sin that we may think of as being small could be the source of God's greatest anger. "Do not look at the smallness of a sin, but look at the greatness of the One whom you are disobeying,"[133] Imam Ali once said. Sins, whether major or minor are a violation against God. Hence, no sin is minor, for you are violating His rights. Let us vow to God to end at least one of our bad habits today.

---

[133] *Bihar al-Anwar*, Al-Allamah Al-Majlisi, v. 14, p. 379

The Roadmap

Chapter 10

﴿فَأَمَّا مَنْ طَغَى ○ وَآثَرَ الْحَيَاةَ الدُّنْيَا○ فَإِنَّ الْجَحِيمَ هِيَ الْمَأْوَى○ وَأَمَّا مَنْ خَافَ مَقَامَ رَبِّهِ وَنَهَى النَّفْسَ عَنِ الْهَوَى ○ فَإِنَّ الْجَنَّةَ هِيَ الْمَأْوَى﴾

As for him who was rebellious and preferred the life of this world, his refuge will indeed be Hell. But as for him who is awed to stand before his Lord and forbids the soul from [following] desire, his refuge will indeed be the Paradise. (79:37-41)

USUALLY WHEN PEOPLE TRAVEL, THEY TAKE WITH THEM A MAP OF THE area that they intend to visit. Guide maps provide the quickest direction, the best scenic routes, and roads that are pleasant and safe to take, and most importantly, they assist people from getting lost. The map of life is a lot like any ordinary map guide, but this map of life has only two roads and the roads are drastically in opposite directions. One road leads to Heaven and the other one leads to Hell. Since life is a quick bridge that we are passing through, we need a map to guide us to what is important so we do not miss anything in these fleeting seconds. Fortunately, God who created us also gave us this map to guide us. Nothing is ambiguous in this map guide. As these verses above say, rebelling against God and living for this life will lead one to

Hell, and fearing God and controlling the self will lead one to Heaven. Some people examine it and take heed, whereas others cast it aside.

There are two traits that people have that will send them towards Hell. One is *athar*, to prefer the life of this world to the hereafter; and the other is *tagha*, to transgress or rebel against the orders of God.

Satan was the first one to rebel against God. In the beginning, he was good, in fact, very good. He worshipped God in the foremost ranks of the angels. However, when God tested him and asked him to respect Adam he refused. He thought he was better than Adam was and did not want to bow down to him. Satan's fall from grace was his obstinate superiority of himself [race], a lot like the racism that we witness around the world today. He destroyed all of his work, for true faith only comes from submitting to God's every command.

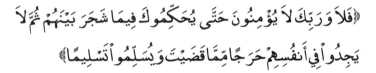

But no, by your Lord! They will not believe until they make you a judge in their disputes, then do not find within their hearts any dissent to your verdict and submit in full submission. (4:65)

Every aspect of our lives needs to be for the sake of God. Even love and hate must be only for His sake. When Satan changed his priorities, he fell from God's grace.

Initially, Satan had been carrying out the external aspect of faith. His internal faith had not yet been tested. Faith has two aspects: one is interior and the other is exterior. We see the exterior every day in the way people pray, fast, give alms, and abstain from open sins. Inner faith is not visible to the naked eye. You can measure your faith by how subservient you are before God. If you acknowledge that you are completely and absolutely nothing before Him, then you have faith. This is also the meaning of love. When you truly love someone, the first thing that you do is obey them. If they tell you to call them at 2 a.m., then you stay awake until 2 a.m. to call them. If they tell you to stand on the corner under the bitter cold rain, then you wait on the corner under the downpour. If they tell you to text message them, you text message them. You never say no. You enjoy doing whatever they want because you love them.

One day, Prophet Solomon was traveling through the desert and saw an ant carrying dust from one heap to another. Solomon, who could talk to animals, asked her why she was carrying the dust. She told him it was because someone she loved asked her to do it. Solomon warned her that there was an entire mountain of dust and she will kill herself before she had finished carrying it and not even make a dent in the pile. She said, "Solomon, dying in the line of duty for someone that I love makes me happy."

Solomon got the message; we do what we have to do for the love of God, even if we have to give our lives, still we will enjoy it. Hence, our life and death should all be for the sake of God and doing whatever He loves from us.

$$﴿قُلْ إِنَّ صَلَاتِي وَنُسُكِي وَمَحْيَايَ وَمَمَاتِي لِلَّهِ رَبِّ الْعَالَمِينَ﴾$$

Say, "Indeed my prayer and my worship, my life and my death are for the sake of God, the Lord of all the worlds." (6:162)

The more you submit to God, the closer you are to Him. This is why the best posture in the Muslim prayer is *sujud* (prostrating the forehead on the ground). *Sujud* exemplifies the meaning behind our prayers. When we do *sujud*, we convey to God that we surrender and humiliate ourselves before Him by putting the highest point and the most respectable part of our body (the face) on the dust for His sake. We tell him that we accept everything that He tells us. This is why the hadith reads, "If a person praying knew how much divine grace overwhelmed him in *sujud*, he would never raise his head up from that position."[134] He would stay there forever. I am sure that everyone who takes the time to attend religious services prays, so try to extend your time in the *sujud*. If it takes 30 seconds, make it 60 seconds, especially the last prostration before you complete your prayer. Tell God in your heart that you are doing this for Him, and that He is the source of power. Our hopes do not rest on our parents, money, college, education, or business - only on Him.

Take care of your prayers; this is the message of Imam Husayn. Since you are the guests of Imam Husayn during the nights of Muharram, ask him to help you stand before God. You will see your life change. Once you start saying your prayers sincerely, your entire life will be transformed.

In contrast, rebellion is the mother of all crimes. Rebellion does not begin with murder, fornication, or alcohol. It starts off very small. You think that whatever you are doing is nothing because everyone else is doing it. Everyone was also sharing in the same sins that caused the wrath of God to descend upon the civilizations of the past. Thus, never underestimate any sin because even the smallest sin violates God's sanctity. It is a crime against Him.

Furthermore, major sins develop over time. A murderer does not begin killing in cold blood overnight. It starts with killing insects or animals and then people. Murder takes a few moments but it leads one to eternal Hell. One is not even selling the Hereafter to enjoy the rest of their lifetime because one cannot rest after committing such a horrendous crime. Criminals do not live easy lives; they live in fear and guilt. They lose out in this world and in the next. They will be in eternal misery.

Do not think that any sin is meaningless and God will forgive it. Unless you truly seek forgiveness and really try to reform yourself, a sin will

---

[134] *'Uyoon Al-Hikam Wal Mawa'idh*, Al-Wasity, p. 417

only magnify itself. A classic example is chatting on the Internet. Some people have the habit of engaging in disgraceful conversations online. They do not even realize that they are sinning or putting themselves in danger. Try not to be naïve into thinking that it is "just chatting," it may begin with casual talk, but it will eventually lead to something you did not plan. This is how the problems begin.

Rebelling against God is the first entrance to the highway towards Hell. The next thing is to prefer the life of this world to the Hereafter. Giving into the vanities and lusts of this temporary life makes one forget the Hereafter. If one owns a painting worth millions of dollars and sells it for ten dollars, would people think that they are wise? This is what someone is like who sells the permanent afterlife for the temporary abode of this life.

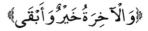

While the Hereafter is better and more lasting. (87:17)

Even if you buy the most luxurious car and the most extravagant house, you will still know that those things are temporary. Certainly, one day all of your material possession will be taken away from you, either before your death or afterwards by your family. However, in Paradise, no one can take the keys away from you. Even if you are driving a Lexus here, you will eventually get tired of it and replace it, but in Paradise, you will never get bored of anything. God will always create something new and exciting.

He warns us not to sell something valuable for something cheap. He also warns us not to favor this life over the next when our next life is where we will permanently reside. One day, the Prophet was walking down the street in Madinah when he came across some Muslims who were surrounding a man and mocking him. When he asked what was going on, they said, "He is crazy, and we are having fun with him." The Prophet replied, "That man is not insane, rather he is afflicted. The person who is truly insane is the one who sells the Hereafter for the life of this world."[135] On another occasion, the Prophet said, "The worst person is the one who sells his afterlife for this life."[136]

Those who favored this life and those who favored the next were both present on the day of Ashura. One of those who chose this life was Umar b. Sa'd, the commander of the enemy forces. Trying to avert the battle from taking place, Imam Husayn called him to a private meeting in his tent right before the fighting broke out. He advised him, "Umar, you know me and my history. You know what I represent. You know how much my grandfather the Prophet adored me and you know that he called me and my brother the 'chiefs of the youth of Paradise'. You are committing a grave crime. Take your army and go back to Kufa. Save yourself from what you are doing. You are not only committing a crime against me, but you are also committing a crime against God, humanity, Islam, and the prophets."

"If I do not arrest you," Umar replied, "then they will destroy my house in Kufa."

"I will rebuild your house," the Imam promised.

"They will confiscate my property," he said.

"I will give you property," the Imam said.

"They will kill my children," Umar objected.

The Imam asked, "Does that give you the right to harm me and my children, the children of the Noble Prophet?"

Umar b. Sa'd was traveling too fast on the highway towards Hell to be saved. In fact, he met his destination before he even died. After fulfilling his mission, he returned back to Ibn Ziyad and asked for his reward. Ibn Ziyad had promised to make him the governor of Rey (a

---

[135] *Mustadrak Al-Wasael*, v. 8, p. 239

[136] *Man La Yahdharuhul Faqih*, v. 4, p. 353

city near Tehran) in return for killing Imam Husayn. When he came with the head of Imam Husayn in his hand, Ibn Ziyad retorted, "How can I trust you with Rey after you killed the son of the Prophet?" So he lost out in this world and in the next, he will be in eternal damnation.

On the other hand, people like Hurr chose the Hereafter. Hurr was traveling fast on the same highway as Ibn Ziyad. Just like the story of a man who was traveling south in California near the border of Mexico. He was driving so fast that he did not pay attention to the last exit sign that warns drivers to return to the USA, otherwise they will end up in Mexico. It was too late for that man, and thus, he ended up in the wrong country. However, Hurr at the last minute turned around - he read the warning sign carefully. He was a high-ranking commander in the enemy army, and was sent to lead the onslaught against Imam Husayn, but then he saved himself. The enemies heard him say, "I see myself wavering between Heaven and the Fire. Finally, he chose Imam Husayn. The Imam did not rebuke or remind him that it was his fault that he had been forced to languish in Karbala. Instead, he assured him, "If you are sincere about repenting, God will forgive you." Within minutes, Hurr decisively rode out to fight against the enemy, who had been his own soldiers only moments before. After he fell, Imam Husayn eulogized him with these immortal words, "Be glad, Hurr[137], for as your mother named you, you are truly free in this world and happy in the next." He escaped the two main entrances to Hell which are rebellion and choosing this life. He became one of those who feared God's tribunal and hence triumphed because of it.

﴿يَا أَيُّهَا النَّاسُ اعْبُدُواْ رَبَّكُمُ الَّذِي خَلَقَكُمْ وَالَّذِينَ مِن قَبْلِكُمْ لَعَلَّكُمْ تَتَّقُونَ﴾

---

[137] The meaning of *hurr* in Arabic is one who has the freedom to choose.

O mankind! Worship your Lord, who created you and those who were before you, so that you may be conscious of God. (2:21)

Everyone will stand before the court of God and it is like no other court in this world. No one can lie or run away from it. All of our deeds will be exposed to others. Our friends and enemies will all watch the grotesque mistakes that we committed in our lifetime.

﴿يَوْمَئِذٍ تُعْرَضُونَ لَا تَخْفَى مِنكُمْ خَافِيَةٌ﴾

That day you will be exposed: none of your secrets will remain hidden. (69:18)

No one will have any privacy and no one will be able to hide anything from our loved ones. God will judge and His will be the final decision. That will be a day of great remorse.

﴿وَأَنذِرْهُمْ يَوْمَ الْحَسْرَةِ إِذْ قُضِيَ الْأَمْرُ وَهُمْ فِي غَفْلَةٍ وَهُمْ لَا يُؤْمِنُونَ﴾

Warn them of the Day of Regret, when the matter will be decided, but they are [yet] heedless and do not have faith. (19:39)

Imagine how you would feel if your fiancé found you with someone else. Some people claim that they love God, but on that Day He will show them proof that they loved others or things more than Him. Ask yourself, is your mind and heart always with God during the prayer? Were you with God during the month of Ramadan? Were you doing that which He forbade you to do? You might be able to deceive your parents or other people, but you can never hide anything from God. He knows everything and will make it plain for everyone to see one day.

Fear God to save yourself. Be conscious of His presence at all times. When Cain raised his hand to kill Abel, Abel swore, "I will never stretch my hand out to kill you because I fear God, the Lord of the

Worlds."[138] Cain's heart was emotionless and thus he murdered his own brother.

Do not let your desires get the better of you. A father once asked me to remind the young Muslim brothers to be careful with other people's daughters and sisters. They are not toys for public use. Do not abuse or misuse them. Remember that whatever you do today, your own daughter will be in danger of it tomorrow. Would you want someone to do the same thing to her that you are planning to do with someone else?

When Zulaykha was chasing after Prophet Joseph through the palace trying to persuade and seduce him, she cornered him in her room, bolted the door, took off her clothes, and then stopped. Joseph thought that maybe she had changed her mind, but instead she said, "I am embarrassed in front of this statue which has been in our palace for years. I want to cover it with my dress." Joseph asked her why she wanted to cover the statue that could not see and could not hear, yet they were both standing before God who was aware of everything that was going on. Imam Ali said, "Fear God as if you see Him, but if you do not see Him, then know that He sees you."[139]

The Qur'an beautifully puts it:

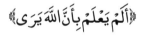

Does one not know that God sees? (96:14)

Let this verse echo in your mind; carry it with you; put it in your car; read it in the morning and in the evening. Whenever Satan whispers anything to you, repeat it. Remember that God always sees you whether you are in public or private.

---

[138] *Al-Qur'an,* 5:28
[139] *Al-Kafi,* v. 2, p. 68

If you have absolute certainty that God is always with you, then you will be able to restrain yourself. Your parents should not be the only ones to tell you what not to do. Since God has given you an innate sense of right and wrong, then curb your desires. Since your soul always asks you to do what it wants, try for one week to say no to it. God has given you the will power to resist the evil temptations of it. Sometimes you see two brothers, one who smokes and the other who does not. The one who smokes cannot stop himself; he feels that if he does not smoke a cigarette then he will die. However, this is only a myth, you will not die. In fact, if you quit this bad habit, your health will get better. If you are involved in an illegitimate relationship, then resolve to end it tonight. Send her an e-mail tonight and tell her that you are going to stop this illicit relationship because you respect her, her parents, and your religion. Tell her if we can marry permanently, then we will be together, but being a boyfriend and girlfriend does not work in the eyes of God. When you slam the door in the face of Satan, he will think twice about returning to you.

Try to use the nights of Ashura and other religious times to strengthen your relationship with the Ahlul-Bayt. God takes note of even the smallest sacrifices and attempts that anyone makes. There are people who drive long distances just to come to the gatherings of Ashura. He will reward you for every penny and every moment that one spends for Imam Husayn.

Due to the fact that we emphasize Ashura so much, some people think that it took place over a long span of time. However, the battle of Ashura ended in less than six hours. It may have been the shortest battle in history, but it has had the deepest effect. It was not a battle between kings but a battle between two opposing principles - good and evil, truth and falsehood, tolerance and barbarism. This battle continues eternally and it has been immortalized. Every year hundreds of thousands of sessions go on all around the world for Imam Husayn. People gather for Imam Husayn because he represented truth, justice, and all of the good in humanity; whereas Yazid personified evil, licentiousness, and every imaginable, disgraceful evil.

Islam was suffering under the rule of Yazid. Read the Islamic history. History has written, "Nothing remained from Islam except its name." Islam was bleeding profusely, in fact, it was nearly dead. Muslims were suffering anarchy and being misled. The only thing that saved Islam was Imam Husayn. He knew that his blood would revive this religion. We can now sit and listen to the genuine Qur'an and tradition of the Prophet because of Imam Husayn's sacrifice. He is the universal icon of sacrifice and revival. Even today, read how Imam Husayn inspires people of other faiths. No one can speak of him other than with reverence and respect. After the fall of Saddam, we saw millions of people walk thousands of kilometers to visit the shrine of Imam Husayn on foot. Every major newspaper in America became fascinated by what was happening. They asked what was so special about him. They were intrigued and inspired by him and his cause. Surely no one can ever extinguish the light of Husayn.

The Timeline

Chapter 11

﴿مِنَ الْمُؤْمِنِينَ رِجَالٌ صَدَقُوا مَا عَاهَدُوا اللَّهَ عَلَيْهِ فَمِنْهُم مَّن
قَضَى نَحْبَهُ وَمِنْهُم مَّن يَنتَظِرُ وَمَا بَدَّلُوا تَبْدِيلاً﴾

*Among the believers are men who are true to the covenant which they made
with God: so of them is he who accomplished his vow, and of them is he who yet
waits, and they have not changed in the least. (33:23)*

ONE OF THE MOST REWARDING ACTS OF WORSHIP IN ISLAM IS *ZIYARAH*,
visiting the resting places of the Holy Prophet and the infallible imams.
The Prophet himself even advised the believers to visit his grave; and he
himself used to visit the graves of his loved ones and the Muslim
martyrs. Although visiting all of the imams is meritorious, visiting the
shrine of Imam Husayn is highly emphasized.

Some schools of thought within Islam consider visiting the graves of
the imams (or anyone for that matter) an "innovation" (*bidah*), and
brand those who do this as heretic. How can we prove that they are
wrong? How can we analyze whether *ziyarah* is an unlawful innovation
or if it is a true Islamic practice?

One must look to the Qur'an. In *Surah al-Kahf*, God tells a story of the
Companions of the Cave who were found alive after spending 300
years in a suspended state of animation. After they returned back to
life, they finally died of natural deaths, and the community disagreed

over what to do with them. One group said to seal off the cave and forget about them, while another said to build a monument over them. God speaks about this as follows:

$$﴿ إِذْ يَتَنَازَعُونَ بَيْنَهُمْ أَمْرَهُمْ فَقَالُوا ابْنُوا عَلَيْهِم بُنْيَانًا رَّبُّهُمْ أَعْلَمُ بِهِمْ قَالَ الَّذِينَ غَلَبُوا عَلَى أَمْرِهِمْ لَنَتَّخِذَنَّ عَلَيْهِم مَّسْجِدًا ﴾$$

When they disputed among themselves about their affair and said, "Erect an edifice over them" - their Lord best knows them. Those who prevailed in their affair said, "We will certainly raise a place of worship over them." (18:21)

Some of the people realized that the Companions of the Cave were special and decided to build a place of worship at their burial site, so that it could be frequented by visitors.

From the tone of this verse, it is clear that God favored the opinion to build a mosque over the area where they were buried, and for people to visit it. If some people claim that visiting the shrine of a prophet or an imam is heresy, then they are implying that the Qur'an is wrong, since it condones building a similar shrine over the graves of the Companions of the Cave.

Other examples are also scattered throughout the Qur'an, and the last Prophet lived this principle. Frequently, he was reported to visit the grave of his mother, where he cried and made others cry. His mother was laid to rest in Mecca, and if you go there today, you will see a cemetery dedicated to the ancestors of the Prophet. He would also visit the cemetery of Al-Baqi and the graves of the martyrs who were killed in the Battle of Uhud. Therefore, it is not *unlawful* to visit the graves of the deceased, especially the graves of the righteous ones, let alone the Prophet or the imams.

The companions of the Prophet also demonstrated the attraction towards wanting to perform *ziyarah*. After the Prophet passed away, the companions used to pay tribute to him at his mosque. Whenever they wanted to leave Madinah, they would visit him, and whenever they returned, they would greet him.

The opposition to paying respect to those buried in the graves began early in our history. One day, a companion, Abu Ayyub al-Ansari went to Madinah to visit the shrine of the Prophet during the rule of Marwan b. al-Hakam. Marwan was a person who had a long history of animosity towards the Prophet and his family, and he had rejoiced when he saw the head of Imam Husayn being carried into Damascus. He was the caliph at that time. When Abu Ayyub al-Ansari put his forehead on the grave of the Prophet (as there was no mausoleum at that time), which was bare and open, Marwan came from behind and accosted him saying, "What are you doing?" Raising his head, Abu Ayyub replied, "I am not worshiping the stones. My intention is to pay homage to the one who is buried here, the Messenger of God." Then he added, "Let me tell you, Marwan. You may consider yourself the legitimate leader, but I heard the Prophet say, 'Do not feel sorry when the right people assume the leadership of Islam. Feel sorry when you see the unqualified people assume the leadership of Islam.'"[140]

Thus, *ziyarah* had its opponents even before the time of Ibn Taymiyyah. I mentioned before that Ahmad b. Taymiyyah, who walked the earth 700 years ago, was one of the founding fathers of bigotry in Islam. He was a harsh anti-*ziyarah* advocate. He branded anyone who visited the grave of the Prophet as a heretic. However, this encounter with Marwan happened in 64 AH, around 3 years after the martyrdom of Imam Husayn. It proves that the enemies of the Prophet and the Ahlul-Bayt have a long history of opposing *ziyarah*.

One may question that how is *ziyarah* an opportunity to renew our covenant? When you go to visit Imam Husayn or Imam Ali, you renew your vows with them. You refresh your soul and renew your allegiance. The ruling powers have always feared that. They wanted people to

---

[140] *Musnad Ahmad*, v. 5, p. 422

forget about the Prophet. This is why, even today, when one goes to Hajj, the religious establishment there discourages everyone from visiting the Prophet. They tell you to go to the mosque to perform the prayers but not to visit the Prophet. They want everyone to believe that visiting the Prophet is *bidah*, innovation. Why? They maintain that the Prophet never visited his own grave. Imagine that! The Prophet never visited his own grave, hence we should not either. What sort of logic is this?

However, the school of the Ahlul-Bayt emphasizes *ziyarah* very much, in particular, visiting Imam Husayn. For example, the imams left us traditions that recommend us to take off our shoes and walk barefoot when we go to visit Imam Husayn. No other imam has that kind of status. Or when one is about to leave the shrine of Imam Husayn, we are instructed to say, *"Wa alayka as-salam ya Rasulullah,"* to return the greeting of the Prophet, since Imam as-Sadiq told us that the Prophet sends a special greeting to whoever is leaving the courtyard of the shrine of Imam Husayn. Therefore, if the Prophet greets you, you must respond because returning a greeting is mandatory in Islam.

These sorts of narrations are not found with the other imams, only with Imam Husayn. Why? The answer is simple, because you are paying homage during the first eleven nights of Muharram. Islam teaches us that the rewards are in proportion to the sacrifice. Since Imam Husayn dedicated everything to God, God's reward to him is unlimited. Therefore, both Sunnis and Shias narrate from the Prophet that, "God has given Husayn three unique characteristics that no one else has: healing in the dust that surrounds his grave; acceptance of the prayers made under the dome of his shrine; and that the other imams will all be from his descendants."[141]

God has declared that He has put healing in certain things. First off, take the example of honey in the Qur'an:

---

[141] *'Udat Al-Da'ee*, Ibn Fahad Al-Hilli, p. 48

$$\textarabic{﴿فِيهِ شِفَآءٌ لِّلنَّاسِ إِنَّ فِي ذَٰلِكَ لَآيَةً لِّقَوْمٍ يَتَفَكَّرُونَ﴾}$$

In which there is healing for men; most surely there is a sign in this for a people who reflect. (16:69)

Therefore, God may sometimes put the cure of a person in honey, sometimes in meat, sometimes in bread, and sometimes in the dust of the grave of Imam Husayn. This is a tradition, and I will say personally as well, that many times I have given the dust from his grave to a person who is sick and they recovered completely by the permission of God.

Underneath the dome and above the grave of Imam Husayn, there is a special place where you can stand next to his head and recite special prayers. God will never reject your prayers, and you have to believe that He will never turn you down either; but sometimes, the answer to your request may come in a different way. Once a person realizes this, one will not go home empty-handed. It is narrated that one time Imam as-Sadiq fell ill in Madinah, so he hired a man to go to Karbala and pray for him beneath the dome of the shrine of Imam Husayn. As that man was leaving Madinah, he met a friend who asked him where he was going. He said that he was going to Karbala; and so the man asked him why? He said that Imam as-Sadiq wanted him to go and pray for him there. Perplexed, the man went to Imam as-Sadiq and asked him, "O son of the Messenger of God, you are the infallible Imam, God will never refuse your prayers, so why are you sending a man 1,500 kilometers from Madinah to Karbala to pray for you there?"

The Imam replied, "Don't you know that God has special places on earth where He likes to be called upon and where He will respond? One of them is the grave of my grandfather Husayn."

Anyone who feels uncomfortable about this has to ask why we pray in Arafat. Nothing is really special about Arafat; it is just a patch of desert. Some people during Hajj ask why we have to go and pray in Arafat.

They have been hearing about it for years, but it does not look like anything special. One may not see anything unique about it with their physical eyes, but God gave this land special property and wants the worshippers to stand within its borders and pray, and not be an inch outside it. He chose this land for us to stand within its parameters, thus we have to obey His commands.

The shrine of Imam Husayn is the same, which is unique to Imam Husayn. It is well worth your time and money to travel all the way to Iraq just to say one prayer for yourself, your parents, or your community.

That was the second gift that is unique to Imam Husayn. The third is for the remaining imams to derive from his lineage. Although Imam Ali had two male children from Fatima al-Zahra, Imam Hasan and Imam Husayn, the remaining nine infallible imams are all descended from Husayn. God granted him this as a gift.

A tradition reads, "Whoever visits Husayn and is aware of his status and acknowledges his virtues, then God will grant him the reward of one Hajj and one umrah for every step that he takes."[142] Hence, it is not enough to go and visit Imam Husayn. You have to know who he is and what he represents, and then of course follow his example.

Even the text of the *ziyarah* of Imam Husayn is unique. In the most common one read by his grave we say, "Peace be upon Adam, the *sifwat* (chosen one) of God. Peace be upon Noah, the Prophet of God…" When we greet Imam Husayn, we first pay homage to all of the universal messengers: Adam, Noah, Moses, Abraham, and Jesus. This is not done to visitations of the other imams, only to Imam Husayn. We do this because Imam Husayn represented the messages of all of the prophets, which became entombed during those three to four hours in the Battle of Karbala, on the day of Ashura.

---

[142] *Fadhl Ziyarat Al-Husayn*, Al-Shajari, p. 65

All of the prophets taught one theme; and thus Islam is nothing new. It is not an exotic philosophy or an aberration. It is a continuation of prior scriptures. It is almost identical to previous religions. This is why Imam as-Sadiq says that if a Muslim believes in all of the prophets except one, then it is as if he has disbelieved in all of the prophets.

Although Muslims respect others, others tend to mock us. While they believe that they have their own way of life, we also believe that we have our own way of life. Although we differ in some issues, we share the same principles. They may scoff at us but we are not allowed to ridicule them. Muslims address other people who have divinely revealed scriptures, namely the Jews and Christians, as "People of the Book." even though their books have been distorted over time. If the time for prayer comes and there is no mosque, a tradition tells us to find a church or a synagogue and obtain permission to pray in it because it is a place built for prayers. It is forbidden for Muslims to harm churches or other places of worship. Although we do not share the exact belief, we still must respect other people and their religious centers, despite our religious differences.

$$﴿وَلَوْلَا دَفْعُ اللَّهِ النَّاسَ بَعْضَهُم بِبَعْضٍ لَّهُدِّمَتْ صَوَامِعُ وَبِيَعٌ وَصَلَوَاتٌ وَمَسَاجِدُ يُذْكَرُ فِيهَا اسْمُ اللَّهِ كَثِيرًا﴾$$

And had there not been God's repelling some people by others, certainly there would have been pulled down cloisters and churches and synagogues and mosques in which God's name is much remembered. (22:40)

This verse proves that the Qur'an intends for these places of worship to be protected. We respect all of the prophets. We love and revere Moses, Jesus, Abraham, Solomon and David as much as the Jews and Christians do. We do not ridicule any of them. However, when it comes to how others treat Muslims, the Qur'an, and the Prophet Muhammad we see the civility of the civilized nations. Indeed, some people are fomenting this tension on purpose.

Nevertheless, I am confident that the stance of the Muslims will be victorious and that the final code of the teachings of God, as given through the Prophet Muhammad (the Qur'an and the Sunnah), will eventually dominate, but not through violence. We have the truth; and we have an excellent message. It makes sense. If we can spread it, then people will accept it. Others do not have what we have. They cannot succeed, but we will be triumphant. The Qur'an tells us how we can achieve victory:

﴿أُدْعُ إِلَىٰ سَبِيلِ رَبِّكَ بِالْحِكْمَةِ وَالْمَوْعِظَةِ الْحَسَنَةِ وَجَادِلْهُمْ بِالَّتِي هِيَ أَحْسَنُ﴾

Invite to the way of your Lord with wisdom and good advice and dispute with them in a manner that is best. (16:125)

﴿وَلَا تَسْتَوِي الْحَسَنَةُ وَلَا السَّيِّئَةُ ادْفَعْ بِالَّتِي هِيَ أَحْسَنُ فَإِذَا الَّذِي بَيْنَكَ وَبَيْنَهُ عَدَاوَةٌ كَأَنَّهُ وَلِيٌّ حَمِيمٌ﴾

Good and evil [conduct] are not equal. Repel [evil] with what is best. [If you do so,] behold, he between whom and you was enmity, will be as though he were a sympathetic friend. (41:34)

Violence solves nothing. Look at the terrorists in Iraq. For almost three years, they have been slaughtering innocent people. What have they accomplished? Even the Sunnis in Iraq have distanced themselves from these killers. The harder they fight, the more they sink into defeat.

Islam wants us to use logic. Why resort to the sword or the bomb when we have logic? This was the approach of the Messenger of God. This was the approach of Imam Husayn. Even though enemies surrounded him, Imam Husayn tried to negotiate until the very end. He refused to be the one who would start the battle.

On the day of Ashura, Imam Husayn was seen crying. Someone asked him if he was crying out of fear of death. He replied, "No, I do not fear death. Death is my ultimate aim. I am crying for this army who came to kill the son of the daughter of their Prophet, for they are going to kill me, and God will throw them into the Hellfire because of me." He was crying over their ignorance.

This is Imam Husayn and this is Shia Islam. We have to have compassion even for our enemies.

$$﴿لَقَدْ أَرْسَلْنَا رُسُلَنَا بِالْبَيِّنَاتِ وَأَنزَلْنَا مَعَهُمُ الْكِتَابَ وَالْمِيزَانَ لِيَقُومَ النَّاسُ بِالْقِسْطِ﴾$$

Certainly We sent Our apostles with manifest proofs, and We sent down with them the Book and the Balance, so that mankind may maintain justice... (57:25)

All of the prophets were sent to establish justice. This is what Imam Husayn stood for. When he left Madinah, he asserted, "I have not risen out of self-conceit or arrogance, nor to spread injustice and corruption. I have risen for one purpose alone, to reform my grandfather's community."[143] His intention was not to reform Islam, but to reform Muslims.

This is an important point. Today, America is asking us to revise the Qur'an. They promise to make it a best-seller, if only we remove the "anti-Semitic" verses. In Los Angeles, they removed the Qur'an from public schools under the premise that it is anti-Semitic. They promised to put the Qur'an back as soon as it is reprinted with no mention of the Jews or jihad.

Jihad does not mean murder; rather, it means struggle, such as to build a country or oneself. When the Prophet saw his battalion returning

---

[143] *Manaqib Al Abi Talib*, v. 3, p. 241

from a war, he said to them, "Today you have completed the minor jihad, and now have come to embark upon the major jihad." When they asked him what he meant by the "major jihad," he said, "fighting the ill-ways of the soul."[144] Self-restraint is the greatest jihad that there is. It is difficult, but the best thing for me, is to be a good person to others, as well as to myself.

Imam Husayn did not seek to change the Qur'an or Islam. He knew that the Muslims had been brainwashed by Bani Umayyad. Their view of Islam had been distorted. He wanted to present Islam in its original form; and once Islam is presented in its original form, people will flock to it.

Islam is like a beautiful painting. In some art galleries, they shine light on paintings from a special angle to bring out the details in the art. If they change the lighting, they will ruin the painting. They have not only changed the direction of the light, but they have turned Islam upside down. It is intrinsically beautiful, but the way that some people have presented it is horrible. Imam Husayn said in response to this, "I came to reform my grandfather's community. I want to enjoin good and forbid evil."

The message of Ashura will never end, it will continue forever. Every day is Ashura, and every land is Karbala. Every day is a day of struggle and tomorrow will be no different.

﴾يَا أَيُّهَا الْإِنسَانُ إِنَّكَ كَادِحٌ إِلَى رَبِّكَ كَدْحًا فَمُلَاقِيهِ﴿

O man! You are laboring toward your Lord laboriously, and you will encounter Him. (84:6)

We cannot rest or waste time. Life is too short to accomplish what we want, and so we must try our best.

---

[144] *Sharh Usool Al-Kafi*, v. 8, p. 53

$$\text{﴿وَسَارِعُوٓاْ إِلَىٰ مَغْفِرَةٍ مِّن رَّبِّكُمْ وَجَنَّةٍ عَرْضُهَا ٱلسَّمَٰوَٰتُ}$$
$$\text{وَٱلْأَرْضُ أُعِدَّتْ لِلْمُتَّقِينَ﴾}$$

And hasten to forgiveness from your Lord; and a Garden. (3:133)

Life is a race, and we have to run, we cannot walk. This is why God made an area between Safa and Marwah in Mecca where even the weakest person has to run. This is for us to realize how we have to live in this life - running and struggling to better ourselves.

Imam Husayn gave everything he had on the day of Ashura. Many people, even non-Muslims, have heard the tragic and horrific story. Nonetheless, we must question ourselves, what will we give back to him? Say to yourself, "I love Imam Husayn. I have listened to his story. I believe in it. I cry for him. Now what can I give in return?" He gave up his life; he gave up his children; he gave up his wealth; he gave up his companions. He gave everything for the sake of God. Now it is our turn to give back to him.

I want to remind you about what happened in America and in England. In America we had the tragedy of 9/11. This may have been the largest attack on American soil since the Civil War. In England it was 7/7 (2005). The Americans and Europeans put the blame squarely on Islam. No one can blame them. They hold Islam responsible because "Abu so-and-so," with his turban and beard came and spoke on behalf of God and Muslims, and claimed the responsibility. You cannot tell the average person that this man does not represent Islam. He will tell you that this man is the imam of an important mosque, and so they believe him.

So how do we respond? We have a responsibility. Muslims are well educated. Most hold graduate degrees from reputable western universities. Hence, one cannot just sit idle and do nothing, for that would be an offense. Shouting and yelling in the streets will not suffice.

That is not what Muhammad, Ali, Fatima, Hasan, and Husayn would have done. We all have to contribute and we all have a responsibility to contribute in whatever way we can. God did not create us to just eat, drink and have fun. If anyone has an 18-year-old son and all he did was eat and sleep, eventually the parent will tell him that he has to go out and do something productive.

We too have to give back to the faith. One who is in the university can do a lot. Initiate dialogue with other people. Do not conclude that they will not speak to you or discuss the matter. After the fallout of 7/7 and 9/11, we have to be the ones to approach non-Muslims. We have to tell them that we are peaceful Muslims and what is being said in the media does not represent our faith. God has endowed each person with the ability to be powerful speakers. If you are not ready for that, then at least write an article, or give them a documentary film about Islam. Designate an Islamic awareness week at your mosque or university, and invite non-Muslims to listen. We have to go after them; we cannot just sit and wait around.

Sometimes it bothers me when on Sunday mornings the doorbell rings and missionaries are at my door. One time, I told them to come back the following week, and I forgot about it, but they did not. The next week came and they were right back at my door. I felt embarrassed, but I told them I had work to finish and for them to come back the week after. They did, and believe me they were so humble when they spoke to me. They are not poor or uneducated. It is not like they do not have other things to do in life. They are busy, but they make time for their faith. They know that I will not become a Mormon, but still they came to share their faith with me. They brought me two Bibles, one in English and the other one in Arabic. I was flabbergasted - a Bible in Arabic, in America! How many of us give the Qur'an in English to our neighbors? I am not asking that you to go door to door and annoy people, but how many Muslims have ever given the Qur'an to their immediate neighbor, if not the Qur'an, then even an article about Islam or a small book?

One day, I was invited to a Mormon church. They have built a giant temple in Orange County, California. The Mormons are the richest community in the world because they give 20% of their gross income, not their surplus, to the church. Before entering the church they asked me to take off my shoes but they had a man sitting at the door whose job was to take the shoes off for the visitors. I wonder, do we ever offer to take off our parents' shoes let alone our guests?

Contribute towards your faith at your school. You do not have to go far. Do something positive for God and for Imam Husayn in your classroom. You can also volunteer in the Islamic community. Go wherever you think that they need help. Donate some hours to God and refuse to take money for your work. God will reward you. Give your time to an Islamic center, for they all can use the help. Islam is estranged today because a few people representing Islam are evil. They are misrepresenting Islam.

Our sisters need to step forward. Why do we ostracize the sisters from Islamic activities? As I mentioned, if a Muslim woman stands up and says that hijab is not imprisonment, but rather freedom, in every sense, then her words would echo across the entire campus. They will believe her because she is a woman speaking on her own behalf, not a Muslim man speaking for her.

We are not trying to convert America or Europe to Islam. Nevertheless, what we want is to tell them that what they see does not represent true Islam. Bombing, killing, and bloodshed do not represent the message of our Prophet. The message of our Prophet is peace, love, and respect for all people. We respect all human beings regardless of their religion, gender, or race.

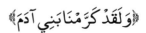

245

And surely We have honored the children of Adam. (17:70)

Part Three

2007 CE / 1427 AH
London, England

Prayers: The Act of Spiritual Ascension

Chapter 1

﴿ٱلَّذِينَ إِن مَّكَّنَّاهُمْ فِى ٱلْأَرْضِ أَقَامُواْ ٱلصَّلَوٰةَ وَ آتَوُاْ ٱلزَّكَوٰةَ
وَأَمَرُواْ بِٱلْمَعْرُوفِ وَنَهَوْاْ عَنِ ٱلْمُنْكَرِ وَلِلَّهِ عَاقِبَةُ ٱلْأُمُورِ﴾

(They are) those who, if We establish them in the land, establish regular prayers and give regular charity, enjoin the right and forbid wrong: with God rests the end (and decision) of (all) affairs. (22:41)

PROPHET MUHAMMAD ONCE SHOOK A DRY BRANCH OF A TREE SUCH that all of the leaves of the branch fell off, and then he said, "The sins of those who pray drop off as the leaves of this branch fell off."[145]

In the thick of the battle of Karbala, on the day of Ashura, Abu Thumamah al-Saydawi advised his commander, "Aba Abdullah, the time for noon prayer has come."

The Imam did not rebuke him for interrupting; instead, he replied, "You have remembered the prayer. May God make you steadfast in your prayers. Yes, the time for noon prayer has just begun."

Prayers are the pillars of our faith. Our entire religion has been condensed into the prayers. If our prayers are accepted, then all of our good deeds will be accepted. When sincerity, honesty, and humbleness are shown in the prayers, then certainly the prayers will be heard by

---

[145] *Wasael Al-Shi'a*, Al-Hur Al-Amili, v. 1, p. 398

the Almighty and our other good deeds will be accepted. However, if the prayers are carelessly performed, then perhaps God may overlook our good deeds.

When we recite the *ziyarah* of Imam Husayn, we highlight his dedication to the prayers, "I bear witness that you established the prayers, and gave charity, and enjoined good, and forbade evil." Beyond politics, these four aims, also encapsulated in verse 22:41 summarize the main message of Imam Husayn. Therefore, we must uphold them, particularly the prayers; for they are what Imam Husayn stood for, and they are what he wants from his followers.

Nevertheless, a fallacy has spread that one does not have to pray because the intercession will come to their aid. This is a complete misconception. As Imam as-Sadiq warned us on his deathbed, "Our intercession will not reach those who take their prayers lightly." Hence, loyalty to Islam begins with your prayers. Nothing can substitute for the prayers. Improving our relationship with God deepens our understanding of the prayers, and similarly improving the prayers deepens our connection with God.

Praying is not unique or exclusive to Islam. All religions encourage some form of meditation or prayer, no matter who they consider the divine to be. Even the pre-Islamic idol worshippers of Arabia prayed.

﴿وَمَا كَانَ صَلَاتُهُمْ عِندَ ٱلْبَيْتِ إِلَّا مُكَاءً وَتَصْدِيَةً فَذُوقُوا ٱلْعَذَابَ بِمَا كُنتُمْ تَكْفُرُونَ﴾

Their prayer at the House is nothing but whistling and clapping. So taste the punishment because of what you used to defy. (8:35)

True, their prayers were lacking and it was not what God wanted from them; but nonetheless, they did pray.

Therefore, the concept stated by the Prophet that "abandoning the prayers marks the division between faith and disbelief"[146] is not limited to Islam. Even if in your heart, you truly believe in God, the prophets, the imams, and the Last Day, you cannot call yourself a true believer if you do not recite the obligatory prayers, for the Prophet has said, "Whoever makes light of his prayers is not from me."[147] Thus, those who do not pray are not recognized as being remotely close to the Prophet.

Unfortunately, the latter tends to be our case these days. Some Muslims are neglecting their prayers because they are too busy working, or studying, or engaged in family or social affairs. They claim that there is no time to perform the five daily prayers. Perhaps, we may live in a very fast-paced and demanding world that requires much of our time and energy, but we have to remember our essence and why we were created. The prayers act as a healthy "time-out" throughout the day to listen to our heart and soul. If we listen carefully, they are telling us that we need to remember God and include Him in our daily life; and the best way to do this is through the obligatory prayers.

One of the beauties of this universe is that God has provided us with many spiritual parables in life. When you love someone, you think about that person all the time. You might spend only one hour a day talking to that person, but the rest of your day is spent in thought about them. You will find any way to communicate with the person you love, no matter what the barriers are. Thinking and talking to the one that you love preoccupies your time. God wants us to feel that way about Him, even more. After teaching Prophet Moses the prayers, God ordained:

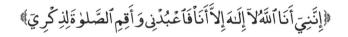

---

146 *Al-Khilaf, Sheikh Al-Toosi*, v. 1, p. 690
147 *Al-Hada'iq Al-Nadhirah*, Al-Bahrani, v. 1, p. 84

"Indeed I am God - there is no god except Me. So worship Me, and maintain the prayer for My remembrance." (20:14)

He wanted Prophet Moses to maintain this sort of relationship with Him, to think about Him and talk to Him continuously. God wants this for us as well.

Remembering God gives us strength and helps us to remain optimistic. Imam Zain al-Abideen said in *Dua Abu Hamzah*, "O Lord, through remembering You, my heart became alive."[148] Everything else for the Imam - money, food, family, socializing, and entertainment - became secondary. He thrived on praising Him.

You will not realize what you are missing out on if you neglect your prayers. You will feel empty inside but will not know why. You will feel lost and hopeless like someone who has lost a loved one. Besides, who is closer to our soul than God? When you have Him near, then you have everything, but when you lose Him, you lose everything.

Rectifying our prayers is also the first step in redressing the social ills of our communities. God will help us stem the tide of these mounting problems, but only if we seek help from Him. Belief is the key. In order to be assuring of His help, we have to believe, not just in Him, but that He will indeed help us; all we have to do is ask Him.

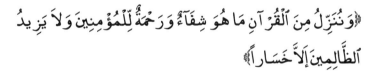

We send down in the Qur'an that which is a cure and mercy for the faithful; and it increases the wrongdoers only in loss. (17:82)

---

[148] Even if it is not the month of Ramadan, I still urge you to reflect on the *duas* (supplications), these are beautiful treasures we have inherited from our infallible imams. Once during Hajj, I saw a group of youth from the West circling the Ka'bah and reciting this *dua*. What a beautiful way to address Allah.

Nevertheless, despite the vast mercy of God, many despair of His aid. Losing hope in God is considered a cardinal sin in Islam. Murder and adultery are not the only major sins; despairing of God's mercy is at the same level. Imam as-Sadiq was sitting near the Sacred Mosque as Hajj ended when a man inquired as to what sort of person has the greatest sin. He replied, "Whoever circumambulates this House, walks between the two mountains of Safa and Marwah, witnesses the two stands in Arafat and Muzdalafah but still doubts God's forgiveness." After going through that course of spiritual purification, if you are still unsure about God's forgiveness, then you doubt Him. From the very beginning, God created, shaped, sustained, and guided you. If after all this you still mistrust His intentions, then that mistrust may become your destruction.

Often more times than we would like to admit, we forget about God, but God never forgets about us. Prophet Joseph was jailed under the orders of the *Aziz* of Egypt. When one of his companions in the jail was being released, Prophet Joseph requested him to recommend his matter to the Aziz so that he too could be released. At this time, the Angel Gabriel appeared to him in the jail and made him look at the floor of the jail. When Prophet Joseph did so, he could see the bottom of the earth and the sea. He saw in the bottom of the earth an ant with a particle of grain in its mouth. The angel said, "Do you think that your God who has not even forgotten this ant at the bottom of the earth, takes care of it and feeds it, would forget or disregard you?"

Still at times, our trust in God wavers. Praying offers us a vital link to keep up that hope and connection. For years, I have repeatedly spoken about the subject of the prayer and I will continue to address it for the rest of my life. If you are young, I urge you to rectify your prayers. Commitment to the prayer only gets harder as you grow older and your responsibilities increase, though your strength decreases. Train yourself to perform all of the prayers, particularly the morning prayer.

When you begin your day with God, then you will stand poised and energized throughout the day.

$$\lbrace أَقِمِ ٱلصَّلَاةَ لِدُلُوكِ ٱلشَّمْسِ إِلَىٰ غَسَقِ ٱلْلَّيْلِ وَقُرْآنَ ٱلْفَجْرِ إِنَّ قُرْآنَ ٱلْفَجْرِ كَانَ مَشْهُودًا \rbrace$$

Maintain the prayer from the sun's decline till the darkness of the night, and [observe particularly] the dawn recital. Indeed the dawn recital is attended [by angels]. (17:78)

As much as possible, say your prayers on the exact time, not just within the time frame allowed for them, but at the beginning of the prayer time. When Imam Husayn's companion reminded him about the prayer on the day of Ashura, the Imam praised him for remembering the prayer at its onset. "Yes, the time for noon prayer has just begun." You will see the effect of praying on time in your life if you make it a continuous habit.

Of course, you also need to remember that your prayers need to come from the heart. A tradition says, "None of a servant's prayers will be accepted except for that which comes from the heart."[149] One has to have spiritual presence of the heart (*hudhur al-qalb*) while praying. Losing focus only takes a split second and Satan will do his best to distract you. The moment you think about food, finals, or your fiancée, your prayers are not worth as much. You need to try as hard as you can to pay full attention to what you are saying and doing, for only those portions that you are paying attention in will be credited to your account.

One day, the Prophet saw a man praying inside the mosque who was rushing through his *ruku* (bowing) and *sujud* (prostration). He said that if this man died praying like that, he would not die on the path of Islam. While in *sujud* we should try to remember the following

---

[149] *Al-Kafi*, v. 3, p. 363

tradition from the Prophet, "If one only realized how many blessings of God encompass a person when they put their forehead on to the dust, a person would never raise their head from the ground." If we tried to keep this in our thoughts then perhaps one would extend the *sujud* and enjoy the grace and mercy that God is showering upon us.

It must be remembered that the rewards of prayers are not confined to this world only. In return for the sincerity of your prayers, God will grant you an eternal home in the highest level of Paradise. Therefore, try your utmost to take care of your prayers. You will be rewarded for your prayers, just like you will be rewarded for attending any religious session. You will reap the fruits of your choice at a time when you are all alone and afraid, and at that time, you will suddenly sense the Divine aid coming to you.

So from now on, make sure that you stand for all of your prayers and on time. Pray with your family if you can; but if that is not possible then pray alone. It will not take you more than a few minutes. Once you begin, you will find yourself wanting to spend more and more time with God, as you taste the sweetness of the prayers. Once you have grown accustomed to that, then you would never want to substitute anything else in exchange for it.

The Final Departure & the Four Fears

Chapter 2

Featured Themes:
Despair; Expectations of Death

﴿تَبَارَكَ ٱلَّذِى بِيَدِهِ ٱلْمُلْكُ وَهُوَ عَلَىٰ كُلِّ شَىْءٍ قَدِيرٌ. ٱلَّذِى خَلَقَ ٱلْمَوْتَ وَٱلْحَيَاةَ لِيَبْلُوَكُمْ أَيُّكُمْ أَحْسَنُ عَمَلاً وَهُوَ ٱلْعَزِيزُ ٱلْغَفُورُ﴾

Blessed is He in whose hands is all sovereignty, and He has power over all things. He, who created death and life that He may test you [to see] which of you is best in conduct. And He is the All-Mighty, the All-Forgiving. (67:1-2)

NOTHING STRIKES MORE TERROR INTO OUR HEARTS THAN DEATH. WE shriek from death in revulsion, yet we all are marching towards the same fate. No matter how far we flee, it will soon catch up to us.

Death is part of life because it is the next step in the human life cycle. Interestingly, the Holy Qur'an interprets death differently than life because it puts death before life. Without death, we would not be able to recognize life, nor would we be able to progress towards our final goal. The Noble Prophet said, "You were created to abide eternally."

Many cringe from death because they fear that it will be their annihilation. However, others look forward to it because they believe that it will bring rest. Both are mistakenly wrong in their approach about death because everyone's experience at death will be different. Some people may draw comfort from the notion that their loved ones are now "at peace" after their passing away from this world, but in reality this may not be the case. Some people, who denied the existence of the Hereafter, may not even reach Heaven because according to the Prophet they "erred when they thought they would cease to exist."

There is good reason why our inner nature abhors death. For most of us, entering the boundary between life and death will be a traumatic moment, according to the Prophet. Further, he says, "They are being transferred from the abode of deeds to the abode of torment or prosperity." When we die, the Angel of Death will take our souls from our bodies. We may try to scream for help, but our tongues will be paralyzed; our connection to this world will be severed. We will have iron vision and we will see the reality of what is before us. The veil between the two worlds, the world of the living and the dead will disappear.

﴿وَجَاءَتْ سَكْرَةُ الْمَوْتِ بِالْحَقِّ ذَٰلِكَ مَا كُنتَ مِنْهُ تَحِيدُ ۝ وَنُفِخَ فِي الصُّورِ ذَٰلِكَ يَوْمُ الْوَعِيدِ ۝ وَجَاءَتْ كُلُّ نَفْسٍ مَّعَهَا سَائِقٌ وَشَهِيدٌ ۝ لَّقَدْ كُنتَ فِي غَفْلَةٍ مِّنْ هَٰذَا فَكَشَفْنَا عَنكَ غِطَاءَكَ فَبَصَرُكَ الْيَوْمَ حَدِيدٌ﴾

Then the agony of death brings the truth: "This is what you used to shun!" Then the Trumpet will be blown: "This is the promised day." Then every soul will come accompanied by a driver and a witness: "You were certainly oblivious of this. We have removed your veil from you, and so your sight is acute today." (50:19-22)

Although the transition will be physically and psychologically challenging, the Prophet taught us to say, "O God, help me against the stupor of death:

$$\text{اَللَّهُمَّ اَعِنِّى عَلَى سَكَرَاتِ الْمَوْتِ. اَللَّهُمَّ خَفِّفْ عَلَيْنَا سَكَرَاتِ الْمَوْتِ.}$$

Allahumma, ainna alaa sakaraat al-mawt; Allahumma, khaffif alayna sakaraat al-mawt.

O Allah! Help me at the time of the stupor of death! O Allah! Lighten upon us the stupor of death!

We need to repeat his words in our prayers in order to lighten that moment, which will come upon all of us.

$$\text{﴿كَلَّا إِذَا بَلَغَتِ التَّرَاقِيَ. وَقِيلَ مَنْ رَاقٍ. وَظَنَّ أَنَّهُ الْفِرَاقُ. وَالْتَفَّتِ السَّاقُ بِالسَّاقِ. إِلَى رَبِّكَ يَوْمَئِذٍ الْمَسَاقُ﴾}$$

No indeed! When the soul reaches up to the collar bones, and it is said, "Who will take him up?" and he knows that it is the [time of] parting, and each shank clasps the other shank, that day he shall be driven toward your Lord. (75:26-30)

After the stupor of death lifts from us, we will find ourselves all alone, in a new and confusing world, a world in which we will come face to face with the consequences of our deeds that we performed in this worldly life.

Are we prepared for this?

$$\text{﴿قُلْ يَا أَيُّهَا الَّذِينَ هَادُوا إِنْ زَعَمْتُمْ أَنَّكُمْ أَوْلِيَاءُ لِلَّهِ مِنْ دُونِ النَّاسِ فَتَمَنَّوُا الْمَوْتَ إِنْ كُنْتُمْ صَادِقِينَ﴾}$$

Say, "O Jews! If you claim that you are God's favorites, to the exclusion of other people, then long for death, should you be truthful." (62:6)

If we have truly prepared ourselves rightfully for the Hereafter, then we will not hesitate in the slightest to meet the consequences of our actions because we want to be rewarded with Paradise. However, most of us are afraid because of the fact that we know very well all of the secret thoughts and misdeeds that we performed throughout our lives. As Voltaire, the French philosopher said, "Fear follows crime and is its punishment." No one needs to instill this dread into us; for we feel it ourselves. It is the most direct result of our mistakes. Rather than living in terror or denying the reality of the Hereafter, if we fear and recognize the next world, then we must take this opportunity now to reform ourselves while we still can before it is too late.

﴿وَأَمَّا مَنْ خَافَ مَقَامَ رَبِّهِ وَنَهَى ٱلنَّفْسَ عَنِ ٱلْهَوَىٰ. فَإِنَّ ٱلْجَنَّةَ هِىَ ٱلْمَأْوَىٰ﴾

But as for him who is awed to stand before his Lord and forbids the soul from [following] desire, his refuge will indeed be Paradise. (79:40-41)

Not all of our fear comes from guilt; for some of our fear is simply of the unknown. Death is the "undiscovered territory." Nothing we hear about it now can fully prepare us for our life after death. Despite all of our religious teachings, the amount that we understand about the next world is still vastly unknown.

As Thomas Hobbes, the English philosopher who lived over 400 years ago said, "I am about to take my last voyage, a great leap in the dark." During his lifetime, he supported the monarchy brutally and fearlessly, but when it came time for his own death, he found himself helpless. He was unprepared to face death.

Plato held the same view, that we fear death primarily because we fear the unknown. If we were to reflect upon it, we would realize that death is only a natural progression of our existence. Like we believe, his thought was that the soul is trapped in the body and held prisoner to its excesses.

Through dying, the soul will be set free and allowed to move onto its final destination. It is as the poet Abu Ala al-Maari commented in his final days when blindness and infirmity confined him indoors. When someone asked him how he was doing, he replied he was held captive through three things: his blindness, his confinement, and his body, and he was waiting for death to come and set his soul free.

Nonetheless, despite how little we understand about death, reflecting upon it is invaluable. We learn poignant lessons when we visit the cemetery. Today, we may bear the weight of a coffin but tomorrow we will be inside of it. I knew a man once who had committed many terrible sins. Suddenly, one day he decided to correct his life. I never heard of him committing a sin again. I asked him what led him to change his life so drastically. He replied that he had been to a funeral for someone who was his own age, and it struck him that death can even approach him without warning. Therefore, he decided to prepare himself; he asked the caretaker a cemetery to sell him a grave. Initially, the caretaker thought that the grave was for his parents. Then, he thought that maybe the man had a terminal illness. Finally, he sold him the plot, and the man began digging his grave with his own hands. After he fashioned a hole, big enough for himself, he put himself inside of it for several hours and imagined what it would be like when his family, friends, and neighbors would heap the earth over him and bury. After that image, he was a changed man.

I am not trying to frighten you needlessly. Reflecting on death does terrify us, but it also awakens us, just like it did with this man. It shocks us into reforming ourselves. In this life, we fear just standing before an ordinary traffic judge. On that Day, the stakes will be much higher and we will have no friends, supporters, or attorneys to defend us. Most of us will be so scared that we will be not be able to stand.

$$﴿وَتَرَىٰ كُلَّ أُمَّةٍ جَاثِيَةً كُلُّ أُمَّةٍ تُدْعَىٰٓ إِلَىٰ كِتَابِهَا ٱلْيَوْمَ تُجْزَوْنَ مَا كُنتُمْ تَعْمَلُونَ﴾$$

And you will see every nation fallen on its knees. Every nation will be summoned to its book: "Today you will be requited for what you used to do." (45:28)

The knowledge of that moment helps us maintain self-control and repel the whispers of Satan.

Another thing which will help us remain on the path of the truth is knowing that God is constantly watching us.

$$﴿أَلَمْ يَعْلَم بِأَنَّ ٱللَّهَ يَرَىٰ﴾$$

Does he not know that God sees? (96:14)

Although He is the most Merciful, but His punishment will also be the most merciless to those whose evil was grand, so much so that "even the heavens and earth will not be able to withstand it."[150]

$$﴿وَلَوْ أَنَّ لِلَّذِينَ ظَلَمُواْ مَا فِى ٱلْأَرْضِ جَمِيعًا وَمِثْلَهُۥ مَعَهُۥ لَٱفْتَدَوْاْ بِهِۦ مِن سُوٓءِ ٱلْعَذَابِ يَوْمَ ٱلْقِيَامَةِ وَبَدَا لَهُم مِّنَ ٱللَّهِ مَا لَمْ يَكُونُواْ يَحْتَسِبُونَ﴾$$

Even if the wrongdoers possessed all that is on earth, and as much of it besides, they would surely offer it to redeem themselves with it from a terrible punishment on the Day of Resurrection, and there will appear to them from God what they had never reckoned. (39:47)

Therefore, reforming ourselves should be the most important task while we are still alive.

---

[150] Dua Kumayl

In many instances, the Prophet taught us ways to alleviate the sufferings of death. One of the most effective ways is to cultivate loyalty towards the Prophet and his Ahlul-Bayt. He foretold, "Love for me and my Ahlul-Bayt aids in three situations: when beholding the Angel of Death; when being placed in your grave; and when standing before God, the Almighty."[151]

Despite all of the terror, God gives the believers glad tidings about death:

$$\text{﴿يَا أَيَّتُهَا ٱلنَّفْسُ ٱلْمُطْمَئِنَّةُ ۞ ٱرْجِعِى إِلَىٰ رَبِّكِ رَاضِيَةً مَّرْضِيَّةً﴾}$$

"O soul at peace! Return to your Lord, pleased, pleasing!" (89:27-28)

True believers will experience no fear at the moment of death, and they will be spared from the Hellfire.

$$\text{﴿إِنَّ ٱلَّذِينَ سَبَقَتْ لَهُم مِّنَّا ٱلْحُسْنَىٰ أُوْلَـٰئِكَ عَنْهَا مُبْعَدُونَ ۞ لَا}$$
$$\text{يَسْمَعُونَ حَسِيسَهَا وَهُمْ فِى مَا ٱشْتَهَتْ أَنفُسُهُمْ خَالِدُونَ ۞ لَا}$$
$$\text{يَحْزُنُهُمُ ٱلْفَزَعُ ٱلْأَكْبَرُ وَتَتَلَقَّاهُمُ ٱلْمَلَائِكَةُ هَـٰذَا يَوْمُكُمُ}$$
$$\text{ٱلَّذِى كُنتُمْ تُوعَدُونَ﴾}$$

Indeed those to whom there has gone beforehand [the promise of] the best reward from Us will be kept away from it. They will not hear even its faint sound and they will remain [forever] in what their souls desire. The Great Terror will not upset them, and the angels will receive them [saying]: "This is your day which you were promised." (21:101-103)

In particular, books of *tafseer* (exegesis) specify that "those for whom the good from Us has gone before" refers to those in the *wilayah* (embracement) of the Prophet and Ali b. Abi Talib. Befriend them in

---

[151] *Mizan Al-Hikmah,* v. 1, p. 518

your lifetime, and be loyal to him in this life, and you will be freed from the anxiety and loneliness on that day of the great terror. Rather than fearing to meet your Lord, you will long to meet your Lord, like Imam Husayn, and the other imams were.

Repentance & Ethical Obligations

Chapter 3

Featured Themes:
God's Mercy; God's Love; Repentance

﴿ٱلتَّائِبُونَ ٱلْعَابِدُونَ ٱلْحَامِدُونَ ٱلسَّائِحُونَ ٱلرَّاكِعُونَ ٱلسَّاجِدُونَ ٱلْآمِرُونَ بِٱلْمَعْرُوفِ وَٱلنَّاهُونَ عَنِ ٱلْمُنكَرِ وَٱلْحَافِظُونَ لِحُدُودِ ٱللَّهِ وَبَشِّرِ ٱلْمُؤْمِنِينَ﴾

[The faithful are] penitent, devout, celebrators of God's praise, wayfarers, who bow [and] prostrate [in prayer], bid what is right and forbid what is wrong, and keep God's bounds - and give good news to the faithful. (9:112)

THOUSANDS OF YEARS AGO, PROPHET MOSES WAS CROSSING THE SINAI Desert when he encountered a man living in the barren wilderness.

"Where are you going?" the man inquired.

"On top of Mount Tur to speak with God," Moses replied.

"Will you take a message to Him from me?" the man asked.

Moses questioned him, "What is the message?"

The man's eyes angered. "Tell your Lord that I am very angry with Him!" he grumbled. "Tell Him that He should be ashamed of Himself! I do not want to be His servant, and I do not want Him to be my Lord! I do not want His sustenance, food, health, or assistance! He can keep them for Himself! I am very disappointed in Him, and I do not want to have anything to do with Him!"

Outraged, Moses parted from the man and resolved never to report this rude message to God. After winding his way up the treacherous slope, he reached the pinnacle of the mountain and had nearly completed his communion with God when he was asked by the Almighty whether he had something else to convey.

There was no way he could lie to God. "I have a message to give You," he said, "but it is very impolite, I cannot bring myself to deliver it."

"Is it from your servant or Mine?" asked God.

"It is from Your servant," Moses admitted, and grudgingly repeated the message.

After he had finished reiterating that man's tirade, God spoke to him and replied, "Moses, hasten to this man. Send him My peace and greetings. Tell him that even if he does not love his Lord, his Lord still loves him. Even if he does not care about Me, I, his Lord still care about him. I am not doing him a favor by providing for him, this is my obligation. He may feel ashamed of being My servant, but I do not feel ashamed of being his Lord. I still want him to return to Me. I will welcome him back whenever He decides to return."

Moses rushed from the mountaintop bearing this message of overwhelming generosity to the man. Completely taken aback, the man fell to the ground and cried out, "Oh God, I thought You hated me. Now, I know that You are my true friend."

Every person is born with an immaculate heart according to God. When the heart of a person is clean, it can contain God within it, for God says that neither the heavens nor the earth can contain God, only the heart of a believer can. It is through the heart that we can feel God's presence, His warmth, and His love inside of us. When God is in our hearts, we sense a form of communion with Him. We feel Him guiding and protecting us, but sometimes we force Him out of our hearts when we continuously commit immoral acts. For God is immaculate, thus He can only reside in a virtuous heart, not one that is tarnished with sin or filth. Nonetheless, God has provided a way for Him to return into the heart of a person that has sinned, and that is through repentance.

Repentance cannot be a hallow confession. One cannot stand in the market, and steal an item, whether hastily or deliberately, and then immediately seek repentance; for this is not a sincere admittance. One has to feel the intense remorse throughout his entire body and vow never to repeat that act again.

Unfortunately, there are people who perpetually repeat offenses without recognizing the gravity of their actions. They view their acts as minute, private or inconsequential; but in fact, they have become immune to their sinful ways. They have tainted their heart with so much sin that it has become hardened and blind to the reality. Even worse, the evil act eventually becomes insignificant for them. The Qur'an declares that the most severe punishment against a habitual sinner is the hardening of the heart. If a sinner continues the offenses, without true repentance, then one will suffer in this life and in the next. It can almost be compared to a smoker. A smoker knows that cigarettes will cause damage to their body and if they persist, then their entire health will suffer and deteriorate.

In order to save a troubled soul, sincere repentance must be performed. A committed vow not to repeat the offense again should be binding. Allow yourself the opportunity for God to reside in the center of your heart. Without His presence there, one will feel empty, unloved, and abandoned. It is the heart that communicates with God; and He will not reject a sincere repenter, for God is full of mercy and compassion.

In another instance, Prophet Moses asked, "God, are you close enough to me that I can whisper to You, or are you far away from me that I have to call out to you?"

"I am a close companion of whoever remembers Me,"[152] came the reply.

---

[152] *Al-Kafi*, v. 2, p. 496

﴿وَإِذَا سَأَلَكَ عِبَادِى عَنِّى فَإِنِّى قَرِيبٌ أُجِيبُ دَعْوَةَ الدَّاعِ إِذَا دَعَانِ فَلْيَسْتَجِيبُوا لِى وَلْيُؤْمِنُوا بِى لَعَلَّهُمْ يَرْشُدُونَ﴾

When My servants ask you about Me, [tell them that] I am indeed near. I answer the supplicant's call when he calls Me. So let them respond to Me, and let them have faith in Me, so that they may fare rightly. (2:186)

No matter what our crimes are, God still wants us to return back to Him. He showers His limitless blessings on believers and atheists alike.

يَا مَنْ يُعْطِي مَنْ سَأَلَهُ، يَا مَنْ يُعْطِي مَنْ لَمْ يَسْأَلْهُ وَمَنْ لَمْ يَعْرِفْهُ تَحَنُّنًا مِنْهُ وَرَحْمَةً

O You who gives to the one who asks. O You who gives to the one who does not ask and does not even recognize You - out of His compassion and mercy.153

As we pray to God through the blessed words of our Imam, this shows us that He loves us despite our misdeeds.

الْحَمْدُ لِلهِ الَّذِي يُجِيبُنِي حِينَ أُنَادِيهِ، وَيَسْتُرُ عَلَيَّ كُلَّ عَوْرَةٍ وَأَنَا أَعْصِيهِ، وَيُعَظِّمُ النِّعْمَةَ عَلَيَّ فَلَا أُجَازِيهِ،

All praise be to God Who answers me whenever I call upon Him, and hides my secrets even though I transgress, and grants me His blessings even though I do not deserve them.[154]

His mercy is infinite. He has no reason to take vengeance on us, because He does not want to see us suffer. However our suffering is often due to our own actions.

Still, we rebuke Him by persisting in our rebellion.

---

[153] *Dua Rajab*
[154] *Dua al-Iftitah*

وَأَنَّكَ لاَ تَحْتَجِبُ عَنْ خَلْقِكَ إلاَّ أَنْ تَحْجُبَهُمُ الأَعْمَالُ دُونَكَ

And You do not hide Yourself from Creation except that they hide themselves from You through their deeds.[155]

Sinning impairs the functioning of our hearts. God created our hearts as tools to communicate with Him. Nevertheless, whenever we sin, a dark stain settles on our hearts and interferes with our ability to perceive the light of God.

﴿كَلاَّ بَلْ رَانَ عَلَى قُلُوبِهِمْ مَّا كَانُوا يَكْسِبُونَ. كَلاَّ إِنَّهُمْ عَن رَّبِّهِمْ يَوْمَئِذٍ لَّمَحْجُوبُونَ﴾

No indeed! Rather their hearts have been sullied by what they have been earning. No indeed! They will be alienated from their Lord on that day. (83:14-15)

Unless we purify our hearts from sin by truly repenting, the stains will remain as a scar. The heart of a sinner becomes so dysfunctional that it can no longer carry out its original purpose which is communicating with the Creator. "There is no severe punishment for a person than the hardness of the heart,"[156] cautioned Imam al-Baqir. Hardness of the heart does not come easily. It accumulates after many years of sinning. However, God gives us many chances and opportunity after opportunity to turn back to Him before allowing our hearts to become cold and bitter.

﴿قُلْ يَا عِبَادِيَ الَّذِينَ أَسْرَفُوا عَلَى أَنفُسِهِمْ لاَ تَقْنَطُوا مِن رَّحْمَةِ اللَّهِ إِنَّ اللَّهَ يَغْفِرُ الذُّنُوبَ جَمِيعاً إِنَّهُ هُوَ الْغَفُورُ الرَّحِيمُ﴾

---

[155] Imam Ali Zain al-Abideen, *Dua Abu Hamzah al-Thumali.*
[156] *Mustadrak Al-Wasael*, v. 12, p. 93

Say [that God declares,] "O My servants who have committed excesses against their own souls, do not despair of the mercy of God. Indeed God will forgive all sins. Indeed He is the All-Forgiving, the All-Merciful. (39:53)

This verse does not address the average sinner. It addresses those engulfed in sins. Despite how far they have sunk, God still reaches out to them, for He loves us all and does not want us to perish. Nevertheless, if we insist on ignoring His kind warnings, then eventually we will become blind to our own wrongdoings. We will have no guilt over what we do. Should that ever happen, then we will have damaged ourselves beyond recovery.

﴿فَلَوْلَا إِذْ جَآءَهُم بَأْسُنَا تَضَرَّعُوا وَلَـٰكِن قَسَتْ قُلُوبُهُمْ وَزَيَّنَ لَهُمُ الشَّيْطَانُ مَا كَانُوا يَعْمَلُونَ﴾

Why did they not entreat when Our might overtook them! But their hearts had hardened, and Satan had made to seem decorous to them what they had been doing. (6:43)

That point is the point of failure, the end game of life, for God did not create us to live apart from Him. On the contrary, He created us to appreciate His generosity and compassion, for He is the One who is the source of all good; and He has intended for us to cultivate His noble virtues, such as patience and forgiveness, in order to enjoy His presence.

If instead, we sever ourselves from Him by sinning, then we will torment only ourselves. He does not need to exact out His punishment on us. We will suffer inside ourselves, for crimes affect the perpetrator first. We are the first ones who will feel the results of whatever we do to ourselves before it even reaches others.

﴿قُل يَـٰٓأَيُّهَا ٱلنَّاسُ قَدْ جَآءَكُمُ ٱلْحَقُّ مِن رَّبِّكُمْ فَمَنِ ٱهْتَدَىٰ فَإِنَّمَا يَهْتَدِى لِنَفْسِهِ وَمَن ضَلَّ فَإِنَّمَا يَضِلُّ عَلَيْهَا وَمَآ أَنَا۠ عَلَيْكُم بِوَكِيلٍ﴾

Say, "O mankind! The truth has already come to you from your Lord. Whoever is guided, is guided only for [the good of] his own soul, and whoever goes astray, goes astray only to its detriment, and it is not my business to watch over you." (10:108)

It is told that on another occasion, when Prophet Moses was living in the desert, a severe drought struck Bani Israil. As food grew scarce and their animals began to wither away, they began to panic. Some murmured that they were the target of God's displeasure. In desperation, they gathered and prayed, beseeched God to send down rain and implored Him to tell them why He was putting them through this great test.

In response, God revealed to Prophet Moses that something indeed was wrong. He was withholding His blessings from them because a man among them was guilty of slander.

"That is it?" wondered Moses. "All of this because of one man?"

With a heavy heart, Moses conveyed the Divine message. Whispers began to circulate the crowd as to who the man might be. Since Moses did not know for sure who the man was, he commanded the man to take it upon himself to leave the community for the sake of its survival.

Immediately, the guilty man realized his crime. His heart began to beat faster, and his mouth became dry. He was petrified that someone may recognize him. Everyone would come to know that it was him. No one had spread more rumors among the Bani Israil than he did. He was infamous, and so he had to leave from there. It was the right thing to do, the moral thing to do. His people should not have to suffer any more because of his evil deeds.

Nevertheless, how could he humiliate himself in front of all of his people? What would they say? How could he admit to being the cause of God's wrath?

Aside from that, this was the desert. He had no means of livelihood, so where would he go?

As he contemplated back and forth inside of his mind, Moses repeated his request. Hours passed. Frustrated, Moses asked God to reveal the man's identity since he had not identified himself.

"Moses, I despise tale bearing," God revealed. "Do you want Me to be a talebearer?"

They remained at an impasse. Finally, Moses repeated his request one last time and then gave up.

The man felt horrible, for he had never realized the ramifications of his tale bearing before. He had not thought that his innocent slander could bring down the chastisement of God upon everyone. Silently, he began pleading to God for help. He admitted that he had done wrong, and he promised never to repeat his mistake; if only He would give him another chance.

Out of nowhere, lightning crashed. Moses blinked. Giant, dark clouds rumbled overhead, and the Children of Israel were suddenly soaked with rain.

Amazed, Moses asked God what had happened.

"I sent the rain because of the repented slanderer," came the reply. "He atoned himself and sought forgiveness."

That one man's crimes brought catastrophe to the entire community; however, his sincere repentance immediately drew the blessings of God. This is why we address God as "the Compassionate, the

Merciful." We teach our children this phrase, and thus we fully have to believe in it ourselves.

God has given us many ways to repent to Him, but the fastest way to return to God is through the Ahlul-Bayt, in particular, Imam Husayn. A tradition reads, "All of us (the Ahlul-Bayt) are ships of salvation, but the ship of Husayn is the fastest." The Prophet assured, "Husayn is the light of guidance and the ship of salvation."[157] No matter how deeply one may be drowning in worldly sins, one can cling to Imam Husayn and find their way back to God. He has granted that honor to the Imam and has informed us about this great blessing.

Therefore, we need to thank God for offering us the opportunity to repent, and we have to take advantage of it. He has invited us to seek his forgiveness and He is waiting for us. So let us turn back to Him and sincerely repent for the mistakes that we have committed in our lives.

---

[157] *Madinat Al-Ma'ajiz,* Al-Bahrani, v. 4, p. 51

﴿سُبْحَانَ ٱلَّذِى خَلَقَ ٱلْأَزْوَاجَ كُلَّهَا مِمَّا تُنبِتُ ٱلْأَرْضُ وَمِنْ أَنفُسِهِمْ وَمِمَّا لَا يَعْلَمُونَ﴾

Immaculate is He who created pairs of all kinds of what the earth grows, and of themselves, and of what they do not know. (36:36)

ONE DAY A MAN DECIDED TO RAISE BIRDS. HE BOUGHT A MALE AND female bird and began to care for them. By nature, the male bird was dominating and would aggressively chase after the female bird, and she naturally would run away, but once he caught her, she succumbed to his wants. One day, the female bird got very sick. All day she lay lifeless, unable to move. The male bird would stand by her side and peck at her neck, and nudge her to get up, but she remained still. For several days she remained like this until one day, in the middle of the night, the male bird screeched a haunting cry, which woke the man up. The man went to check on the birds and found that the female bird had died. The following morning the male bird seemed withdrawn and quiet. Two days later, the male bird also died due to his intense grief of losing his mate.

This is a true story about two birds who loved each other so much that one could not live without the other. As human beings, we also long for such a love in our life partner; the type that is inseparable; full of tenderness, compassion, and tranquility.

However, finding a suitable partner has become a Herculean task. Establishing a family is only a dream for some people. This phenomenon is not limited to the West; it is also a worldwide phenomenon. It is not due to lack of money, nor is it due to a lack of jobs. Rather, it is due to a lack of pure, refined human beings; and as a result, we are suffering and so is our society.

What is more is that the rate of happy marriages seems to have drastically declined. Before getting married, you need to ask yourself, why do you want to get married in the first place? Why do you want another person in your life? Look at the social upheaval of unhappy marriages. You do not want to be another statistic. From the beginning, one should try to make their marriage different and invest in its success by conducting it according to the teachings of the Qur'an and the Ahlul-Bayt.

Some people get married only to fulfill their fantasies of physical enjoyment. Others marry to parade their husband or wife to the public; to show how attractive of a "catch" they have found. Still others marry to remove the financial burden from their shoulders, and some, unfortunately, only marry to obtain immigration status.

However, only a select few marry for the reasons described in the Holy Qur'an. Only a few sincerely seek a soul mate to share in the happiness with them for the rest of their lives. Only a few think of finding a partner not only for themselves, but also a proper parent for their children; a father or mother who can nurture their children into excelling above themselves.

These are the Islamic reasons for marriage. As such, an increasing number of people are finding it very difficult to search for a like-minded husband or wife, who is ready to undertake the responsibilities of the family life.

Many married people complain that they have been miserable for decades. From the beginning, they were disappointed in their marriage because they did not make the right choice. Either they blindly fell in love, or they were forced to marry against their wishes, or they met each other at unsuitable places. A marriage that begins in the street will end in the street. A marriage that begins in a nightclub will end in a nightclub. A marriage that begins with text messaging will end with text messaging. One day he will send you a message saying, "Goodbye, I am dumping you!" A marriage that begins because of money will end because of money. The physical beauty that enticed one into marriage will become a curse and lead to divorce.

When one intends to get marry they should solely put the satisfaction of God above their own satisfaction or the satisfaction of their parents. Ask yourself whether your marriage is Islamic or not? Will God share His happiness with you on your wedding night, or will He turn His face away from you? If He is happy, then your marriage will be blessed; but if he's not, then no wealth or connections can save you.

Today, those people who can admit that they chose the wrong spouse are a lesson for you. We must learn from their mistakes in order to avoid them. Study your potential mate's character and commitment before marriage. Ask yourself whether you really want to stay with that particular person for the rest of your life or not? If you just get married because you are enjoying the romance, then you will wake up one day and realize that this relationship has no future. You will go to the religious leader and ask for a divorce. Divorce may take five minutes, but its ramifications will last an entire lifetime. Your mental health and reputation are at stake, so one must be very careful before entering into a marriage. Islam encourages marriage, but it also encourages rationality and caution when choosing a partner.

When I was a child, I would occasionally accompany my father to solemnize marriages, the bride used to take her time to approve the marriage. My father would have to ask her repeatedly whether or not she conceded to marry the groom. Eventually, she would say yes, but it would take time because it is a lifetime decision. Nowadays, when I solemnize marriages, sometimes even before I finish the question, the bride hastily says, "Yes!" I hope one takes the time to understand the true meaning of marriage when a person says yes.

The Holy Qur'an discusses two purposes of marriage, the first of which is procreation:

﴿وَٱللَّهُ جَعَلَ لَكُم مِّنْ أَنفُسِكُمْ أَزْوَٰجًا وَجَعَلَ لَكُم مِّنْ أَزْوَٰجِكُم بَنِينَ وَحَفَدَةً وَرَزَقَكُم مِّنَ ٱلطَّيِّبَٰتِ أَفَبِٱلْبَٰطِلِ يُؤْمِنُونَ وَبِنِعْمَةِ ٱللَّهِ هُمْ يَكْفُرُونَ﴾

God made for you mates from your own selves and appointed for you, from your mates, children and grandchildren, and We provided you with all of the good things. What, will they believe in falsehood while they deny the blessings of God? (16:72)

Soon after marriage comes parenthood. To be a good parent is a huge responsibility. You may say now that you do not want children, but you will change your mind as you mature and the marriage progresses. Having children is a natural part of married life. If you can have children but choose not to, then you will suffer, and so will the marriage.

The Qur'an also describes marriage as a way for one part of the soul to fulfill its yearning for the other:

﴿يَٰٓأَيُّهَا ٱلنَّاسُ ٱتَّقُوا۟ رَبَّكُمُ ٱلَّذِى خَلَقَكُم مِّن نَّفْسٍ وَٰحِدَةٍ وَخَلَقَ مِنْهَا زَوْجَهَا وَبَثَّ مِنْهُمَا رِجَالًا كَثِيرًا وَنِسَآءً﴾

O mankind! Be wary of your Lord who created you from a single soul, and created its mate from it, and from the two of them, scattered numerous men and women. (4:1)

This is the real reason why you need to get married. You do not need a partner to cook or clean for you; or a partner to bring home money. These things are secondary. Most importantly, marriage is to bring about peace, protection, and comfort to the soul.

$$﴿وَمِنْ آيَاتِهِ أَنْ خَلَقَ لَكُم مِّنْ أَنفُسِكُمْ أَزْوَاجًا لِّتَسْكُنُوا إِلَيْهَا وَجَعَلَ بَيْنَكُم مَّوَدَّةً وَرَحْمَةً إِنَّ فِي ذَٰلِكَ لَآيَاتٍ لِّقَوْمٍ يَتَفَكَّرُونَ﴾$$

And among His signs is that He created for you mates from your own selves that you may take comfort in them, and He ordained affection and mercy between you. There are indeed signs in that for a people who reflect. (30:21)

Marriage is for spiritual and emotional healing. When you are sick, you can go to the doctor. When you are hungry, you can go to a restaurant. However, when you are sad and lonely who else can you go to but your spouse?

It is written in *Bihar al-Anwar* that for a few moments after his creation, Adam felt very alone. Therefore, God created Eve immediately.

Adam was mesmerized. His heart swelled up with joy, hope, and peace. "God," he asked tentatively, "who is this that You just created right now?"

"Adam," God replied, "she is your partner and your intimate friend. You are permitted to live with her."

Adam was very happy.

One cannot truly flourish in this life without a partner. One cannot fulfill their mission on earth alone. One has to marry in order to develop oneself.

Unfortunately, marriage has lost much of its meaning today, and so many people fear marriage. However, one will look forward to marriage if one reflects on what it truly means. When a marriage is based on respect and mercy, not abuse and exploitation, then it will serve its intended purpose; it will become a source of one's happiness.

When one does get married, one has to realize that a giant responsibility lay ahead of you. You are responsible for your husband or wife. This other person that is living with you is a human being with feelings. More than your money, they need your kindness, attention, and good manners. When the Prophet asked what a woman's right on her husband was, he replied, "To feed her, clothe her, be kind and humble towards her,"[158] a man must not be arrogant or demonstrate his force inside of the house.

If you want to prove that you are a man then do it outside of the house; not in the kitchen because the food is not ready. This is not the attitude of a believer who fears standing before God. Your household should be a place where you can show God your sincerity, not your hardheartedness. Some people go home angry and victimize their wife or child, not their real enemy. Do not go home angry. Cool down first and then go home. The Prophet said, "The best of you is the one who has the best manners, and the one who has the best manners is the one who is closest to his family, and compared to all of you (and your closeness to your family), I am the closest to my family." Another time he said, "The closest person to me on the Day of Judgment will be the one who had the best manners with his family." You will not earn the privilege of standing with the Prophet only through prayers, fasting, and charity, but by being the best mannered within your home.

You will gain this privilege by treating your family with kindness and forgiveness, like Ali b. Abi Talib did. Despite his immense responsibilities towards Islam, he used to come home and take care of his wife Fatima, and their children. He used to ask Fatima how he

---

[158] *Al-Kafi*, v. 5, p. 511

could help her with her chores. This is the best etiquette of a husband and a father.

A model example of a good marriage was that of Imam Ali and Lady Fatima. Why was Fatima al-Zahra the best wife? Why did Imam Ali continue to miss and weep for her years after her departure? He summarized the answer in one sentence to Ammar b. Yasir, "By God, I never angered her and never upset her and she never angered me or upset me."[159] That was Fatima, and Fatima was not the daughter of a king who was living in royalty in a grand palace. She worked very hard every day for her family. Back then, in that society it was common for people to have servants. When her hands were cracked and bleeding, she asked her father for a servant to assist her, but he advised her to be patient because our days in this life are numbered and the real happiness is reserved for the next life. She believed in this and continued to live a humble, yet fulfilling marriage.

Many people have asked whether premarital relationships are healthy or risky. The answer depends on what "premarital relationship" means. If it means getting to know your future husband or wife with the intention of marriage, then that is absolutely healthy and it is what Islam asks from us. You should establish mutual understanding before you get married. You should get to know your future partner's personality and lifestyle, so you will not discover unbearable conditions during the marriage, such that it leads to the disintegration of the marriage or family later on. You have a natural right to know your future spouse.

However, if by "premarital relationship," it means having a physical relationship then this is very dangerous. Even if you are engaged and about to be married, you should not have any form of a physical relationship with each other, otherwise this will prevent you from rationally understanding each other. When you are engaged, your

---

[159] *Bihar al-Anwar*, Al-Allamah Al-Majlisi, v. 43, p. 134

emotions are skyrocketing. You are the happiest couple on earth. You would die for each other; and your life seems perfect. You have no serious responsibilities. You see your fiancé at his or her best. You forget about the reality of life, its expectations, responsibilities, and challenges. The real marital life is full of struggles; it will continuously swing from bitterness to sweetness. Once you're married life together begins, you will tell each other how you have changed compared to the engagement time. Before, you were always smiling, but then you became sick and tired of one another. Unfortunately, this is what is happening more and more today. Young couples are not realizing that marital life is about commitment, sacrifice, patience, and responsibility. Marriage should be looked upon as a final sale - non-refundable, non-transferable, and no-exchanges.

Sadly over the years, I have been inundated with many stories about marriages in the community falling apart. What is happening to our community? Where is our faith? Why are we being afflicted with the ills of the society? God wanted us to practice the ways of Islam and to influence the society that we live in, in a positive way, not for us to be contaminated by its social problems. We should be leading the way for others on how to have successful marriages. We are raised on Islamic ethics of patience, sacrifice, and goodness.

Moreover, the best ones to show us how to carry that responsibility and practice of marriage was the Noble Prophet and the Ahlul-Bayt; and among them was Imam Husayn, a man who had the best family and the best children. Imam Husayn did not only teach us how to die in honor, but he also taught us how to live an honorable life.

Marriage Series: Qualities to Search for in a Partner before Marriage

Chapter 5

﴿يَـٰٓأَيُّهَا ٱلنَّاسُ ٱتَّقُوا۟ رَبَّكُمُ ٱلَّذِى خَلَقَكُم مِّن نَّفْسٍ وَٰحِدَةٍ
وَخَلَقَ مِنْهَا زَوْجَهَا وَبَثَّ مِنْهُمَا رِجَالًا كَثِيرًا وَنِسَآءً﴾

O mankind! Be wary of your Lord who created you from a single soul, and created its mate from it, and from the two of them, scattered numerous men and women. (4:1)

"NO INSTITUTION HAS BEEN FOUNDED MORE BELOVED TO GOD ALMIGHTY than marriage,"[160] said Imam al-Baqir, the fifth Imam from the Ahlul-Bayt. To preserve the sanctity of marriage, one needs to seek the right qualities in a potential partner. Although one may look for innumerable traits, six of them should be focused on the most. When you find someone with these qualities then forego the rest, as they are not as crucial. However, if someone lacks one of them, then be cautious.

The first factor that one needs to consider is the background of the family; it is not enough to just look at the individual. Human beings are like goods in the market; some are genuine, while others are counterfeit. A tradition says, "People are minerals like gold and silver."[161] Some are plentiful and cheap, while others are valuable and

---

[160] *Wasael Al-Shia*, v. 20, p. 14
[161] *Al-Kafi*, v. 8, p. 177

scarce. Therefore, search for someone from a sincere family, not necessarily a rich or famous family, but a family that is known for their generosity and faith. Thus, seek out families that are genuine, not pretentious; one that is known for their morals and ethics.

We have all heard the Prophet's warning, "Beware of a flower that is growing in the trash (meaning a beautiful woman who has grown up in an indecent environment)."[162] Aside from the inherited influence of the family, one also needs to keep in mind of the social atmosphere. This is another important quality when choosing a life partner; where were they raised; what was that society like; did it have a negative influence on that individual? These are some important questions to ask yourself in regards to your prospective partner.

The extended family is also critical. Not only did this person spend his or her formative years with the extended family, but these relatives will not disappear after your wedding. In fact, you will be adopting them as your extended family. They will become your aunt, uncle, and grandparent, and more importantly, they will become the aunt, uncle and grandparent of your children. One must be very cautious of who your children's relatives will be.

Of course, you should not just look at the family and ignore a great individual. Exceptions are always there. From time to time, you do meet people whose demeanor vastly exceeds that of their blood relatives and vice versa. You should also not reject someone who has no family, or who is orphaned, or separated.

In addition, converts (or reverts as they are often referred to as) to Islam forms another giant exception. We tend to find that the Muslim community has wronged them, and many converts find it nearly impossible to marry. This is terrible and completely contrary to the teachings of Islam. Only piety distinguishes us from one another. Despite not coming from Muslim families, most converts are

---

[162] *Al-Kafi*, v. 5, p. 332

completely dedicated to the religion, some even more so than born Muslims. They can be compared to Salman al-Farsi, who although his parents were not Muslim, the Prophet included him as his family (*ahlul bayt*). Islam does not have a caste system. God's love and compassion encompasses all of His creatures. A tradition notes, "He has hidden His friends among His servants, so do not disrespect any of His servants."[163] In such cases, you need to evaluate the individual, not the family.

In any case, despite the importance of investigating the family, you still need to scrutinize the individual. Character, integrity, manners, and morality are the building blocks of an exceptional person. The number one personal characteristic that you should check for is honesty. Mutual trust forms the basis of a stable marriage. You need to be able to trust your partner in order to focus on your duties as a spouse and as a parent. Without trust, your marriage will fall apart. The road to divorce begins with suspicion. You cannot live with someone whom you do not trust. You will not be happy together. The Prophet said, "The core of faith is trustworthiness, and the worst trait is treachery,"[164] and "The center of hypocrisy is dishonesty."[165] So inquire about a person's honesty. If you cannot ask them yourself then have someone else ask for you. Do not waste your time with a person who is dishonest, a liar or an illusionist, unless you want to live the rest of your life in suspicion and fear.

Another quality to look for in a person is that they are devoted to God and the family. I knew a religious woman who married a very devout man. He did not drink, smoke, or do drugs, and he prayed five times a day, sometimes even more. However, two years later, they divorced. When I asked her why, she said that he was devoted to his friends but not to the marriage. Rather than paying attention to her and their little daughter, he would invite his friends over after work. She would cook

---

[163] *Al-Khisal*, Sheikh Al-Sadooq, p. 209
[164] *Mizan Al-Hikmah*, v. 4, p. 214
[165] *Mustadrak Al-Wasael*, v. 14, p. 15

for them, and they would eat and socialize all night. She hardly ever saw him. In reality, he was religious to himself. He prayed, but neglected his wife and child. He did not understand the true meaning of marriage. A man who is truly devoted to God will never abuse or neglect anyone, let alone his wife and child. The Prophet said, "A Muslim is the one whose hand and tongue people are safe from," and "One will not enter Paradise until you believe, and you will not have believed until you love and respect each other."[166] Caring about one another is the essence of religion.

The prospected person needs to be devoted to God and to you. People become more devoted to each other when they are impressed by each other's inner characteristics. Everything else disappears eventually, but our essence remains. Some Muslim philosophers maintain that the human personality is immutable. While our motivations may change, our essence will remain the same. In most cases, someone who is prone to envy will remain envious; someone who is cowardly will most likely remain a coward. Religion helps us ease and suppress our undesirable traits, but it cannot eradicate them completely. Even children display completely different personalities at a very young age. Some want to share while others are selfish. Who taught them this? Of course, parents must do their best to instill socially appropriate values into their children, but many of these characteristics are innate. Therefore, search for a spouse whose innate characteristics please you. Look at their essence, not merely their physique. Money, beauty, authority, and fame will all come and go, but the character of a person will remain true.

Of course, you should not completely neglect physical attraction either. You do not have to emphasize moral beauty at the expense of ignoring physical beauty. You should enjoy looking at your spouse. It is not fair to yourself or to your spouse that you marry someone whom you are

---

[166] *Mustadrak Al-Wasael*, v. 8, p. 362

not attracted to. Nevertheless, beauty is in the eyes of the beholder. All mothers will tell you that her child is the most beautiful child in the universe - even though you might have to recite a prayer before you look at them! Keep in mind that physical beauty may be felt at the first glance, but inner beauty will endure. Whoever you love will appear beautiful to you. However, someone that you hate will seem to be the ugliest person alive, no matter how beautiful you once thought that person was.

Lastly, one needs to consider the intelligence and open-mindedness of a person. Your future partner needs to be intelligent. Marriage is about spending quality time with your partner. In order to enjoy that time, one needs to have an intelligent and open-minded husband or wife. You and your future family will suffer if you marry someone who is unintelligent. As Imam Ali warned, "Don't befriend someone who is dim-witted, for that person will want to help you but (because of his/her incapacity) they will harm you." Along the same line, avoid someone who is mentally unstable or easily angered. One needs to have a stable environment to raise a good family.

A critical note to remember is that do not expect to change your husband or wife after marriage. It rarely happens. Most compromises need to take place before the marriage, not afterwards. If you want your potential mate to start praying, or quit smoking, or wear hijab, then wait for him or her to reform themselves beforehand, and make sure that the change comes from inside, not a superficial change. If that person loves you, then he or she will truly change.

It is my hope that these few words will guide the single ones among you, and assist you to embark on a most successful journey that beholds you. By choosing the right spouse, you will have the potential to reform society and the perception of marriage. Work towards a blessed union, instead of being another modern statistic.

We ask for God's help in every aspect of our lives.

Marriage Series: Ingredients for a Healthy Marriage

Chapter 6

Featured Themes:
Forgiveness; Listening; Arrogance; Sharing; Honor/Respect; Sacrifice

﴿وَٱللَّهُ أَخْرَجَكُم مِّن بُطُونِ أُمَّهَاتِكُمْ لاَ تَعْلَمُونَ شَيْئاً وَجَعَلَ لَكُمُ ٱلسَّمْعَ وَٱلأَبْصَارَ وَٱلأَفْئِدَةَ لَعَلَّكُمْ تَشْكُرُونَ﴾

God has brought you forth from the bellies of your mothers while you did not know anything. He gave you hearing, eyesight, and hearts so that you may give thanks. (16:78)

SIX ESSENTIAL INGREDIENTS WILL BE DISCUSSED IN ADDRESSING AN Islamic marriage; a marriage that will help one lead a stable and productive life, one which would please God.

The first ingredient is forgiveness. We all make mistakes. Although God created us physically perfect, our spiritual side is left for us to develop in order to reach relative moral perfection. We all have faults and shortcomings. Some of us realize our errors quickly and try to make amends; others take time to realize their mistakes; while some never realize their mistakes at all, nor do they ever apologize.

﴾قُلْ هَلْ نُنَبِّئُكُم بِالْأَخْسَرِينَ أَعْمَالًا ۞ الَّذِينَ ضَلَّ سَعْيُهُمْ فِي الْحَيَاةِ الدُّنْيَا وَهُمْ يَحْسَبُونَ أَنَّهُمْ يُحْسِنُونَ صُنْعًا﴾

Say, "Shall we inform you about the biggest losers in regard to works? Those whose endeavors go awry in the life of this world, while they suppose they are doing good." (18:103-104)

Such people may live their entire lives thinking that they are always right, and do not ever want to be corrected. This is very sad indeed. The ability to recognize our mistakes through our "self-reproaching soul (*al-nafs al-lawwamah*)" is one of God's greatest gifts to mankind.

﴾وَلَا أُقْسِمُ بِالنَّفْسِ اللَّوَّامَةِ﴾

And I swear by the self-reproaching soul! (75:2)

If one is fortunate, then before going to sleep, one's soul will nag them about their errors and evil deeds which they performed that day. One should listen to it and try the next morning to compensate for whatever wrong was done. However, if one is unfortunate, then they will tell their self that they did not really do anything wrong. Whoever was harmed by me deserved what they got. In this case, one will continue to repeat the same mistakes. This kind of an attitude is a form of arrogance. When it comes to marriage, if one cannot recognize their mistakes or forgive their partner's mistakes, then the marriage will become a source of unhappiness and bitterness

In contrast, forgiveness holds a double reward. When you forgive someone, you allow that person to realize his or her mistakes gently and you increase in wisdom yourself. Your relationship with them becomes enjoyable again.

You may object that your spouse (or former spouse) ruined your entire life. You may ask how you are supposed to forgive a person when you are still suffering because of him or her. That is exactly why you should forgive that person. When you truly forgive people, nothing stays in your heart against them. If you can forgive someone who damaged you for many years, then your inner capacity for mercy and compassion will increase; and you will feel relief instead of distress. The moment you cleanse your heart of grudges, you will be set free.

As an example, one day Malik al-Ashtar, the commander-in-chief of the armed forces under Imam Ali was walking through the market in Kufa when an ignorant man threw a date pit at him. Malik turned his face away and left without involving himself in the situation. The other shopkeepers gathered around that man and asked him if he knew who he had struck. He said he did not know and did not care. They told him that it was Malik al-Ashtar, the commander-in-chief, and that Malik could easily ruin his entire life for this act!

Terrified, the man abandoned his shop and chased after Malik. People told him that Malik had gone to the main mosque of Kufa. When he got to the mosque, he saw Malik praying. He waited impatiently for Malik to finish his prayers and then threw himself at his feet, begging for forgiveness and saying that he did not realize who he was.

After the man finished pleading, Malik told him, "The only reason I came to the mosque at this time was to pray for your forgiveness."

A forgiving person will always be filled with happiness and peace. When the Quraysh used to stone the Prophet, he would ask God to forgive them. He never bore hostility in his heart. When Abdul Rahman b. Muljam struck the poisonous sword on the head of Imam Ali and was then brought before him, Imam Ali felt sorry for him. This is a sign of genuine forgiveness. When you truly forgive someone, you will pity that person. You will sympathize with that person because of the generosity in your heart.

Conversely, when you harbor resentment inside of yourself, your capacity for hatred and estrangement will grow. Day by day, you will hate more and more. You will never find inner peace. You will not be able to sleep properly, nor cope with things throughout the day.

God created your heart to be the center of love and compassion. If you fill it with hostility and hatred, then it will malfunction. Your heart is the only avenue of spiritual connection, so you need to keep it clean. Do not pollute it with grudges. This is why forgiveness is very important.

Without forgiveness, one's marriage will never survive. If your spouse does something that bothers you (and everyone is guilty of this), then try to teach them lovingly rather than punish them. People need time to learn. Some people spend twenty years in school working towards their post doctorate degree, and even afterwards they continue to be like a student in their field. We all learn from our mistakes, and thus we need to master the art of forgiveness.

$$﴿وَلْيَعْفُوا۟ وَلْيَصْفَحُوٓا۟ أَلَا تُحِبُّونَ أَن يَغْفِرَ ٱللَّهُ لَكُمْ وَٱللَّهُ غَفُورٌ رَّحِيمٌ﴾$$

...and let them excuse and forbear. Do you not love that God should forgive you? And God is All-Forgiving, All-Merciful. (24:22)

The second vital ingredient in a marriage is communication. You need to be able to hear each other's frustration and grievousness. Only the inconsiderate are not willing to listen.

$$﴿وَإِنِّى كُلَّمَا دَعَوْتُهُمْ لِتَغْفِرَ لَهُمْ جَعَلُوٓا۟ أَصَـٰبِعَهُمْ فِىٓ ءَاذَانِهِمْ وَٱسْتَغْشَوْا۟ ثِيَابَهُمْ وَأَصَرُّوا۟ وَٱسْتَكْبَرُوا۟ ٱسْتِكْبَارًا﴾$$

Indeed whenever I have summoned them, so that you might forgive them, they would put their fingers into their ears and draw their cloaks over their heads, and they were persistent [in their unfaith], and disdainful in [their] arrogance. (71:7)

Your marriage will fall apart if you refuse to listen; it will not be able to prosper. In order for a marriage to develop, one needs to listen to the other person.

Third, one needs to remove any kind of arrogance. Conduct yourself with humility, not stubbornness. Open yourself up to new ideas (as long as they are within the boundaries of Islam). Never assume that you are right and your partner is always wrong. Never assume that you are perfect and have to teach everyone else. Do not force your preferences on your partner. You cannot make your wife believe in ideas that she disagrees with. Marriage is all about mutual understanding and respect.

Do not force your customs on your spouse. Just because your great-grandmother did something one way does not mean that you need to do it that way also. Your great-grandmother lived back in the old country. Times are changing; circumstances are different; and customs are diverse.

Do not assume that just because you are older or more educated, you know better than your spouse. Wisdom has nothing to do with education. You may meet people with a high education who are not wise; and others who are less educated yet prudent. We can all learn from each other.

Fourth, marriage needs to be about sharing. One needs to share in the other partner's pain, happiness, goals and dreams. One needs to be willing to sacrifice for each other.

I knew a very respectable scholar whose wife fell sick and went blind. He stayed home to take care of her. When people told him that he had a responsibility to spread Islam, he replied that he had a human being at home who needed his help. For fifty years, his wife had been there for him, and now it was his turn to care for her, thus he stayed home, cooked for her, served her, and cleaned her.

One also needs to honor and respect their spouse. One should never belittle or insult their partner.

$$﴿يَٰٓأَيُّهَا ٱلَّذِينَ ءَامَنُواْ لَا يَسْخَرْ قَوْمٌ مِّن قَوْمٍ عَسَىٰٓ أَن يَكُونُواْ خَيْرًا مِّنْهُمْ وَلَا نِسَآءٌ مِّن نِّسَآءٍ عَسَىٰٓ أَن يَكُنَّ خَيْرًا مِّنْهُنَّ وَلَا تَلْمِزُوٓاْ أَنفُسَكُمْ وَلَا تَنَابَزُواْ بِٱلْأَلْقَٰبِ بِئْسَ ٱلِٱسْمُ ٱلْفُسُوقُ بَعْدَ ٱلْإِيمَٰنِ وَمَن لَّمْ يَتُبْ فَأُوْلَٰٓئِكَ هُمُ ٱلظَّٰلِمُونَ﴾$$

O you who have faith! Let not any people ridicule another people: it may be that they are better than they are; nor let women [ridicule] women: it may be that they are better than they are. And do not defame one another, nor insult one another by nicknames. An evil name is transgression after faith! And whoever is not penitent - they are the wrongdoers. (49:11)

Think about the effects of what you say. Comparing your wife's food to your mother's will not make her a better cook. Comparing your husband's salary to your neighbor's will not help him earn more. You will just drag each other down. When you see faults in each other, try to overlook them, or encourage each other to improve them. The Prophet said, "If you distress a believer, then even offering him or her everything in the world as a form of retribution would still not compensate them for the grief they went through."[167] Insulting them has no benefit.

In particular, watch yourselves when you get angry, for anger is a branch of insanity. Conflicts used to arise for the Prophet at home, but he would restrain his anger and we must do the same. A man asked the Prophet to advise him about something, and so the Prophet repeated

---

[167] *Mustadrak Al-Wasael*, v. 9, p. 99

three times, "Do not get angry, do not get angry, and do not get angry."[168]

$$ ﴿ٱلَّذِينَ يُنفِقُونَ فِى ٱلسَّرَّآءِ وَٱلضَّرَّآءِ وَٱلْكَاظِمِينَ ٱلْغَيْظَ $$

$$ وَٱلْعَافِينَ عَنِ ٱلنَّاسِ وَٱللَّهُ يُحِبُّ ٱلْمُحْسِنِينَ ﴾ $$

Those who spend in ease and adversity, and suppress their anger, and excuse [the faults of] the people, and God loves the virtuous ones. (3:134)

Especially restrain yourself from quarrelling in front of the children. A mother who disrespects the father in front of their children will bring disrespect upon herself as well. First, the children will imitate her and disrespect their father, and then they will also disrespect her. Solve your personal problems privately; and while in front of the children and other people, respect your partner.

Sixth, before you marry, you need to understand that marriage involves hard work and sacrifice. Once you get married, you can no longer be lazy or idle. You will eventually become a mother or father and your responsibilities will grow. If you are a man, then you have to realize that you are supposed to be the main breadwinner of the family. You have to go to work early in the morning every day. One cannot stay home and be lazy. A tradition says, "There are some sins that God will only forgive when you exert yourself in seeking livelihood."[169] Prayers are not enough; one must work hard in this life.

The home requires responsibility too. Your house needs to be presentable. A husband once complained that his wife spends the entire day watching T.V. or going shopping. His home was not tidy and meals were rarely prepared. This is irresponsibility on the wife's part. Marriage is a huge responsibility and involves great sacrifice. One needs to learn to take responsibility for their family's needs.

---

[168] *Al-Kafi*, v. 22, p. 303
[169] *Kanzul 'Ummal*, v. 6, p. 482

Some wives rightfully complain that their husbands come home late at night. After you get married, you have to realize that a human being is at home waiting for you. A wife does not only need money or material things; she needs companionship as well. Do not just think that by giving her a credit card you are fulfilling your responsibility. One must not stay out all night with their friends. Before it gets late in the evening, say goodbye to your friends and go home. Your wife should be your first priority.

One also needs to be moderate in their expectations. Marriage is not about extravagance, consumerism, or materialism. It is about partnership and raising the next generation. Avoid comparing yourself to others. Do not overburden your husband with demands that he cannot afford, nor expect from your wife things that she cannot perform.

﴿وَلاَ تَتَمَنَّوْاْ مَا فَضَّلَ ٱللَّهُ بِهِ بَعْضَكُمْ عَلَىٰ بَعْضٍ لِّلرِّجَالِ نَصِيبٌ مِّمَّا ٱكْتَسَبُواْ وَلِلنِّسَآءِ نَصِيبٌ مِّمَّا ٱكْتَسَبْنَ وَٱسْأَلُواْ ٱللَّهَ مِن فَضْلِهِ إِنَّ ٱللَّهَ كَانَ بِكُلِّ شَيْءٍ عَلِيماً﴾

Do not covet the advantage which God has given some of you over others. To men belongs a share of what they have earned, and to women a share of what they have earned. And ask God for His grace. Indeed God has knowledge of all things. (4:32)

Be happy and content with what you have; you can never be content if you compare yourself to what others have. Even if you are living in a grand palace, you will one day find a more beautiful and larger palace. A tradition says that in the matters of this world, look to those who are below you; and in matters of the Hereafter, look to those who are above you. Aspire to attain what they have.

May God bless us all with happy marriages that bring joy and blessings for us in this life and in the Hereafter.

Leadership in Islam
Chapter 7

﴿يَوْمَ نَدْعُواْ كُلَّ أُنَاسٍ بِإِمَامِهِمْ فَمَنْ أُوتِيَ كِتَابَهُ بِيَمِينِهِ فَأُوْلَٰئِكَ يَقْرَؤُونَ كِتَابَهُمْ وَلاَ يُظْلَمُونَ فَتِيلاً﴾

That day We shall summon every group of people with their leader (imam), then whoever is given his book in his right hand - they will read it, and they will not be wronged so much as a single date-thread. (17:71)

IN RECENT DECADES, THE QUESTION OF POLITICO-RELIGIOUS LEADERSHIP in Islam has risen to the forefront of debate. From the East to the West, from academics to policymakers, world attention has shifted to the subject of who truly holds authority in Islam.

As followers of the Ahlul-Bayt, we know the answer. Although we can explain to other Muslims (through the Qur'an and the tradition of the Prophet) how the current Imam, Imam al-Mahdi, is leading us in his absence, still a deeper explanation on his leadership in the broader context of rational proof is needed, particularly because the subject of our Imam has piqued much interest, even outside of the Islamic community.

It must be noted that if God willed, He could control the minutest workings of the universe firsthand. However, for reasons unknown to us, He created intermediaries to act on His behalf. For example, although all light emanates from Him, He Himself does not shine light directly on the planet. He created the sun to carry out this task.

$$﴿وَسَخَّرَ لَكُمُ ٱلشَّمْسَ وَٱلْقَمَرَ دَآئِبَيْنِ وَسَخَّرَ لَكُمُ ٱلَّيْلَ وَٱلنَّهَارَ﴾$$

He disposed the sun and the moon for you, constant [in their courses], and He disposed the night and the day. (14:33)

Although He sustains us, He does not give us food with His own hands, nor does He put it into our mouth for us. He assigns our means of sustenance to others, such as the fields or our parents.

$$﴿وَٱلَّذِى هُوَ يُطْعِمُنِى وَيَسْقِينِ﴾$$

...and provides me with food and drink... (26:79)

He is the source of healing. No doctor can save a person whom God has decreed to take. Yet, in order for Him to heal us, we need to seek medical help. Otherwise, we will remain sick.

$$﴿وَإِذَا مَرِضْتُ فَهُوَ يَشْفِينِ﴾$$

...and when I get sick, it is He who cures me. (26:80)

Likewise, although God guides us, He does not inform or speak to us directly. Anyone claiming to be in a direct, two-way communication with God is a liar. It is said that Saint Paul was on his way to Damascus to persecute the Christians when he saw a vision of God. Such stories are difficult for Muslims to believe because when Prophet Moses asked to see God, He replied:

﴿وَلَمَّا جَآءَ مُوسَى لِمِيقَاتِنَا وَ كَلَّمَهُ رَبُّهُ قَالَ رَبِّ أَرِنِي أَنظُرْ إِلَيْكَ قَالَ لَن تَرَانِي وَ لَـٰكِنِ انظُرْ إِلَى الْجَبَلِ فَإِنِ اسْتَقَرَّ مَكَانَهُ فَسَوْفَ تَرَانِي فَلَمَّا تَجَلَّىٰ رَبُّهُ لِلْجَبَلِ جَعَلَهُ دَكًّا وَخَرَّ مُوسَىٰ صَعِقًا فَلَمَّآ أَفَاقَ قَالَ سُبْحَانَكَ تُبْتُ إِلَيْكَ وَ أَنَا أَوَّلُ الْمُؤْمِنِينَ﴾

When Moses arrived at Our meeting and his Lord spoke to him, he said, "My Lord, show [Yourself] to me, that I may look at You!" He said, "You shall not see Me. But look at the mountain: if it abides in its place, then you will see Me." So when his Lord disclosed Himself to the mountain, He leveled it, and Moses fell down swooning. And when he recovered, he said, "Immaculate are You! I turn to You in penitence, and I am the first of the believers." (7:143)

Instead, God sends intermediaries such as prophets, imams, and Divine scriptures to teach us.

﴿إِنَّكَ لَا تَهْدِي مَنْ أَحْبَبْتَ وَلَـٰكِنَّ اللَّهَ يَهْدِي مَن يَشَآءُ وَهُوَ أَعْلَمُ بِالْمُهْتَدِينَ﴾

You cannot guide whomsoever you wish, but [it is] God [who] guides whomsoever He wishes, and He knows best those who are guided. (28:56)

All of His prophets and messengers are linked, one after the other.

﴿قُلْ آمَنَّا بِاللَّهِ وَمَآ أُنزِلَ عَلَيْنَا وَمَآ أُنزِلَ عَلَىٰ إِبْرَاهِيمَ وَإِسْمَاعِيلَ وَإِسْحَاقَ وَيَعْقُوبَ وَالْأَسْبَاطِ وَمَا أُوتِيَ مُوسَىٰ وَعِيسَىٰ وَالنَّبِيُّونَ مِن رَّبِّهِمْ لَا نُفَرِّقُ بَيْنَ أَحَدٍ مِّنْهُمْ وَنَحْنُ لَهُ مُسْلِمُونَ﴾

> *Say, "We have faith in God, and in what has been sent down to us, and what was sent down to Abraham, Ishmael, Isaac, Jacob and the Tribes, and that which Moses and Jesus were given, and the prophets, from their Lord. We make no distinction between any of them, and to Him do we submit." (3:84)*

Islam did not begin with Prophet Muhammad. It began with Prophet Adam, the first human being to worship God on earth, and then it culminated the belief in the last prophet, Muhammad. If you remove one prophet from the chain, then you lose the continuity. You have only two choices: accept all of them or accept none of them. You cannot exclude anyone of them merely because you do not like him. This is our belief as Muslims.

In addition to this, all of the prophets, not just Prophet Muhammad, had successors. Prophet Moses had a successor; Prophet Jesus had a successor; and Prophet Muhammad had twelve successors who God Himself had appointed. He did not leave the matter open for the general public to decide or to elect. Every era of human history had either a prophet or an imam alive on earth. Hence, you cannot exclude the successors - the chosen successors (*imams*) - from the chain, any more than you can exclude any of the prophets.

Therefore, when God revealed the final verse of the Qur'an about the succession to the Prophet (*Imamah*), He used two specific words: *akmaltu* (completed) and *atmamtu* (perfected).[170] Without *Imamah*, Islam is neither complete, nor perfect; without believing in *Imamah*, even our faith is neither complete, nor perfect. Refusing to believe in *Imamah* leaves a giant gap in our faith.

Another prime requisite of the faith is belief in the unseen. Even if we cannot see the final successor (*khatim al-awsiya*), meaning the 12th Imam, whose leadership we are living under, we must still have conviction in his existence. In the Qur'an, belief in the unseen supersedes everything else:

---

[170] *Al-Qur'an*, 5:3

$$﴿ذَٰلِكَ ٱلْكِتَابُ لَا رَيْبَ فِيهِ هُدًى لِّلْمُتَّقِينَ. ٱلَّذِينَ يُؤْمِنُونَ بِٱلْغَيْبِ وَيُقِيمُونَ ٱلصَّلَاةَ وَمِمَّا رَزَقْنَاهُمْ يُنفِقُونَ﴾$$

This is the Book, there is no doubt in it, a guidance to the God-conscious, who believe in the Unseen, and maintain the prayer, and spend out of what We have provided them with. (2:2-3)

God equipped us to believe in the unseen Reality. He wants us to see Him with our inner eyes, not our physical eyes. There is no point in praying or fasting if you refuse to believe in the unseen.

Although God is the core of the unseen, He created more invisible entities. In the Qur'an, He talks about the angels and the spirits (*jinns*) and other beings that exist outside of our sensory boundaries. In addition, the past has become part of the unseen. We have faith that the prophets are part of our history. There have been those who questioned whether Muhammad or Jesus ever existed. Yet, when we look inside of ourselves, we can find confirmation that they did exist. God created many aspects of the spiritual world invisible to our physical eyes but visible to our hearts and spiritual eyes. As the Qur'an says, "The heart is not deceived by what it sees."[171] Our eyes may deceive us, but our hearts never do. Therefore, we view God with our hearts and our minds. We view the prophets with our hearts. Even more, we see Imam Mahdi with our inner vision. We understand him clearer that way than we would if we saw him in person because using our spiritual vision renders us immune from delusion.

However, believing in Imam Mahdi requires strong faith and a strong heart. A heart weakened by sins first needs to be purified of the impurities by ceasing to sin, not just for a day or two, but at least for 40 days. Recovering from inner filth requires patience and steadfastness, but it is necessary in order to ascend to the levels of faith; the first of

---

[171] *Al-Qur'an*, 53:11

which is monotheism (*tawhid*), and the last of which is belief in the authority of the Imam.

We are presently being tested with the absence of the Imam.

﴿أَحَسِبَ ٱلنَّاسُ أَن يُتْرَكُوٓا۟ أَن يَقُولُوٓا۟ ءَامَنَّا وَهُمْ لَا يُفْتَنُونَ﴾

Do the people suppose that they will be let off because they say, "We have faith," and they will not be tested? (29:2)

When some newly converted Muslims informed the Prophet that they had become believers, God instructed him to reply that these people have only verbally accepted and have yet to put their belief into practice. Indeed, real faith requires practicing the message not just verbally attesting to it.

God promises to help the sincere.

﴿وَٱلَّذِينَ ٱهْتَدَوْا۟ زَادَهُمْ هُدًى وَءَاتَىٰهُمْ تَقْوَىٰهُمْ﴾

As for those who are [rightly] guided, He enhances their guidance, and invests them with their God-consciousness. (47:16)

God will also test our sincerity. We all know the story of Bani Israil when they were ordered to sacrifice a cow. It sounded ridiculous to them and they tried to evade it. In the end, they reluctantly sacrificed the cow. They failed in their test.

Today, 3,000 years later, although God is not testing the Muslims with a sacrificial cow; he is testing us with belief in the Ahlul-Bayt, and in particular, Imam Mahdi. Not everyone will pass this test. Many have failed despite the overwhelming body of literature describing the Imam. Asides from the fact that hundreds of Qur'anic verses allude to him, a thousand traditions from the Prophet describe him and his reappearance, still many reject him. Some of these resources were compiled by Al-Kanji al-Shafi. These traditions relate the Imam's first name, last name, nickname, description, and the circumstances around his reappearance. It is said that he will be from the line of the Prophet, through his daughter Fatima and his grandson Husayn, and more specifically, the son of Imam Hasan al-Askari, the 11th Imam. Throughout history, only a few Muslims on the fringe have ever rejected these traditions, such as Ibn Taymiyyah, who bore enmity against the Ahlul-Bayt. Otherwise, the vast majority of Muslim scholars have considered them reliable.

From these sources, we learn that the Imam will reappear when two conditions are met. One is the will of God.

$$﴿وَلِلَّهِ غَيْبُ ٱلسَّمَاوَاتِ وَٱلْأَرْضِ وَمَآ أَمْرُ ٱلسَّاعَةِ إِلَّا كَلَمْحِ ٱلْبَصَرِ أَوْ هُوَ أَقْرَبُ إِنَّ ٱللَّهَ عَلَى كُلِّ شَيْءٍ قَدِيرٌ﴾$$

To God belongs the Unseen of the heavens and earth. The matter of the Hour is just like the twinkling of an eye, or [even] swifter. Indeed God has power over all things. (16:77)

The Prophet foretold, "When the Mahdi, who is from us, comes, God will settle the matter overnight."[172] It will happen that fast; and no one knows when the final phase of the world will begin; only God knows. He will then grant permission for the final Imam to reappear when the followers themselves are prepared. When we are ready to stand with him and not against him, then He will send the Imam to our aid.

Muslims are not alone in waiting for him; all of humanity is waiting for a savior, but we have not proven our worthiness yet for his return. His absence is our problem; it is not his problem or God's problem.

It is not just that we are reluctant to sacrifice ourselves for the truth and justice. We still need to work on our own manners (*akhlaq*). Our Imam wants quality followers, not just anyone who faces the *qiblah* (direction of the prayer in Mecca) and prays. He wants followers who

---

[172] *Bihar al-Anwar*, Al-Allamah Al-Majlisi, v. 13, p. 42

will stand with him even if what he ordains contradicts our own desires. If he tells us to change, then we must be willing to listen to him, and not follow our own wishes.

Before he went into his occultation, the Imam said, "What prevents us from returning to them is the bad news of (them performing the evil things) that we detest from them." He is aware of what we do. Our own sins are driving our Imam away from us. We may not have power over cosmic events, but we do have power over our own selves. This is something that we can rectify, and should try our hardest to do.

Contrary to popular imagery, the Imam will not base his conquest on violence. The Imam should not be presented to the world as a warrior, since there is enough conflict on the earth today. People are waiting for him to bring peace and justice, not violence and bloodshed. One of the verses that apply to him reads as follows:

$$\text{﴿ٱلَّذِينَ إِن مَّكَّنَّٰهُمْ فِى ٱلْأَرْضِ أَقَامُواْ ٱلصَّلَوٰةَ وَ آتَوُاْ ٱلزَّكَوٰةَ وَأَمَرُواْ بِٱلْمَعْرُوفِ وَنَهَوْاْ عَنِ ٱلْمُنكَرِ وَلِلَّهِ عَاقِبَةُ ٱلْأُمُورِ﴾}$$

Those who, if We granted power to them in the land, maintain the prayer, give the zakat, and bid what is right and forbid what is wrong; and with God rests the outcome of all matters. (22:41)

His mission is not to kill, but to combat moral decadence with righteousness, to use justice to counter the inequity, and to end injustice, tyranny, prejudice, hostility, and hatred that has overwhelmed our world. You cannot fight prejudice with prejudice, nor hatred with hatred. You have to combat prejudice with tolerance, and hatred with mercy. If only some Christian world leaders would obey Jesus' teachings in this matter:

> But I tell you who hear me: Love your enemies, do good to those who hate you, bless those who curse you, pray for those

who mistreat you. If someone strikes you on one cheek, turn to him the other also. If someone takes your cloak, do not stop him from taking your tunic. (Luke 6:27-29)

Therefore, we need to make ourselves ready. Our situation on earth is desperate, and we need the help of our Imam. In order to speed up his return, we need to prepare our souls and our dwellings, and make sure that everything in our lives is acceptable to him, and that we do nothing to be ashamed of. After doing all of this, we need to pray for God to hasten the Imam's appearance and grant us the privilege to see the light of the family of Muhammad walking upon the earth again.

Principles of Parenting
Chapter 8

Featured Themes:
Faith; Mission of Life; Restoring Islam; Pride in our Faith; Respecting Children;
Hajj; Bringing up Balanced Children

﴿فَبَشَّرْنَاهُ بِغُلَامٍ حَلِيمٍ. فَلَمَّا بَلَغَ مَعَهُ السَّعْيَ قَالَ يَٰبُنَيَّ إِنِّيٓ أَرَىٰ فِى الْمَنَامِ أَنِّيٓ أَذْبَحُكَ فَانظُرْ مَاذَا تَرَىٰ قَالَ يَٰٓأَبَتِ افْعَلْ مَا تُؤْمَرُ سَتَجِدُنِيٓ إِن شَآءَ اللَّهُ مِنَ الصَّابِرِينَ. فَلَمَّآ أَسْلَمَا وَتَلَّهُ لِلْجَبِينِ. وَنَادَيْنَاهُ أَن يَٰٓإِبْرَاهِيمُ. قَدْ صَدَّقْتَ الرُّءْيَآ إِنَّا كَذَٰلِكَ نَجْزِى الْمُحْسِنِينَ﴾

So We gave him the good news of a forbearing son. When he was old enough to assist in his endeavor, he said, "My son! I see in a dream that I am sacrificing you. See what you think." He said, "Father! Do whatever you have been commanded. If God wishes, you will find me to be patient." So when they had both submitted [to God's will], and he had laid him down on his forehead, We called out to him, "O Abraham! You have indeed fulfilled the vision"! Thus indeed do We reward the virtuous! (37:101-105)

ONCE, A MAN WHO HAD BOUGHT A TON OF GOODS HIRED A PORTER TO carry his new purchases home. As they went along, the man struck up a conversation with him and asked what family he came from.

When the porter gave his name, the man was shocked.

"You're *his* son?" he rebuked. "What a wonderful father he is and what a despairing son you are!"

The porter, who had revealed that he was the son of a wealthy prominent man set down his load and said, "Don't say that. Instead say what a wonderful grandfather and what a horrible father. My grandfather sacrificed his life for my father. However, when I came along, my father neglected me. All he cared about was his own wealth and reputation. So what else was I supposed to do?"

Our concerns about raising children in the West run much deeper than whether they will become servants or not. We have to be concerned about whether or not they will practice their religion or will they abandon it. Although we have no guarantees, what we do to steer them towards staying on the path of the religion lies on our shoulders; and we will be questioned about it in the next world.

﴿إِنَّا نَحْنُ نُحْيِي ٱلْمَوْتَىٰ وَنَكْتُبُ مَا قَدَّمُوا۟ وَءَاثَٰرَهُمْ وَكُلَّ شَىْءٍ أَحْصَيْنَٰهُ فِىٓ إِمَامٍ مُّبِينٍ﴾

Verily We give life to the dead, and We record that which they send before and that which they leave behind (aatharahum), and all of the things have We taken account in a clear Book (of evidence). (36:12)

Aatharahum ("that which they leave behind") in this context, according to some commentators, refers to our children. A righteous child is the best legacy that a parent can leave, for a tradition says that a righteous child is one of only three things that can benefit the parents in the Hereafter. Sacrificing ourselves for their moral growth is well worth it, not only for this world, but more so for the next life.

Many parents invest their time and money into trying to make their children happy. As Muslims, we should amend that objective to making them righteously happy. Without following God's path, your children will never truly be happy.

In particular, help your children understand why God created them. No one has come to earth accidentally. God made all of our souls for a reason; otherwise, without understanding the meaning of life, our children will wander confused, not realizing their purpose for which they were created.

$$﴿أَفَمَن يَمْشِى مُكِبّاً عَلَىٰ وَجْهِهِ أَهْدَىٰ أَمَّن يَمْشِى سَوِيّاً عَلَىٰ صِرَاطٍ مُّسْتَقِيمٍ﴾$$

Is then one who walks headlong, with his face groveling, better guided, - or one who walks evenly on a Straight Way? (67:22)

No one would ever think of going to a university without knowing why they are there and what they are supposed to do, so how can a person be expected to live life clueless?

Other religions give different answers to the eternal question of human existence. Christianity for example, teaches that our earthly life is a punishment for the original sin. It teaches that childbirth itself (which is the process of bringing new life into this world) is a curse as well.

However, the Qur'an rejects these ideas. It teaches us that we are sent to this world with a mission. All of us, no matter who we are, or where we come from, have been sent to be God's representatives on earth and to carry out His plan.

$$﴿وَإِذْ قَالَ رَبُّكَ لِلْمَلاَئِكَةِ إِنِّى جَاعِلٌ فِى ٱلأَرْضِ خَلِيفَةً قَالُوا أَتَجْعَلُ فِيهَا مَن يُفْسِدُ فِيهَا وَيَسْفِكُ ٱلدِّمَاءَ وَنَحْنُ نُسَبِّحُ بِحَمْدِكَ وَنُقَدِّسُ لَكَ قَالَ إِنِّى أَعْلَمُ مَا لاَ تَعْلَمُونَ﴾$$

When your Lord said to the angels, "Indeed I am going to set a viceroy on earth," they said, "Will You set in it someone who will cause corruption in it,

and shed blood, while we celebrate Your praise and proclaim Your sanctity?"
He said, "Indeed I know what you do not know." (2:30)

We were not meant to live miserably on earth as a punishment. Instead, God wants us to be happy, and fosters our happiness by teaching us the most wholesome way to live through His messengers. Therefore, it is imperative that you teach your children about their mission in life, and it is very important for you to think about it yourself as well.

One individual can change the world. Many world leaders and reformers hailed from humble backgrounds. Some were hungry, fatherless, homeless, and uneducated, but at a crucial point in their lives, they had an inner revolution and realized that they were capable of changing the world.

These goals of course, can be both positive and negative. A few lawless people changed the face of Islam in the West through terrorist acts. They killed many and wounded others, and as a result, Muslims are still suffering today, particularly our sisters. This handful of people created a mass hysteria about Islam. They were deluded into thinking that by attacking Britain or America they could raise the banner of Islam in those lands. Islam presents a message of tolerance and peace, not violence and hatred. They tried, but they erred.

Each one of us can effect enormous change for the good, not for evil. Although it is easier to destroy than it is to create, we all have the responsibility of restoring the true image of Islam in the West. No one else will do it for us. The media will not one day wake up and decide to portray Muslims in a favorable light. We are the ones who need to intervene and dedicate our time and efforts to reviving Islam in those areas; not by violence, but by education and by our good manners.

We need to be dedicated, and to believe that our work will bear fruit. One time, I was on a boat in Alaska with nearly forty youths clutching Bibles. They were on their way to Bible camp for the summer. I was very impressed and admired them for spending their entire summer break at Bible camp studying religion, when in America they could have gone anywhere else. Those youth were on their way to make a change. We can do the same too; we need to find our way. Reflect and meditate and perhaps you will find your way. We must all ask ourselves what is our purpose in this life. Is it just to eat, have fun, and drive a nice car? God has placed the answer inside all of us.

After helping our children understand their mission in life, parents also need to assist their children to take pride in their religious identity. Make them feel proud to be Muslim, not ashamed of it, as if they are doing something wrong. Religious knowledge alone does not suffice. We also need to have a strong sense of self-esteem, so you will be able to influence others and not be influenced in the face of social pressure. Although many youth know Islam extensively, they hide their Muslim identity out of embarrassment. In addition, some immigrant youth suffer from an inferiority complex. They imagine that because they came from Iran, Iraq, Syria, or Afghanistan they are less intelligent, less capable, and even less innovative than Westerners are. Nothing could be further from the truth. In fact, although there is no need to justify our own worth, Islamic history disproves such a notion. The scientific and cultural legacy of Islam is extensive and glorious. Advances in science, chemistry, medicine, astronomy, mathematics, philosophy, and art used to radiate from the Islamic world. The royalty of Europe used to travel to Muslim Spain to partake in their medical accomplishments. Numerous European textbooks have been translated from Arabic.

Today of course, the situation has reversed, not because we are inherently inferior, but because we have picked up an inferiority complex after being colonized and ruled over by adversaries. That is however changing, no longer is it an era for Muslims to feel embarrassed about who they are. Stand tall when you tell people that you are Muslim. Let them learn about Islam through your behavior and make sure that your behavior qualifies you to be an ambassador of Islam. In society, one of us represents all of Islam.

Aside from confidence in our religion, in order to help our children develop high self-esteem, we need to avoid three mistakes in raising them: humiliation, overprotection, and perfectionism.

As parents, we need to realize our children are not our private property. They are a trust from God, and He will ask us about how we treated them. Never put them down or disrespect them. We are the closest people to them. Just as we have the ability to shape them, we also have the ability to harm them. Do not degrade them because they have poor grades or are overweight. Humiliating them will not help them to excel. In fact, it will only discourage them. You need to teach them how to do things right, not just tell them what they are doing wrong.

This was the approach of the Prophet. Although he always knew who was responsible for what, whenever he saw something in his community that he disliked, he would address it indirectly from the pulpit (*minbar*), even if the offenders were sitting in front of him. He never named them directly because he wanted to avoid embarrassing them. He encouraged them to change by preserving their dignity.

﴿فَبِمَا رَحْمَةٍ مِّنَ ٱللَّهِ لِنْتَ لَهُمْ وَلَوْ كُنْتَ فَظًّا غَلِيظَ ٱلْقَلْبِ لَاَنْفَضُّوا۟ مِنْ حَوْلِكَ﴾

It is by God's mercy that you are gentle to them; and had you been harsh and hardhearted, surely they would have scattered from around you. (3:159)

Overprotecting our children will also stunt their growth. Although we need to look after our children because they are unaware, inexperienced, and vulnerable, but to keep them from venturing into the outside world at all will impede their progress in life. We need to develop a sense of mutual trust and encourage them to communicate

314

with us so that we can let them explore life safely. For instance, do not prevent your sons or daughters from traveling to study if you feel that they will be safe and in good company.

Do not prevent them from going to Hajj, especially if they save their money to go while they are teenagers. As soon as they become financially able, Hajj becomes mandatory upon them. They are religiously obligated to go, but many parents forbid them and tell them to enjoy life now and go for Hajj later.

Hajj is a phenomenal experience. It will open the eyes of our children who are being raised in the West. We are spoiled in the West. We can buy whatever we want from the market. In some countries, people have to put their names on a waiting list to get a soft drink! Therefore, when they leave the comfort of their homes for Mina, Arafat, and Muzdalafah, and sleep on the dust surrounded by millions of strangers, they will realize the meaning of this verse:

$$﴿مِنْهَا خَلَقْنَاكُمْ وَفِيهَا نُعِيدُكُمْ وَمِنْهَا نُخْرِجُكُمْ تَارَةً أُخْرَىٰ﴾$$

From it did We create you, into it shall We return you, and from it shall We bring you forth another time. (20:55)

Hajj can revolutionize the thinking of someone who has lived nowhere but the West. It hammers in the meaning of life and a sense of human equality and deep consideration for others. During the winter season of Hajj it is bitter cold. Most of the people cannot sleep due to the cold. This is for one night; but it should make us wonder, how many homeless people suffer like this every day?

Do not deprive them of the beauty of these realizations. Let them travel. Yes, be prudent, but if you do everything for them, they will internalize the idea that they are incapable of doing anything on their own and they will suffer because of this.

Finally, although we should encourage our children to excel, we should not expect them to be perfect. For some parents anything less than an A+ is a disaster. Life is a learning experience. We are all humans, not superhuman. A young man once told me that his parents had taught him about the "15" *Masoumeen* (Infallible Imams). I asked him who the 15 were (because there are only 14) and he told me they were the Prophet, Fatima al-Zahra, the twelve Imams, and then himself because his father always told him that he had to be the fifteenth *infallible*.

No one is perfect. Do not overburden your children with these expectations. Use their mistakes as an opportunity to teach them. No one will ever be perfect, so be lenient on them. Even God is All-Forgiving and Merciful. Otherwise, they will run away from the family once they are able to.

The family atmosphere has a lot to do with how the children's personalities form. One can easily tell whether a child has been raised in a caring or a violent environment. Children are unwritten books. They will thrive on love and tolerance, but will shrivel at harshness and neglect. If you are too hard on them, they will rebel.

Both the father and the mother need to share disciplinary responsibilities. Neither parent should undermine the other's efforts to discipline the children. If they disagree, they need to discuss their differences in private, not in front of the children. Otherwise, their disunity will counter their efforts and manifest itself in the child's personality. Do not victimize your children. An overwhelming number of criminals and dictators had disturbed upbringings. If you and your spouse do not get along, then take care of your problems outside the earshot of your children. Do not make them pawns in your arguments. Children need a stable and peaceful family environment in order to flourish.

The mother is the centerpiece of the family. The elegance and beauty of the family rests upon her. The stability of the family depends much more on the mother than on the father. She is the one who nurtures the children in their early years. When she breastfeeds her child, she holds them close to her heart and builds their character from her own. Those first two years are very decisive in shaping the character of the baby. Most of the time, when the mother is moral the entire family will likely be moral as well. So women should not underestimate their responsibilities. Although, some people believe that motherhood is a curse, we believe it is a privilege and an opportunity. "Heaven lies beneath the feet of the mothers."[173] Our mothers offer us a passport to Paradise.

Spiritually, we have two major responsibilities towards our children. One is to connect them to the Ahlul-Bayt, not just God, for the Ahlul-Bayt are the quickest routes to reach God.

We need to inculcate the love for Muhammad, Ali, Fatima, Hasan, Husayn, and the imams in our children from an early age. They will understand God's mercy through the Ahlul-Bayt.

Traditionally, we tend to instruct children in the mechanics of religion first before addressing the spirit. We usually teach our children how to pray before inspiring in them the essence of prayer. Some Muslims ask why they do not enjoy praying. Probably, they do not enjoy it because they learned the actions before the feelings. We need to know why we pray before we pray. Therefore, we need to convey to our children the emotions, as well as the actions of spirituality.

Lastly, we need to be careful about how we present God. Many parents are tempted to present God as frightening, threatening, and angry, for instance, saying to our children, "God will punish you!" A youth once told me that when he was growing up he only heard about the Hellfire, and the first time he heard about Heaven was at Disneyland. Do not scare your children away from God. We teach them every day to say, "In the Name of God, the Infinitely Compassionate, the Most Merciful

---

[173] *Mustadrak Al-Wasael*, v. 15, p. 180

(*Bismillahir Rahmanir Raheem*)," sometimes several times a day. Portraying Him as their disciplinarian is an oxymoron. Teach them instead about God's infinite mercy and love; teach them about His protection and forgiveness. This is how we will link them to God. Make religion pleasant for them so they will want to hold onto it. Help them to understand that God is their closest friend, so when they are alone or in any type of need they will not hesitate to turn to Him.

Youth Predicaments

Chapter 9

Featured Themes:
Ways & Customs; Holy Qur'an; Islam's Way; Mosque & Women; Mosque &
Youth; Religious Institutes

﴿يَٰٓأَيُّهَا ٱلَّذِينَ ءَامَنُوا۟ ٱتَّقُوا۟ ٱللَّهَ وَلْتَنظُرْ نَفْسٌ مَّا قَدَّمَتْ لِغَدٍ
وَٱتَّقُوا۟ ٱللَّهَ إِنَّ ٱللَّهَ خَبِيرٌۢ بِمَا تَعْمَلُونَ. وَلَا تَكُونُوا۟ كَٱلَّذِينَ نَسُوا۟
ٱللَّهَ فَأَنسَىٰهُمْ أَنفُسَهُمْ أُو۟لَٰٓئِكَ هُمُ ٱلْفَٰسِقُونَ. لَا يَسْتَوِيٓ أَصْحَٰبُ
ٱلنَّارِ وَأَصْحَٰبُ ٱلْجَنَّةِ أَصْحَٰبُ ٱلْجَنَّةِ هُمُ ٱلْفَآئِزُونَ﴾

O you who have faith! Be wary of God, and let every soul consider what it
sends ahead for tomorrow, and be wary of God. God is indeed well aware of
what you do. And do not be like those who forget God, so He makes them
forget their own souls. It is they who are the transgressors. Not equal are the
inmates of the Fire and the inhabitants of Paradise. It is the inhabitants of
Paradise who are the successful ones. (59:18-20)

OUR YOUTH SHOULD BE THE ONES WHO ARE REVIVING AND
transmitting Islamic values. Unfortunately though, practically, they
have fled from our institutions. Our traditional Islamic programs hold
little, to no interest for them. Although they should be in the forefront,
they are nonetheless absent. Normally, people (mostly men) from their
40's to their 80's dominate most of the mosques. We have to ask
ourselves why this is. One problem may be the ever-increasing,
unbridgeable gap between Islamic and Western culture. Another may

be our own cultural habits that disenchant the youth and drive them away.

Perhaps our parents who migrated to the West should have considered heavily that they would be bearing children into a society that may not be welcoming towards Islam. One may not fully realize the depth of disparity between these two lifestyles. All of the adults in our community, whether parents, elders, religious leaders, or civic leaders need to familiarize themselves with the negative realities of American culture in order to educate the younger generation of the dangers that are present in the society.

Let me give you some basic examples. In the American culture, from the time that the children are in elementary school, the society is gearing them towards dating, having a boyfriend or girlfriend. For most American parents and society, this is socially acceptable. If they do not partake in this, then others think there is something wrong with them. Alcohol is omnipresent. In Europe, toddlers are sometimes given sips of alcohol drinks in order to familiarize them with the taste. When I was flying back from an Islamic country, the couple behind me kept asking for wine for themselves and their children, and imagine we were coming from an Islamic country. Women's fashions and clothes are designed to reveal their bodies, rather than conceal it. Hiding one's attractiveness is unheard of. Nothing is protected and nothing is covered.

Perhaps the most important difference between our cultures is that Islamic culture still promotes adherence to the sources of ethical and conservative values - the Qur'an and the Sunnah. It is not a culture of moral resistance.

Following the teachings of the Prophet is praised.

$$\lambda \text{ فَلَا وَرَبِّكَ لَا يُؤْمِنُونَ حَتَّىٰ يُحَكِّمُوكَ فِيمَا شَجَرَ بَيْنَهُمْ ثُمَّ لَا}$$

$$\text{يَجِدُوا۟ فِىٓ أَنفُسِهِمْ حَرَجًا مِّمَّا قَضَيْتَ وَيُسَلِّمُوا۟ تَسْلِيمًا} \lambda$$

*But no, by your Lord! They will not believe until they make you a judge in
their disputes, then do not find within their hearts any dissent to your verdict
and submit in full submission. (4:65)*

However, modern Western culture has more of a tendency towards
rebellion. Muslims are not the only ones who feel this pull. Even
Christians are suffering in such an environment today. Some Christian
leaders have confided that even they are finding themselves defamed
and marginalized, since Western culture tries to outcast religion.
Individualism forms a major pillar of an American society. Popular
culture teaches people that the individual comes first, and then the
society is second. The individual is more important than the society.
You should not restrict yourself. You should do whatever you think is
good for you no matter what your parents think. You should enjoy
yourself. Unfortunately, the new generation is being indoctrinated
with this idea.

On the other hand, Islam teaches us not to be selfish. It teaches us to
put God first before everything else. We are His slaves. He put us on
earth to test us and to see whether or not we will follow Him.
Eventually, we will return back to Him.

$$\lambda \text{ قُلْ إِن كَانَ آبَاؤُكُمْ وَأَبْنَآؤُكُمْ وَإِخْوَانُكُمْ وَأَزْوَاجُكُمْ}$$

$$\text{وَعَشِيرَتُكُمْ وَأَمْوَالٌ ٱقْتَرَفْتُمُوهَا وَتِجَارَةٌ تَخْشَوْنَ}$$

$$\text{كَسَادَهَا وَمَسَاكِنُ تَرْضَوْنَهَآ أَحَبَّ إِلَيْكُم مِّنَ ٱللَّهِ وَرَسُولِهِ}$$

وَجِهَادٍ فِى سَبِيلِهِ فَتَرَبَّصُواْ حَتَّىٰ يَأْتِىَ ٱللَّهُ بِأَمْرِهِ وَٱللَّهُ لَا يَهْدِى
ٱلْقَوْمَ ٱلْفَٰسِقِينَ ﴾

Say, "If your fathers and your sons, your brethren, your spouses, and your kinsfolk, the possessions that you have acquired, the business you fear may suffer, and the dwellings you are fond of, are dearer to you than God and His Apostle and to waging jihad in His way, then wait until God issues His edict, and God does not guide the transgressing lot." (9:24)

We recognize that if we put anything above God, whether it is our parents, spouses, children, siblings, business, or wealth, then we will feel the setback. These morals are limited to the Islamic culture; American society tends to hold an opposite view from Islam; facing all of these odds, we are raising our children in this society. Without proper Islamic guidance from an early age, Muslim boys and girls will have no choice but to join the mainstream culture. If this happens, then naturally our children will not want to come to the mosques because it represents a reality which they do not want to live in.

However, that is not the only reason why our youth are estranged. Despite the society that we live in, many of our youth do have a strong Islamic identity, but still they do not want to associate themselves with the Islamic centers. They have two concerns: one is called "orthodoxy," and the other is "orthopraxy." By "orthodoxy," I mean that some of our youth are uneasy about some of our ideas; and by "orthopraxy," I mean that some are uneasy with some of our customs.

It must be noted that the Qur'an itself is not the problem. I have yet to meet a Muslim youth who rejects the Qur'an. Although some youth I meet do not understand the Qur'an, but they do still accept it as the word of God. My advice is for those youth who are confused about it should study it. The Qur'an has a unique peculiarity that once a person dedicates their time to reading and understanding it, it will open up, and we will enjoy it. However, if a person is bored with it, then it will become inscrutable. It depends on our intention.

$$﴿وَنُنَزِّلُ مِنَ ٱلْقُرْآنِ مَا هُوَ شِفَآءٌ وَرَحْمَةٌ لِّلْمُؤْمِنِينَ وَلاَ يَزِيدُ ٱلظَّالِمِينَ إِلاَّ خَسَاراً﴾$$

We send down in the Qur'an that which is a cure and mercy for the faithful; and it increases the wrongdoers only in loss. (17:82)

The Qur'an has healing, salvation, and mercy for those who appreciate it; but others are driven farther and farther away. It is like the ocean. Some people swim on its shores, some go further out, and others dive deep into it. An average person who has no time for the Qur'an will understand nothing but the initial meaning; but those who want to expand their knowledge can study it their entire lives and never exhaust its supplies.

Therefore, we see that the Qur'an is not the problem. However, some of our youth have issues with the sanctity of the hadith collections. At school in the West, children are taught critical thinking from an early age. They are taught to use their reason to attack the text. Even the Bible is open for criticism. However, in the mosque, Sunnis are told to accept the six books of hadith unquestioningly, even if what they read contradicts their common sense. They are reminded that criticizing the Companions is blasphemous and are drilled with hadiths like, "My Companions are like stars and whichever one you follow you will be guided."[174] This hadith makes no sense at all. Hundreds of thousands of people became "Companions" by merely seeing the Prophet, but how did that make them flawless? They criticize the Shia for having 14 Infallibles; but with this hadith, they made a hundred thousand people infallible and they see nothing wrong with it.

---

[174] *Fath Al-Bari*, Ibn Hajar, v. 4, p. 49

The Shia are not the only ones who reject this particular tradition. Even many prominent Sunni scholars have denied it. Yet it is commonly repeated; however, it does not work for our youth. It drives them away from Islam. They ask simple questions like, "Why, if all of the Companions were "rightly guided" did some of them kill each other or call each other heretics?" Rather than receiving an intelligent answer, they are warned against investigating that part of history. They are told that these traditions are sacred; and the thinking youth are unconvinced. Some even leave Islam, not knowing if there is an alternative path

Many other youth are driven away by our habits. They do not have a problem with Islam, but they have a problem with how it is implemented. For example, some of the mosque cultures in the West tend to be hopelessly misogynistic. Count the number of women inside a mosque in the West. Women are not welcomed; the mosque is mainly catered for the older men. Some, in fact, discourage women from visiting the mosque altogether. When they do go, they are often relegated to dark, ill-kept corners. I wonder how we expect our wives to be our children's first teachers if we ban them from the mosque. I wonder how we can expect our youth to come to the mosque when their own mothers cannot bring them there from an early age. Even male youths avoid the mosque. Our youth need to be regularly present in the mosque if we want them to represent Islam. A simple solution is to make Islamic organizations less hostile to women and the youth. Also, in some cases, the mosques are not family-friendly. In contrast, churches welcome the entire family. The entire family goes to church on Sundays; they listen to the sermon and pray together. They enjoy worshipping together and bond with each other. However, in some mosques, the entire family is not present. Everyone should feel a sense of ownership and welcoming in the mosque. Going to the mosque should be pleasant for everyone, and each member of the family should encourage the others to attend.

Additionally, from the early days of Islam, the mosque was always the intellectual center of the community. However, nowadays it has been reduced to a mere place of worship. Although it may be open five times a day for prayers, there is no scholar to learn from or discuss issues with. It is very sad to see the impact of this.

Ironically, 9/11 opened the eyes of many American to the beauty of Islam. Immediately after 9/11, we actually saw more non-Muslims than Muslims in the audience; the mosque became a magnet for them. Unfortunately, they soon realized that they had no place there. They were not welcomed, and they did not learn anything. They left and never came back. Often times, there is a major discrepancy between faith and practice.

Thus, the mosques need to be revitalized into friendly centers of learning for everyone. They need to fulfill the same role that they did during the time of the Prophet. Once, the Prophet found two groups of people in the mosque, one studying and the other one praying. When asked which one was better, he smiled and said that both of them were good, but then pointed to the group that was studying and said, "But I was sent for this." His main mission was to teach. Without learning, one cannot worship properly.

Many Muslims recite their prayers, but their prayers do not restrain them from evil acts, the way that it should. Praying has become a ritual, like brushing your teeth three times a day. God wants our prayers to be meaningful, and that meaningfulness requires knowledge.

We also need to communicate with the youth in a language that they understand without patronizing them. We need to address them at the same intellectual level that they hear at the universities. As Muslims, we are facing some contemporary dilemmas that even the Muslim scholars (*ulama*) have not resolved. When we reveal our ignorance about those issues, then our word loses credence with them.

We also need to stop importing religious leaders from abroad. We need homegrown religious scholars who are familiar with Western culture and lifestyle.

$$﴿وَمَا كَانَ ٱلْمُؤْمِنُونَ لِيَنفِرُواْ كَآفَّةً فَلَوْلَا نَفَرَ مِن كُلِّ فِرْقَةٍ مِّنْهُمْ طَآئِفَةٌ لِّيَتَفَقَّهُواْ فِى ٱلدِّينِ وَلِيُنذِرُواْ قَوْمَهُمْ إِذَا رَجَعُوٓاْ إِلَيْهِمْ لَعَلَّهُمْ يَحْذَرُونَ﴾$$

Yet it is not for the faithful to go forth all together. But why should not there go forth a group from each of their sections to become learned in religion, and to warn their people when they return to them, so that they may beware? (9:122)

The development of traditional Muslim seminaries (*hawzahs*) and seminaries is excellent. We need to combine academic studies at the universities with traditional teachings at the *hawzah* in order to produce future leaders of Islam in the West.

We all need to step up to fulfill these responsibilities. Do not leave it for someone else. When God intends goodness for one of His servants, He opens up his eyes to study religion and serve Islam. Imam Husayn and the Ahlul-Bayt are waiting for us all to volunteer and carry on their message and their mission.

The Spirit of Ashura
Chapter 10

﴿إِنَّ ٱللَّهَ ٱشْتَرَىٰ مِنَ ٱلْمُؤْمِنِينَ أَنفُسَهُمْ وَأَمْوَالَهُم بِأَنَّ لَهُمُ ٱلْجَنَّةَ يُقَاتِلُونَ فِى سَبِيلِ ٱللَّهِ فَيَقْتُلُونَ وَيُقْتَلُونَ وَعْداً عَلَيْهِ حَقّاً فِى ٱلتَّوْرَاةِ وَٱلْإِنجِيلِ وَٱلْقُرْآنِ وَمَنْ أَوْفَىٰ بِعَهْدِهِ مِنَ ٱللَّهِ فَٱسْتَبْشِرُواْ بِبَيْعِكُمُ ٱلَّذِى بَايَعْتُم بِهِ وَذٰلِكَ هُوَ ٱلْفَوْزُ ٱلْعَظِيمُ﴾

Indeed God has bought from the faithful their souls and their possessions for Paradise to be theirs: they fight in the way of God, kill, and are killed. A promise binding upon Him in the Torah and the Injeel (Gospel) and the Qur'an. And who is truer to his promise than God? So rejoice in the bargain you have made with Him, and that is the great success. (9:111)

THE EVE OF ASHURA IS A VERY SOLEMN NIGHT FOR MANY MUSLIMS worldwide. We begin to recall the events of that evening up until the next day. Immediately, grief strikes the heart upon hearing the story. Without compulsion, one joins a wave of mourners remembering the life and sacrifice of Imam Husayn, his family, and his companions; and we all remember them in sadness.

On this night, we share our sympathy with the Ahlul-Bayt and their grandfather, the Prophet, who is cited by Bukhari as saying that the Prophet held Husayn in his arms and said, "Husayn is form me, and I am from Husayn. May God love whoever loves Husayn." Whoever shares in the sorrow of Imam Husayn is beloved in the eyes of God.

On the eve of Ashura, millions of people around the world feel sadness over the events that happened on the plains of Karbala over 1,350 years ago. One gathering ends and then another begins. In the morning, they begin in Australia and the Far East. By the time that program finishes, new commemorations begin in the Middle East and Africa. Still later, more commemorations begin in Europe and America for a noble and innocent man named Aba Abdullah Husayn. No corner of the earth is absent of his remembrance on the eve and day of Ashura.

Three catalysts led to the uprising of Imam Husayn. The first was the pressure to pay allegiance to Yazid. The second was the presence of people of conscience, who in search of freedom pushed him to rise against the Bani Umayyad. Finally, the third was nothing other than the pivotal principle of Islam, "enjoining the good and forbidding the evil." These three factors combined to result in the uprising of the Imam on the day of Ashura.

Before he died in the year 60 AH, Muawiyah b. Abi Sufyan had ruled the Muslim stage for four decades with an iron fist. He was the first person to change the caliphate, the succession to the Prophet, into a monarchy. This is a historical fact, and the Muslim historian, Ibn Khaldun was one of those who mentioned this.

In order to secure his son's succession to the throne, Muawiyah summoned one of his senior aides named Ziyad b. Abihi, as well as, Al-Mugheerah b. Shubah to inform them that before he died he wanted to see his son Yazid crowned as Commander of the Faithful. They advised him against that because people would reject him due to his licentiousness. However, Muawiyah insisted on this.

At the time of Muawiyah's death, Yazid was on a hunting expedition outside Damascus. He hastily returned to the royal palace to take his position. His first action as caliph was to write an urgent letter to his first cousin, Waleed b. Utbah b. Abi Sufyan, the governor of Madinah, instructing him to take oaths of allegiance from the prominent leaders of Madinah - for he knew that Madinah was the intellectual and spiritual center of Islam at that time.

A few days later, the message arrived in Madinah, and immediately Waleed summoned Imam Husayn to his palace. Imam Husayn adamantly refused to give his hand saying, "We are the family of prophethood and the guardians of the message. Yazid is a corrupt licentious man who drinks alcohol and sheds innocent blood, and someone like me will never pay allegiance to someone like him."

Those few words highlighted Yazid's character, who was the personification of sin. Bukhari relates that the Prophet warned the people, "My community (ummah) will perish at the hands of a childish boy from Quraysh,"[175] clearly referring to Yazid b. Muawiyah. Someone like Imam Husayn whose mission was to preserve God's message on earth could never bow to him.

$$\text{﴿وَلَا تَرْكَنُوا إِلَى الَّذِينَ ظَلَمُوا فَتَمَسَّكُمُ النَّارُ وَمَا لَكُم مِّن دُونِ اللَّهِ مِنْ أَوْلِيَاءَ ثُمَّ لَا تُنصَرُونَ﴾}$$

And do not incline toward the wrongdoers; lest the Fire should touch you, and you will not have any friend besides God, then you will not be helped. (11:113)

The pressure mounted, and the Imam could not remain in Madinah any longer. He left Madinah in the month of Rajab and arrived in Mecca in the month of Shaban. He remained there for four months. News spread rapidly that the Imam had been forced to abandon his birthplace. People began to question what was happening. Scores of delegates

---

[175] *Fath Al-Bari*, v. 11, p. 417

came from abroad to encourage him to lead a revolt against the Bani Umayyad. They told him that they were extremely dissatisfied with the government, they wanted to seek guidance, and needed a savior to rescue them from Yazid.

Their fears about Yazid were indeed true, for Yazid left three major legacies during his rule. To start with, in the first year of his rule, he murdered Imam Husayn and his small group of followers. The next year (62 AH), he attacked the city of Madinah and made it a free-zone for three days for his soldiers to rape and pillage as they wished. Historians relate that ten thousand innocent civilians were killed inside of Madinah, and women and girls were raped. Lastly, in the third year of his rule, he destroyed the Holy Ka'bah.

In addition to the visitors, Imam Husayn also received many letters pleading him to aid the people of Kufa, and elsewhere, against the tyrants of the Bani Umayyad. He sent his cousin Muslim b. Aqeel to Kufa to investigate the situation. Within a few days of his arrival, thousands of people paid allegiance to Muslim, and he wrote back to Imam Husayn that 18,000 men were waiting for his arrival. This was the second factor that led to his tragic journey.

The third was nothing other than adherence to the basic principle of faith, "enjoining the good and forbidding the evil." The ummah had neglected that principle.

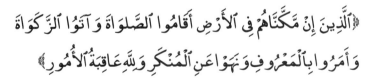

Those who, if We granted power them in the land, maintain the prayer, give the zakat, and bid what is right and forbid what is wrong. And with God rests the outcome of all matters. (22:41)

Islam was not meant to be a faith strictly based on a set of rituals. Moral security comes first. Without moral security, no one can worship in peace. The only way to establish peace and justice on earth is to enjoin good and forbid evil.

However, Islam had become ritualized, and it was on its last breath. It had been stripped of its substance by such a caliph at its head. Imagine how people would react today if a leader of any country went on television and asked the people to abstain from alcohol but he himself held a bottle in his hand. That was Yazid. Even when his father sent him to Hajj to rehabilitate him before he took over the throne, he could not live without wine. "Leave the mosques for the worshippers to inhabit, and let me sit at the tavern and drink my fill," were his exquisite lines about drinking. These were his words; and this was Yazid b. Muawiyah - the "cursed tree" described in the Qur'an.[176] In truth, his entire lineage was cursed.

When Imam Husayn took it upon himself to leave Hejaz, scores of people advised him against heading towards Iraq. They begged him to stay and told him that they needed him there. The Imam had one reply:

> I heard my grandfather the Messenger of God, may the peace and blessings of God be upon him and his family, say that if a person sees an oppressive tyrant ignoring the boundaries of God and betraying the Sunnah of the Prophet of God and treating the servants of God aggressively and wickedly, and that person does not oppose him through his words or deeds, then it is incumbent upon God to give that person the same end as the tyrant (i.e. to send him to the Hellfire).

Keeping quiet under despotic rule is tantamount to aiding a tyrant. Thus, Imam Husayn had no choice but to embark on his mission.

---

[176] "When We said to you, 'Indeed your Lord comprehends all mankind,' We did not appoint the vision that We showed you except as a test for the people and the tree cursed in the Qur'an. We deter them, but it only increases them in great rebellion." (17:60)

Some people argue that Imam Husayn should not have jeopardized his own life and his family's lives to confront Yazid. In response, one would ask, "Was it necessary for the martyrs of Badr or Uhud to give up their lives?" Were all the martyrs throughout history misguided? Our survival depends on sacrifice. All religions believe this, not just Islam.

"The martyrs are the princes of Paradise." Imam Husayn saved Islam for us by sacrificing himself. Otherwise, Islam was fated to go the way of the other major divine messages. God sent the largest contingent of prophets to the Jews, but Judaism was later changed. He sent Jesus who achieved world recognition, but his message was changed. This was exactly what was going to happen to the message of the Seal of the Prophets, Muhammad. It took the blood of Imam Husayn to keep the true message of Islam intact.

During his time, he was the one who took that responsibility on. Now, we also have a responsibility in our time. We must not be indifferent, nor can we be mere spectators. These are difficult times for us, and we have to do whatever we can to aid our religion righteously according to our capacity.

$$﴿كُنتُمْ خَيْرَ أُمَّةٍ أُخْرِجَتْ لِلنَّاسِ تَأْمُرُونَ بِٱلْمَعْرُوفِ وَتَنْهَوْنَ عَنِ ٱلْمُنكَرِ وَتُؤْمِنُونَ بِٱللَّهِ وَلَوْ آمَنَ أَهْلُ ٱلْكِتَابِ لَكَانَ خَيْرًا لَّهُم مِّنْهُمُ ٱلْمُؤْمِنُونَ وَأَكْثَرُهُمُ ٱلْفَاسِقُونَ﴾$$

You are the best nation [ever] brought forth for mankind: you bid what is right and forbid what is wrong, and have faith in God. And if the People of the Book had believed, it would have been better for them. Among them [some] are faithful, but most of them are transgressors. (3:110)

The Muslim ummah has been praised on one condition, "it enjoins the good and forbids the evil." Otherwise, there is no difference between

Muslims and others. Only a person who can carry out that responsibility has true faith; and the others are still aspiring to truly follow their religion. God says about the ancient civilizations that perished:

$$﴿كَانُوا لاَ يَتَنَاهَوْنَ عَن مُّنكَرٍ فَعَلُوهُ لَبِئْسَ مَا كَانُوا يَفْعَلُونَ﴾$$

They would not forbid one another from the wrongs that they committed. Surely, evil is what they had been doing. (5:79)

Due to the fact that they abandoned that duty, they were destroyed.

Today, we have an enormous responsibility. We should not commemorate Ashura just to cry and lament, but rather, we have to learn and reflect. Imam Husayn gave his entire life and family in order to enjoin good and forbid evil. We need to ask ourselves whether we are fulfilling that duty, even if it is just among our families and friends. People ask me sometimes whether they should advise their parents or relatives to pray; and the answer is that of course you should! If you want your family to remain safe and united then you need to remind them. Certainly, you would tell your family and friends to avoid a hazardous road because you care about them. Likewise, when it comes to moral issues, you have to enjoin what is right to those you care about. They may not listen to you immediately, but you need to be patient for it takes time. One has to be consistent.

$$﴿وَأْمُرْ أَهْلَكَ بِالصَّلاَةِ وَاصْطَبِرْ عَلَيْهَا لاَ نَسْأَلُكَ رِزْقاً نَّحْنُ نَرْزُقُكَ وَالْعَاقِبَةُ لِلتَّقْوَى﴾$$

And bid your family to prayer and be steadfast in its maintenance. We do not ask any provision of you. It is We who provide for you, and the outcome will be in favor of the God-conscious. (20:132)

God revealed to Prophet Jethro, "O Jethro! I am going to destroy 100,000 of your people - 60,000 of the good and 40,000 of the bad."

Jethro was shocked. "God," he asked, "I understand why You want to punish the evil ones, but what crime have the good people committed?"

God revealed, "O Jethro, they sided with the evildoers and did not show or express anger at My anger."[177] In other words, they did not side with God. This is how important enjoining good and forbidding evil is.

No one at that time could have stood up for the cause like Imam Husayn. Had he ceded his responsibility and yielded to the Bani Umayyad, Islam would have perished. He could never have allowed that to happen, for he was the son of Imam Ali, the first defender of Islam. His blood revived Islam and the ummah. Mere talk was not enough; and he knew that he had to give his life to save the religion. The survival of Islam depended on him. This was why Imam Husayn was content to give his life for the sake of Islam, and not only his life, but even the lives of his loved ones as well. On the day of Ashura, ten children of Ali b. Abi Talib sacrificed their lives for the sake of Islam.

As a result, today Imam Husayn is the universal icon of reform. Wherever you go, Imam Husayn is honored, and even non-Muslims revere him. Although the actual battle of Ashura only took a few hours, it has been immortalized. Did you ever ask yourself why? Did you ever ask yourself why some may not always come to the Islamic centers during the year, but they always show up during the time of Ashura? Is it just tradition, or is it something else?

The battle of Ashura did not take place between two leaders or two tribes. It was a conflict of truth versus falsehood; justice versus injustice; dignity against disgrace. This is the essence of Ashura, and this is why we keep coming back to our religious centers every year for more inspiration.

---

[177] *Wasael Al-Shi'a*, v. 11, p. 416

Ashura inspires all of us. You will see the effects of remembering it; perhaps not today, perhaps not tomorrow, but definitely sometime during your lifetime. This is the effect of Imam Husayn, and this is why the anniversary of Ashura needs to be commemorated. Promise yourself that every year, no matter where you are, no matter what you are doing, you will take the time to remember Imam Husayn, for the cause that he fought for will never end until we have the honor to witness the illuminating face of Imam Mahdi. That will be the final day of Ashura, and at that time we will witness universal peace.

One should ask themselves "where would I stand?" If there are two camps, one camp is for the truth and the other is for falsehood, which one would you choose? Would you join Imam Husayn if he was standing before you? Most of us would say yes! We must remember that even today, Imam Husayn needs our help; his sister, Lady Zaynab needs our help. I am sure that one of the things that they would ask of us is not to sell our selves short while living in the West. We must all endeavor to live an honorable life; live a clean life. Our lives have a very important role. We have to be ready to sacrifice everything for Islam. We have to work hard as we are the soldiers of Imam Husayn and the future soldiers of Imam al-Mahdi.

Even today, our lives have a meaning and purpose. Each and every person was born with a quality that is meant to be shared with others. We need to tap into those qualities. You have the potential to make positive changes, not only for yourself, but more so, for others. Today, we may not be needed in the battlefield, but we are needed in the classroom, workplace, political offices, soup-kitchens, and neighborhoods; we have a role to play in these and many other walks of life. Today, the sword has become the pen that writes great works about Islam; the armor has become the speech that will protect Islam; the soldiers of Islam are represented by our fortress of ethical and moral values. This is what Imam Husayn wants from all of us; this is the sacrifice of Ashura.

Reformation & Transformation
Chapter 11

﴿وَنَفْسٍ وَمَا سَوَّاهَا ۞ فَأَلْهَمَهَا فُجُورَهَا وَتَقْوَاهَا ۞ قَدْ أَفْلَحَ مَن زَكَّاهَا ۞ وَقَدْ خَابَ مَن دَسَّاهَا﴾

By the soul and Him who fashioned it, and inspired it with [discernment between] its virtues and vices: one who purifies it is certainly felicitous, and one who betrays it certainly fails. (91:7-10)

MILLIONS OF MUSLIMS WORLDWIDE WILL CONTINUE TO MAKE THEIR annual presence at religious institutes' commemorating the life and legacy of Imam Husayn, his family and companions. More so now, we all have to ask ourselves, how will commemorating Ashura change us?

Ashura does not end on the 10th of Muharram just because the main commemorations have ended. The aim of the Ashura sessions is nothing less than the salvation of humanity. We come to be inspired, touched, and motivated by Imam Husayn, but more importantly, to apply his message to our own lives on a daily basis.

These sessions need to be a catalyst for change. One may not see a radical change in their life in only ten days. However, these sessions should open our eyes to show us our way in life and help us to reorganize our priorities. We cannot remain stagnant and continue in our negative ways.

Do not despair if you try to change but are not completely able to. One must keep on trying. At the end of the struggle, when one reaches salvation, then you will be grateful that you did not give up. Meanwhile, you will enjoy and benefit from the journey of reformation.

This path to inner change needs to begin first with ourselves, then our family, and then our society. God created human beings to be the jewel of this universe. A hadith *al-Qudsi* says, "My servant, I have created everything for you, and I have created you for Me."[178] A married couple who have only one child will bequeath everything to that child; we have the same value before God Almighty.

The importance of humanity lies deep in the soul. All of God's messengers came for one reason - to teach us how to refine our souls and make us become true human beings. One of our *maraja*[179], Sheikh Abd al-Kareem al-Haeri went to the shrine of Imam Husayn and told him, "Today I have reached the height of knowledge. People follow me, but I want you to help me become a true human being."

Imam Ali said, "Your first battlefront should be your soul. If you can subdue it, then you can subdue others; but if you succumb to it, then you will succumb to others."[180]

A team that cannot win on its own turf will not be able to win elsewhere. We have to be victorious inside ourselves first. Afterwards, we can venture outside of our own souls into our families and our communities, and then we will be able to go forward easier. However, if we fail inside our own souls, then we will most likely fail in the outside world. If we cannot resist temptations in our lives then how can we expect our children to resist it in theirs? We need to begin with ourselves first.

---

[178] *Sharh Usool Al-Kafi*, v. 4, p. 232
[179] One of the highest levels of religious authority that a person can reach to.
[180] *Nahjul Balaghah*

The Bible has a beautiful verse, "For what shall it profit a man if he shall gain the whole world but lose his own soul?" (Mark 8:36)

$$﴿فَٱعْبُدُواْ مَا شِئْتُم مِّن دُونِهِ قُلْ إِنَّ ٱلْخَاسِرِينَ ٱلَّذِينَ خَسِرُوٓاْ$$

$$أَنفُسَهُمْ وَأَهْلِيهِمْ يَوْمَ ٱلْقِيَامَةِ أَلَا ذَٰلِكَ هُوَ ٱلْخُسْرَانُ ٱلْمُبِينُ﴾$$

You worship whatever you wish besides Him. Say, "Indeed the losers are those who ruin themselves and their families on the Day of Resurrection." Look! That is the manifest loss! (39:15)

True failure in this world is when we will stand before God on the Last Day and will realize that we had lost our soul in this world because we had not been able to restrain ourselves from sin. It has nothing to do with losing our prestige, health, or wealth in this temporary world. We must try very hard not to lose ourselves. Some people try to guide others, but fail to guide themselves. Some people want to try and reform the entire world but fail because they do not have enough willpower to control their own souls. A failed person cannot reform others. This is why we must begin with ourselves.

Think of Prophet Joseph, a major reformer of his time. He was at the peak of glory and power, but he was not interested in either one. He had the wealth of Bill Gates, the charisma of the most famous celebrities, and the inner beauty of a saint. That was Joseph at his time. Yet, at the height of his prestige, he asked God:

$$﴿رَبِّ قَدْ آتَيْتَنِى مِنَ ٱلْمُلْكِ وَعَلَّمْتَنِى مِن تَأْوِيلِ ٱلْأَحَادِيثِ$$

$$فَاطِرَ ٱلسَّمَاوَاتِ وَٱلْأَرْضِ أَنتَ وَلِيِّى فِى ٱلدُّنْيَا وَٱلْآخِرَةِ$$

$$تَوَفَّنِى مُسْلِماً وَأَلْحِقْنِى بِٱلصَّالِحِينَ﴾$$

My Lord! You have granted me a share in the kingdom, and taught me the interpretation of dreams. Originator of the heavens and earth! You are my

> *guardian in this world and the Hereafter! Let my death be in submission [to You], and unite me with the Righteous. (12:101)*

God gave him command over the greatest empire of his time which was Egypt, and bestowed him with supernatural knowledge. Yet, he turned his attention away from the worldly matters; and prayed to be a true slave of God. He wanted to be with the spiritually elite ones, and this is described in the exegesis (*tafseer*) of the Qur'an as being the Prophet Muhammad and his family (the Ahlul-Bayt). He saw beyond his own time.

We need to be very careful with our inner self. Our soul is the closest thing to us, much closer than our family or possessions. Certainly, one may ask, how can we reform ourselves?

Imam Ali said, "The first step to sinning is the assent of the soul." Our soul has two parts to it: one good and the other evil. We need to be careful and vigil of the latter; and must try our hardest not to give into it.

We can control the evil half of our soul by holding it accountable for its deeds. Every night, before we go to sleep, we should review our day. Make time to speak to yourself for ten minutes. Go over what we did from the early hours of the morning (when we woke up to pray), until the nighttime when we are ready for bed. It will only take a few minutes to do this. Some people waste hours on the Internet or on their cell phones. Make a phone call to yourself. The Prophet said, "Strengthen your souls by evaluating them, and guard them by opposing them."[181] Put a restraining order against the part of your soul that tempts you to do evil acts. Follow the advice of the Commander of the Faithful who said, "The best commander is the one who has command over his own soul."[182] Through this process, we will embark on the journey towards salvation; and God will make it easy for us. Our

---

[181] *Mustadrak Al-Wasael*, v. 12, p. 155
[182] *Mizan Al-Hikmah*, v. 4, p. 2927

deeds remain written with Him forever, so we cannot allow ourselves to forget them.

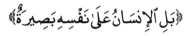

Rather each person is a witness to himself. (75:14)

All of us have bad habits that we must try to quit performing. A young man confessed that he could not stop himself from dating girls. I told him that he is not the only one; and some others his age have the same problem. He asked me how to stop. I told him that the first step is to be honest with yourself, for that shows that you are serious about changing. I told him that if you want to stop dating other people's daughters and sisters, then think of the girls that you are dating as being your own sister, would you want someone else to use your sister as entertainment? Think seriously about the potential consequences before you pick up the phone and ask a girl on a date.

Whenever you are tempted to do anything at all, think about the consequences. Every action has a reaction. This is not just a law in physics, but it also holds true for everything in life. Everything that you do has a price to pay, and sometimes, the price is heavy. Would you charge up your credit card, which has a ten thousand dollar limit on it just because you can do it? Who will pay for it? It is you and only you who will have to pay, and surely, the payback will be very difficult.

Dating has a similar price. First of all, it will distance you away from God because it is a violation of His command. You will lose His blessings and guidance. If you promise to stop, but keep regressing, then your soul will become weakened, and you will wonder why you ever wanted to go back to God in the first place.

In addition to this, dating cheapens men and women. Everyone prefers to buy a brand new car; a new car has a new car smell and clean seats. You know that you are the first driver. A second-hand car is not clean and thus you will not value it like a new car. It is the same with people.

If you cheapen yourself and reduce your moral value, then your future family will not respect you as much. Besides, you need to see it from another perspective as well; would you tolerate someone in the community that tampers with your daughter or sister? Obviously you would not, so think about it before you infringe on the honor of other families.

That is how we must try to keep ourselves away from sins, by examining ourselves and considering the consequences. Imam al-Ridha narrates a story of a monk, at the time of the Children of Israel, who saved himself by holding himself accountable for his deeds. After 40 years of worship, God had asked him to offer a sacrifice. After he gave the sacrifice, God rejected it. The monk was worried; but rather than blaming others, which is usually what we do, he was honest with himself. He blamed God's rejection on himself; for he had indeed betrayed his own soul. God inspired him to realize that those few moments were superior to all the 40 years of his worship.

You should be the first one to realize what is wrong inside of yourself before others mention it. God has provided us with the ability for self-reflection. However, we have to accept others' advice as well. We have to thank them for advising us, even if they are criticizing us. We should not get angry or offended, for sincere advice is the best gift that we can ever get.

﴿إِلاَّ ٱلَّذِينَ آمَنُواْ وَعَمِلُواْ ٱلصَّالِحَاتِ وَتَوَاصَوْاْ بِٱلْحَقِّ وَتَوَاصَوْا بِٱلصَّبْرِ﴾

Except those who have faith and do righteous deeds, and enjoin one another (tawaasaw) to [follow] the truth, and enjoin one another to patience. (103:3)

Tawaasaw refers to mutual advice. True believers should be able reach out to their brothers and sisters and ask what they are doing wrong and get honest advice. A tradition states, "Your friend is the one who tells you the truth, not the one that (just) tells you that you are right."[183] Another tradition says, "A believer is a mirror to a believer."[184] For many people, the mirror is an important piece of furniture in their house because it shows them exactly how they look. We need to cultivate honest friendships with those who will give us sound advice.

Thus, everything that has been mentioned will enable us to continue on the journey of reform; a journey which we renewed at the beginning of this month, and which God willing, we will all continue to tread in the memory of our beloved Imam Husayn who sacrificed everything that he had for the reformation and transformation of the human race.

---

[183] *Al-Eedhah*, Al-Azdi, p. 70
[184] *Mustadrak Al-Wasael*, v. 9, p. 49

Glossary of Terms

Akhirah: An Islamic term referring to the afterlife.

Akhlaq: An Islamic term referring to the practice of virtue, morality and manners in Islamic theology and philosophy. It is also referred to as disposition, nature, temper, ethics, morals or character (of a person).

Aalam al-Barzakh: Sometimes referred to as the astral plane – the world of the planetary spheres, crossed by the soul in its astral body on the way to being born and after death; it is generally said that this world is populated by angels, spirits and other immaterial beings.

Amaanah: Trust or 'free will' which has been given only to humans and jinn, in contrast, other entities do not have this quality.

Aqd: A religious contract.

Aql: Intellect and a term used in Islamic theology or philosophy to the intellect or rational faculty of the soul or mind.

Arhaam: Family members or kin.

Ayah: Arabic word for sign, proof, commandment, law, rule and/or guidance.

Aziz: One who is powerful, strong, or respected.

Bay'ah: In Islamic terminology, an oath of allegiance to a leader.

Bidah: Any type of innovation in Islam.

Dua': In the terminology of Islam, this word means an act of supplication. The term is derived from an Arabic word meaning to 'call out' or to 'summon', and Muslims regard this as a profound act of worship.

Ghaflah: Used in Islamic terminology in the meaning of negligence or heedlessness.

Halal: Means lawful or legal and is a term designating any object or an action which is permissible to use or engage in, according to Islamic law.

Haram: An Islamic term meaning "forbidden"; used to refer to anything that is prohibited by the faith.

Hawzahs: Religious seminaries.

Hidayah: An Islamic term meaning 'guidance' (given by Allah).

Husayniyyahs: Places in which sessions of remembrance of Imam Husayn are conducted.

Imamah: An Arabic word with an English language suffix (ate) meaning leadership. Its use in theology is confined to Islam.

Insaaniyyah: Humanity.

Istihsan: An Arabic term for juristic "preference". Muslim scholars may use it to express their preference for particular judgements in Islamic law over other possibilities. It is one of the principles of legal thought underlying personal interpretation or ijtihad.

Ja'ala: Made or done.

Jahiliyyah: An Islamic concept meaning "ignorant of divine guidance" or "the state of ignorance of the guidance from God"or "Days of Ignorance" referring to the condition that Arabs found themselves in pre-Islamic Arabia, i.e. prior to the revelation of the Qur'an to Prophet Muhammad.

Jihad: An Islamic term which refers to a religious duty for Muslims. In Arabic, the word jihad translates as a noun meaning "struggle".

Jinn: Genies are supernatural creatures in Arab folklore and Islamic teachings which occupy a parallel world to that of mankind. Together, jinn, humans and angels make up the three sentient creations of Allah.

Kafan: White burial shroud used to cover a deceased Muslim.

Kafir: Term used primary by classical Islamic doctrine to refer to those who "disbelieve" in one God - atheists and polytheists.

Khalifah: The calipha or successor to the Prophet Muhammad.

Khalq: Creation.

Laghw: Means "evil, vain talk", vain, dirty, false, falsehood, nonsensical, meaningless and anything which is forbidden by Allah. It refers to anything which serves no purpose or for a goal in a practicing Muslim life and has no room in a proper Muslim's life.

Ma'rifah: Recognition or awareness.

Ma'rouf: Righteousness.

Mahr: Dowry paid by the groom to the bride.

Mahram: Refers to people who are unlawful for a woman or man to marry due to blood relationships or marriage.

Makruh: A disliked or offensive act (literally "hated"). Though it is not haram (forbidden) and therefore not a sin, a person who abstains from this action will be rewarded. Muslims are encouraged to avoid such actions when possible.

Marja' Taqlid: The highest theological authority followed by the common people.

Ma'soom (Pl. Masoumeen): Infallible, Divinely protected against sinning.

Mawali: A word with many meanings in Arabic including: Master, Slave, Servers.

Minbar: Pulpit or podium.

Muharram: The first month of the Islamic calendar. It is one of the four sacred months of the year in which fighting is prohibited.

Mutashabihat: Things which are metaphoric and unclear.

Nafs: An Arabic word meaning self, psyche, ego or soul.

Qawamun: Care-takers.

Qawl al-zur: Deceitful sayings, lying, the untruth.

Qibla: The direction that Muslims face when performing their prayers. It is in the direction of the Ka'bah in Mecca.

Rakah: An individual unit of salat.

Ruku': To bow down. During the prayers, a Muslim performs the act of ruku' before God to express veneration to him, he bows forward at the waist, puts his hands on his knees and his back is parallel to the ground.

Salat: Salat is an Arabic word which means: a spiritual relationship and communication between the servant/being and his Creator. Salat is one of the five pillars of Islam. It is performed five times a day at these times: fajr (pre-dawn or pre-daybreak), dhuhr (noon), 'asr (afternoon), maghrib (just after sunset) and 'isha' (late night).

Shahadah: Martyrdom; it also means testimony, declaration of faith. A person must recite the shahadah in Arabic to convert to Islam.

Shaykh (Shaikh or Sheikh): The word "shaykh" is a title of an elderly person or a religious leader. This title is also given to a wise person, in this case, it means a mentor.

Shirk: Polytheism, the belief in the existence of partners with Allah, (which according to Islam is not permitted).

Shisheh: Waterpipe.

Sujud (Sujood): Prostration to God, it is done during one's daily prayers in which seven parts of the body are placed on the ground: the forehead, two palms, two knees and the two big toes.

Sunna (Sunnah): In general, the word Sunnah means: way of life, habit, practice, customary procedure, action, norm and tradition followed by tradition. Usually, the word Sunnah refers to what Prophet Muhammed had said and done or approved of when said or done, by someone else. It includes the Prophet's sayings, practices, living habits, etc. The hadith reports on the Sunnah. The two major legal sources of jurisprudence in Islam are the Qur'an and the Sunnah.

Tafsir: The exegesis or commentary, usually of the Qur'an.

Tahajjud: Night devotions - the tahajjud prayer is an optional prayer that is supposed to be performed in the middle of the night and it helps one attain higher spiritual stations.

Tajseem: Materialization, personification, incarnation.

Takfir (Takfeer): Labeling someone as "kafir", apostate, unbeliever, excommunicating from the creed. People who do that are called "Takfiris" or Takfeeri". This terms is applied mainly to the most extremist and fanatical offshoots within Islam who loosely apply this term to those who do not follow their own line, ideology or version of "Islam".

Tasbih: A form of dhikr that involves the repetitive utterances of short sentences glorifying God, in Islam. To keep track of counting either the phalanges of the right hand or a misbaha is used. The tasbih is similar to the komboskini of the Eastern Church and the rosary in the Roman Catholic Church.

Tawbah: Literally means 'to return'. In an Islamic context, it refers to the act of leaving what God has prohibited and returning to what He has commanded.

Thawab: Reward or blessing.

'Ulama (Ulema or 'Ulema): Plural of 'Alim which is a scholar-theologian, a learned or knowledgeable person in Islam

Usuliyyah: Fundamentalism.

Wudu: A purification (ablution) which must be performed before one can perform the salat or touch the Qur'an. (There are other instances which also require one to be in this state of purity)

Ziyarah: Visit, social get-together. A pilgrimage to a holy site other than Mecca or Medina is also called Ziyarah.